ALSO BY JOHN LOBELL

Between Silence and Light:
Spirit on the Architecture of Louis I. Kahn

The Little Green Book

Joseph Campbell: The Man and His Ideas
(With Stephen and Robin Larsen)

VISIONARY
CREATIVITY

VISIONARY
CREATIVITY

How New Worlds Are Born

JOHN LOBELL

Visionary Creatives swim in the culture of our day. The things they create—in art, design, science, technology, business—embody our culture and at the same time pull us into the future.

JXJ

A publication of JXJ Productions, Inc

🅙🅧🅙

Published by
JXJ Publications
JXJPublications@gmail.com

ISBN-13: 978-0692430446
ISBN-10: 069243044X

Also available on Kindle
Book information at VisionaryCreativity.com

Printed in the United States of America

1. Creativity. 2. Cultural Theory.
3. Art. 4. Innovation.

Book design by Tony Iatridis

CONTENTS

INTRODUCTION

Poets are the unacknowledged legislators of the world.
~ Percy Bysshe Shelley, English Romantic poet

An Urgent Call

This book is an urgent call for creativity in our Selves, our economy, our society, and our culture.

Western culture is built on creative freedom, but today that freedom has diminished in Europe and is under attack in the United States. As we will see in the course of this book, the loss of that creativity would pose threats to us on many levels: individually, we can be either passive consumers or active creators; economically, we can compete by lowering the cost of labor, or by creating new technologies, goods, and services; socially, we can live in the past or create the future; and most importantly, culturally we can keep alive in the West a moral and creative center in the heart of each individual, or we can surrender that role—that responsibility—that resides in each of us.

You might wonder, why would creativity be under attack? Isn't creativity an unquestioned good? But as we will see in this book, a particular form of creativity that I am calling *Visionary Creativity* can be a serious challenge to the status quo; it has the potential to bring forth new worlds, but in doing so it can also destroy old worlds. Those who remain attached to old worlds are not interested in seeing them destroyed.

Visionary Creativity is a particular type of creativity that is paradigm shifting in its essence. It changes the rules of the

1

game and in this sense it is very different from ordinary, everyday creativity. It is the type of creativity that we associate with figures like Vincent van Gogh, Igor Stravinsky, Albert Einstein, Elvis Presley, J. K. Rowling, and Steve Jobs. It not only created the great works of art, science, technology, and industry of the past, it is at work at this very moment creating our emerging world as we move deeper into the twenty-first century.

Why is Creativity Important?

Let's start by asking two questions and seeing how the answers to them merge: What do we admire in others and aspire to in ourselves? And what do we wish for our society? We might at first be tempted to answer that we admire in others and aspire to in ourselves health, wealth, power, beauty. Perhaps. But what about going beyond these things for a truly fulfilling life? Then we might say that we want engagement with the world, influence over it, and recognition for our accomplishments. In other words, we want a life of creativity.

And for our society? These are times of social, technological, and economic turmoil. Our old institutions are in distress and new ones to replace them are struggling to be born. We are cut adrift in almost every aspect of our lives, shorn of frames of reference, decentered in a world of change. But times of change can also provide opportunities for creativity, and we are becoming aware of new possibilities in our arts, sciences, technologies, institutions, and industries.

So looking at our own lives as well as our social problems, we see that both call out for creativity. We are creative creatures who flourish best in the pursuit of our creativity, and it is precisely in creativity that we will find not only fulfillment for ourselves, but also the visions that our world needs. Hence the title of this book: *Visionary Creativity*. What exactly, then, do we mean by Visionary Creativity?

2

Visionary Creativity: Creating New Worlds

Although creativity is vital to ourselves and our society, and although there is an outpouring of books on the subject, creativity remains poorly understood. There are in fact two kinds of creativity: Ordinary creativity, for example preparing a well-conceived meal, drafting a legal brief, or writing an episode of a sitcom; and the kind of creativity that we see in Albert Einstein's formulation of his theory of relativity or Salvador Dalí's painting of his melting watches. We have a tendency to say that the creativity of Einstein and Dalí is like ordinary creativity, only more, but this is not correct. Einstein's relativity and Dalí's melting watches are examples of Visionary Creativity, a creativity that shatters old worlds and gives birth to new ones.

Let's look very briefly at Einstein and Dalí. For Isaac Newton, space and time were absolute, uniform, and continuous, as though space were marked by a uniform grid and time by a universal clock. This was, of course, a notion in physics, but it was pervasive; space and time represented the *stage* on which all human action unfolded. We see this Newtonian stage in perspective painting with its implied grid converging at a vanishing point, and its figures captured in a moment frozen out of the continuous flow of time. But by the beginning of the twentieth century, that space and time were gone. In Einstein's relativity, space is dynamic, collapsing in on itself, and time is elastic, as conveyed by Dalí's melting watches.

The importance of this? Visionary Creatives like Einstein and Dalí respond to the culture of their day, and at the same time they advance it into an emerging world, creating for us an entirely new stage on which we live our lives. This stage, as we call it in this book, presents us with the nature of our cosmos and our place in it, our newly formed circumstances, the possibilities of our relationships, and the means by which we might fulfill our potentials. It establishes the ways in which we can move about in our world—both figuratively and literally.

Today we no longer live in Newton's world. But we also no longer live in the world of Einstein and Dalí—*that world was born a hundred years ago.* Today we live in a newly emerging world being built right now by our Visionary Creatives, a world of interconnected fractal networks that computationally generate themselves. Visionary Creatives, then, sweep away old worlds as they create new ones, and there is no guarantee we will prefer the new to the old. Visionary Creativity can be discomforting, even dangerous.

We might think of people as generally falling into several groups or combinations thereof in terms of temperament and ability: *leaders,* who organize, motivate, and command; *nurturers,* who care for others; *producers,* who make things; *actives,* who seek physical challenges; *scholars* who contemplate ideas; *mystics,* who experience transcendence; and *somnambulists,* who are content with feelings of wellbeing. And *Visionary Creatives,* bringers of the new, destroyers of the old. All are worthy. All can lead rich lives. But this is a book about Visionary Creatives and for those who seek to encourage them, or perhaps just admire them.

Visionary Creatives swim in the culture of their day and manifest in their work the spirit of their age. The things they create—in art, design, science, technology, business—embody that spirit, and at the same time are a little off center for us, somehow not what we anticipated, thus pulling us into the future.

Three Parts

In the introduction to his highly influential book, *Understanding Media,* Marshall McLuhan writes that his editor was dismayed that seventy-five percent of his material was new. The editor said that a book cannot be successful if more than ten percent of its material is new. In this book you will find an ocean of new material—ideas about our world, ourselves, and our future, but as you read, unities will appear that will help you form your own approach to this material, your own creative narrative.

This book is divided into three parts. *Part One: What is Creativity* describes Visionary Creativity, *Part Two: Becoming a Visionary Creative* addresses how we must challenge established wisdom, and *Part Three: Creating the Future* looks at the stage on which Visionary Creatives are working today.

Part One begins by differentiating Visionary Creativity from mastery, innovation, and ordinary creativity, and then looks at some examples of how Visionary Creativity is expressive of its culture. It is difficult for us to see our own culture, or even to recognize the concept of culture itself—we tend to see our world as "real," and not one of many possible symbolic constructs, which we must do if we are going to understand Visionary Creativity.

There is a continual interplay between culture and individual processes of cognition—that is to say, structures of consciousness—as they make and remake each other. We can see this particularly in art, which, through *discontinuities*—differences between what we anticipate and what we encounter—restructures our consciousness; reorganizes our minds. We go to an art gallery expecting the drip paintings of Jackson Pollack and instead encounter the Campbell soup cans of Andy Warhol. We go to a science fiction movie expecting the visual mythology of *2001: A Space Odyssey*, and instead encounter the sword and ray gun hero journey of *Star Wars*. Later we will look at the basis for such discontinuities in neuroscience.

We will also see that science plays a role similar to art in this respect. We usually think of art and science as two separate things, with art functioning as the product of the individual imagination and science as an objective investigation of the world. But in this book we will see them both as expressions of their cultures, both constituting the vocabularies of Visionary Creatives in their task of building new worlds. For example, if we attempt to understand the world in Newtonian terms and instead find that it reveals itself in quantum terms, we are not only engaging in scientific investigations, we are also experiencing a type of cultural discontinuity, an act of remaking our consciousness and our world. In this book, science does not just provide examples of Visionary Creativity, it also gives us excellent descriptions of the various stages on which we have lived—and today are living—our lives.

In *Part Two* we discuss becoming a Visionary Creative and see that there is no exclusive path. Psychologists have attempted to describe how we can become more creative and perhaps some of their exercises might help with creativity, but for Visionary Creativity we turn to a philosopher. In "The Three Metamorphoses of the Spirit" from his *Thus Spoke Zarathustra*, Friedrich Nietzsche presents his parable of the camel, the lion, and the child. First, as a camel you take on the load of your culture and the traditions and techniques of your discipline. Once loaded, the camel runs out into the desert where it becomes a lion. Your job as a lion is to slay a dragon named "Thou Shalt," thus destroying what you have mastered and overthrowing the established culture. Finally you become a child. As a child, a wheel rolling out of its own center, it is your task to build the new, which you can do only by projecting your own, self-generated vision.

You may have heard that the Harry Potter stories sprang fully formed into the head of their author, J. K. Rowling, while she was waiting for a delayed train. She states: "I had been writing almost continuously since the age of six but I had never been so excited about an idea before. To my immense frustration, I didn't have a functioning pen with me, and I was too shy to ask anybody if I could borrow one. I think, now, that this was probably a good thing, because I simply sat and thought, for four (delayed train) hours, and all the details bubbled up in my brain, and this scrawny, black-haired, bespectacled boy who didn't know he was a wizard became more and more real to me." Rowling had absorbed the stories of Merlin, including those in Malory's *Le Morte d'Arthur*, in which Merlin, who could not be killed, was buried in a cave, to come back when England needed him. And she had read T. H. White's description of the education of young King Arthur in *The Once and Future King*, titled after the inscription on Arthur's tomb, "Here lies Arthur, king once, and king to be." Rowling's years of reading prepared her for what became for both her and the world a great creation and a great adventure. (We mention Rowling here not just because of the phenomenal success of her Harry Potter books, but, as we will see later, for her role as a Visionary Creative—the way in which her work internalizes mythological archetypes.)

For the first twenty-five years of her life, Rowling did not know that she was going to write her Harry Potter novels, so she could not have known what material would be important for her future creativity. The late cofounder and CEO of Apple, Steve Jobs, in his Stanford address, said, "You can't connect the dots looking forward; you can only connect them looking backwards." Jobs could not have anticipated that the calligraphy course he sat in on after dropping out of Reed College would lead to his designing the Mac computer with elegant typefaces, thus not only creating a more pleasing visual experience, but also contributing to the growth of visual thinking, something we will discuss later. So perhaps your preparation should be rather broad.

In *Part Three* we describe the world in which Visionary Creatives are working today and the world they will create in the future. We have a tendency to see ourselves and our world as stable. The commonplace view is that new technologies bring new circumstances and opportunities, but who we are fundamentally, and what our world is fundamentally, remain constant. In this book we challenge that view. From the Renaissance until the mid-nineteenth century, we were discrete individuals, private psychological Selves, existing in a culture—on a stage—of uniform space, time and causality. In the late nineteenth and early twentieth century a new environment of electric media—the telegraph, telephone, radio, television—brought about a new Self in continual self-creating flux living on a stage with no fixed frames of reference, a flow of relativistic space-time, intermingled with our consciousness, a world that was more a great thought than a great machine.

And today's emerging digital world is creating yet again a new Self, one constituted of interconnected fractal networks computationally generating themselves and the world. Okay, that's a lot of jargon, but we will make sense of it as we go along.

Your Own Work

Few of us can aspire in our creativity to be like Einstein, Dalí, Nietzsche, Rowling, Jobs, or the other creative figures we will discuss, so at first we might think that this book would not pertain to our own creativity. But there are in fact many lessons we can all learn from these figures. And a few of the figures we will encounter were exceptional not in their talents, but in their accomplishments. Let's look at Gregor Mendel, who, next to Charles Darwin, is one of the most important people in the development of the theory of evolution. Mendel, a monk who twice flunked his exam to become a teacher, was nevertheless both curious and observant. In simplified terms, he asked what would happen if you crossbred

8

peas that have red flowers with peas that have white flowers. Everybody assumed you would get pink flowers, but nobody had ever tried it and actually paid attention to the results. It turns out that three quarters of the offspring have red flowers and one quarter have white flowers. None have pink flowers. From this Mendel was able to work out the basic principles of genetics, not by having a soaring IQ, but by having the simple curiosity to ask a question to which everyone else thought they knew the answer.

Here is another example of a "What if?" scenario: Of course Einstein was brilliant. But so were the physicist Hendrik Lorentz and the mathematician Henri Poincaré, both of whom were also working on the problem of the Michelson-Morley experiment (which we will discuss later). What differentiated Einstein from these other two was that he made the leap to ask, "What if I assume that there is no absolute reference against which to measure the motion of an observer, and that is why the speed of light is constant for all observers, no matter how they are moving relative to a light source?" The result was the theory of relativity, one of the two pillars of modern physics. (The other is quantum theory. More on both later.)

We see this positing of "What if...?" everywhere in Visionary Creativity. Here are just a few examples in music: Igor Stravinsky's *The Firebird*, produced by the impresario Sergei Diaghilev, was enthusiastically received in Paris. Stravinsky then asked, "What if I use the eroticism of primitive drums driving a human sacrifice in a musical composition?" The audience rioted at the premier of *The Rite of Spring* and Stravinsky's reputation was made. Elvis asked, "What if I take county music classics like "Blue Moon of Kentucky," speed them up, intensify the beat, and back them with an aggressive guitar?" He got Rock and Roll. Johnny Cash asked, "What if I take 'Ring of Fire,' which my future sister-in-law has recorded, and add mariachi-style Mexican horns?" He got the biggest hit of his career. The Beatles asked, "What if we use a symphony orchestra in a rock album?" The result was *Sgt. Pepper's Lonely Hearts Club Band,* now referred to as the most important Rock and Roll album ever made. And Bob Dylan, whose audience had decided he was a folk singer, asked, "What if I put down my acoustic guitar and pick up an electric guitar?" He did at the Newport Folk Festival, where he was booed by his folk music fans. He incorporated the electric guitar in his album *Bringing It All Back Home,* the first cut of which, "Subterranean Homesick Blues," owes more to the "lowbrow commercial" genre Rock and Roll than to folk music, deriving from Chuck Berry's "Too Much Monkey Business." But he found a broader audience and became one of the twentieth century's most important cultural figures.

So one of the lessons of this book is to question the obvious, test your ideas, and pay attention to the results. Ask yourself what in your field is obvious to everyone else but seems somehow not right to you, and then ask, "What if?" Doing so just might open productive lines of exploration.

Valuing Creativity

Why are we so interested in creativity? Let's go back to the question we asked earlier about the qualities to which we aspire. We first suggested that these qualities were things like wealth, power, and beauty, and, then we considered creativity. Could it be that even when we aspire to or admire qualities such as wealth, it is often creativity that we really have in mind?

Think of some of the wealthy people now on our radar screens: the late Steve Jobs, Sergey Brin and Larry Page, Bill Gates, Donald Trump, Richard Fuld. Notice that we have placed this small selection not in the order of their wealth, but in the order of how much we admire them. We admire

Steve Jobs of Apple for his role in bringing computers and other digital devices to "the rest of us" that are easy to use, elegantly designed, and that enrich us. We admire Sergey Brin and Larry Page for creating Google, which is organizing all of the world's information to make it accessible and useful. (Although we are perhaps getting a bit nervous as we realize that *all* of the world's information includes everything about each of us, but more on that later when we discuss the end of privacy.) Bill Gates is further down the list because while we admire his philanthropy, and while the company he founded, Microsoft, has brought us useful software, it was not always focused on the elegance and ease of use of its products. Steve Jobs was asked some years ago what he disliked about Microsoft, at the time Apple's archrival, and after a pause he replied that Microsoft had "no taste—and I mean that in the big sense." Donald Trump is on our list for starting his career by building in New York during bad economic times when others had abandoned the city, but further down because he has also created a brand of crass pseudo sophistication.

Last on our brief list, and least admired, is Richard Fuld, former CEO of the now bankrupt Wall Street banking firm, Lehman Brothers. Banking firms have traditionally been financers of new business, often creating entire industries in the process. For example, Mellon Bank was the driving force behind Alcoa, Gulf Oil, Westinghouse, U.S. Steel, Heinz, General Motors, Standard Oil, and other companies that defined an earlier age of American industrial might. Lehman itself had helped create Radio Corporation of America, a broadcast pioneer; DuMont, one of the first television manufacturers; and Digital Equipment Corporation, a computer pioneer. More recently, venture capital firms have played similar roles in financing the digital technology companies that define Silicon Valley. But most Wall Street banks today, as exemplified by Fuld's Lehman corporation, no longer make their money by backing new businesses, but by trading for their own accounts. Put simply, they gamble. Fuld and other bankers had doubled down their companies' bets until their losses threatened to bring down the entire world financial system.

While many would probably agree with this ranking of the admirability of these wealthy people, they might not realize why they gravitate to some and away from others. I suggest that it has to do with creativity. We admire those who create great things and we are indifferent to those who create things that are not well conceived, while we do not admire at all those who do not create but leach off of those who do.

And power? Of course we remember villains, but we also remember leaders who are associated with periods of creativity: Pericles, who ruled Athens during its golden age; Catherine the Great, who brought the Enlightenment to Russia; and Franklin Roosevelt, who imagined modern America. But more often we remember a period for its creative figures, not its political leaders. For example, we remember Pope Julius II, who commissioned Michelangelo's Sistine Chapel ceiling frescos, because of his tempestuous relationship with his artist, but do we remember Leonardo da Vinci's patron in Milan or the clergyman who commissioned Palladio to build the Villa Rotunda? Do we remember the French nobleman who had Voltaire imprisoned on a personal writ or the rulers of Austria when Mozart and Beethoven composed their music? Do we remember the rulers of France when Pasteur was researching microorganisms and Monet was painting his poplar trees; or when Cézanne was painting his *The Bathers*; or when members of the Lost Generation, including Ernest Hemingway, F. Scott Fitzgerald, Ezra Pound, T. S. Eliot, Sherwood Anderson, John Dos Passos, John Steinbeck, and Cole Porter, were meeting in Parisian salons? Do we remember who the governors of California were when Hewlett-Packard, Intel, Apple, and

Google were launched? For the most part, we do not, but we do remember the leading creative figures of many eras, beginning with Imhotep, the architect of the first Egyptian pyramid.

We could go on and look at beauty. We admired Marilyn Monroe in the 1950s not just for her beauty, but for the way she created a vulnerable femininity both onscreen and off that captured and also helped create her time; Elizabeth Taylor in the 1960s for her tempestuous emotionality also both onscreen and off that captured and also helped create her time; and we admire Angelina Jolie today for the way she plays her asexual onscreen action heroes against her off-screen mothering, philanthropy, advocacy, movie producing and directing, and for her courage dealing with her health problems in a search for a new femininity for our time. And before these stars, we admired Jean Harlow for the way she reflected changing social and economic circumstances in one of America's most tumultuous periods when she moved from blonde bombshell to more serious roles that paralleled her real life problems as the Great Depression wore on, all transpiring in just seven years from 1930 until her death from kidney failure at the age of twenty-six. We admire creativity, and when we admire wealth, political power, or beauty, we are often still admiring creativity.

What distinguishes the figures we have mentioned so far? Of course they are exceptional and they bring us pleasure and illumination. But there is more to it than that. *All of these Visionary Creatives felt that our world was no longer what we had thought it to be and that a new world was struggling to be born. They wondered what was wrong with others that they did not also feel this, and they were driven to produce works that would help others experience what they experienced. Their audiences, on encountering them were changed and they entered new worlds.*

13

PART ONE:
■ WHAT IS CREATIVITY

CREATIVITY IS...

In which we see that Visionary Creativity is a type of creativity that is immersed in its culture and at the same time remakes its culture; and we also see that Visionary Creativity takes place not only in the arts, but also in science, technology, and business. We further see that in our time, our notion of a person is very different from what it was during the Renaissance. And we discover how mastery, innovation, ordinary creativity and Visionary Creativity all differ from each other.

"Yes, that's it! That's what I have been trying to imagine but did not until now have the imagery."
~ *Imagined thought of a sixteenth century Florentine*

Michelangelo and Mark Zuckerberg

What do Michelangelo Buonarroti and Mark Zuckerberg have in common? Yes, this is one of those grabber questions authors sometimes use. To justify it, the author should show that there is a significant commonality, and that this commonality points to something important. Let's see how we will go about doing both.

Michelangelo and Zuckerberg, as well as other figures we will look at in this book, are *Visionary Creatives*. They accomplished not just mastery, innovation, or even ordinary creativity, but *Visionary Creativity*. The work of the Visionary Creative is embedded in its culture, and, in a circular process, it is instrumental in the destruction and re-creation of that culture.

17

We can imagine the morning of September 8 in 1504 when Michelangelo's sculpture, *David*, on which he had worked in secret for three years, was drawn from his studio into Florence's Piazza della Signoria. *David* was seventeen feet tall, truly monumental, and there must have at first been shock, followed by realization: "Yes, that's it! That's what I have been trying to imagine but did not until now have the imagery to do so." David, a symbol of Florentine independence is, of course, an Old Testament figure, but the sculptural style is that of ancient Greece, thus fusing together Biblical and Greek traditions. *David* was simultaneously the embodiment of Renaissance humanism with its focus on the human figure, and a stretching of that idea.

In Europe before the Renaissance, the most important component of one's Self was an eternal soul that was thought to reside temporarily in an ephemeral vessel. The humanists, including Michelangelo and his fellow artists, experienced something new, seeing the Self as a complex unity of body, mind, and soul. The magnificence of *David*'s anatomy celebrates the body and connects the Florentines to the ancient Greeks through its similarity to Greek sculpture, while its piercing eyes are windows into a private mind at work, a psychology. Humanism, born out of the books made possible by the new technology of the printing press, focused its understanding on both who we are as physical beings and on the private mental processes inside of our heads. Still, *David* was a stretch for the Florentines of the day. It was, indeed, a *discontinuity*, the difference between what the Florentines had been anticipating and what they actually encountered, which helped destroy the medieval world view in which the body was only a vessel, and crystallize the new humanist vision that some anachronistically still hold today. As we will see later, we now live in a very different world.

The growth of Mark Zuckerberg's online social network,

18

Facebook, was so spectacular that it has led to the Silicon Valley garage being challenged by the Harvard dorm room as an icon for an innovation incubator. On February 4 in 2004, Zuckerberg, then a Harvard sophomore, pressed the enter key on his laptop computer and launched Thefacebook, later to become just Facebook. Facebook allows users to "link" to and communicate with "friends," and to post profiles, personal updates, photographs, "likes," and other material for their friends to see. While several websites already had many of these features, Facebook brought them together in a compelling way and quickly grew to become one of the world's most valuable companies. Stories of Facebook typically focus on the personalities of its founders and its rapid growth, thus missing its significance, which is that of facilitating our migration from inside our skins out to the digital cloud, thus destroying the individual psychological Self of Michelangelo's humanist world and opening us up to a new and still unfolding world.

We are more than our bodies, minds, and souls. We are also our memories, roles, relationships, friends, papers, photos, etc. Our identities began migrating outside of our skins as soon as we started making art, and the pace of that migration increased with writing and then again with printing. But the pace greatly accelerated in the late nineteenth century as we began to weave an electric net around our planet, and exploded with the Internet as we now deposit vast parts of ourselves—our memories, records, images—in networked server farms around the world, known as the cloud. Zuckerberg's Facebook greatly extends this process of exporting more and more of ourselves into the cloud and facilitates the sharing of this material, thus dissolving the private humanist vision created by the printed book and crystallized by Michelangelo and creating a new vision. This destruction of the old and creation of the new is the role of the Visionary Creative, and the reason the Visionary Creative is both celebrated and sometimes feared. As we will discuss later, the vociferous objections to the Internet in general and Facebook in particular regarding privacy are actually reactions to the ongoing destruction of the private psychological Self that had been a defining feature of the previous culture. Such changes are always threatening.

So what do Michelangelo and Zuckerberg have in common? They both mastered their disciplines, Michelangelo carving stone and Zuckerberg coding; both were innovative and both were creative. But we are linking them here because they were both Visionary Creatives. Both experienced a new world coursing through them, and both were motivated to make apparent to others what was obvious to them: that the world had changed, it no longer was what it had been. Visionary Creatives, as we will come to understand in this book, manifest the spirit of the age in their work and at the same time propel that spirit forward into a continually unfolding future, destroying old worlds and building new ones. And now Visionary Creatives are building our twenty-first century, the most radically different period the human race has ever experienced.

You might wonder about the choice of Zuckerberg to compare to Michelangelo. Why not Steve Jobs? Jobs is a revered creative figure and we will indeed look at him later. But in this example we are looking at our movement out of our skins to become a new kind of creature, and Zuckerberg's Facebook plays a major role in that movement. As we say again and again, the things Visionary Creatives create—in art, design, science, technology, business—embody their culture and at the same time pull us into an unfolding future, a future with which we are not always happy.

From Mastery to Visionary Creativity

As we said in the introduction, creativity is vital to all parts of our lives. Individually, we can be either passive consumers or active creators; economically, we can compete by lowering the cost of labor, or by creating new technologies, goods, and services; socially, we can live in the past or create the future, and most importantly, culturally, we can either keep alive in Western culture the moral and creative center at the heart of each individual, or we can surrender that responsibility. In each case, creativity is crucial. But while creativity is now widely discussed, it is seldom fully understood, and creativity is often confused with mastery and innovation.

Mastery

In the past few years several writers looking at mastery have relied on the work of psychologist K. Anders Ericsson, who shows that mastery of just about any discipline requires ten thousand hours of "deliberate practice"—working on technique, seeking feedback, and addressing weaknesses. The disciplines that have been extensively studied to make this determination include music, painting, poetry, tennis, and chess. It should be obvious that masters of a discipline acquire and maintain mastery through practice, but there is perhaps some usefulness to these studies, as they can both confirm and discredit some of our assumptions. For example, these studies show that dedicated practice that pushes boundaries and leads to mistakes that have to be worked through is highly productive, while practice that endlessly repeats material already mastered is of little benefit.

Besides in Ericsson's own work, you can find references to the ten thousand hours thing in several books, including Malcolm Gladwell's *Outliers* and David Shenk's *The Genius in All of Us*. Gladwell claims that what differentiated the Beatles from other rock groups was their many hours of performing in Hamburg, Germany, and that Mozart's work when he was young was unexceptional; he did not excel until he had put in ten thousand hours. But this is questionable. It may indeed have taken

Mozart and the Beatles ten thousand hours to acquire their mastery, but it was not just mastery that made their music great rather than merely accomplished. When Mozart's rival Antonio Salieri reached ten thousand hours, his work did not then equal Mozart's in luminous insight. And Elvis Presley did not put in ten thousand hours before doing his first and best work, the Sun Recordings. Practice certainly helped Mozart and the Beatles to convey their insights, but the more interesting question is, what were these insights and how did they achieve them?

Mastery is not innovation.

Innovation

One can master one's discipline and perform well without ever creating anything new. Creating something new is innovation.

In *Outliers* Gladwell looks at exceptional people, but mostly attempts to debunk exceptionalism. One of his portraits is of a girl who attended a special inner city school that required long hours and lots of homework. After graduation, the girl got a good job as a bookkeeper. A laudable achievement, but it did not make her a mathematician. Gladwell could have told the story of George Bernard Dantzig. One day Dantzig, a graduate student at Berkeley, arrived late to a class in statistics and quickly copied down two problems from the blackboard that he thought were the homework assignment. The problems seemed harder than usual, and he struggled with them for a few days but was finally able to solve them and turn in his long overdue "homework." His professor informed him that he had solved two of the most famous unsolved problems in statistical mathematics and Dantzig went on to make important contributions to linear programming. Try to assign seventy people to seventy jobs. The number of possible combinations is larger than the number of particles in the universe, and no computer can tackle the problem by brute force. But with Dantzig's simplex algorithm (an algorithm is a systematic approach to a problem that proceeds through a series of prescribed steps), regarded as one of the top ten algorithms of the twentieth century, such problems, which are fundamental to the distributions of just about all goods and services, are now solvable. (As in finding the shortest route for a FedEx truck in making its deliveries.) Gladwell's bookkeeper achieved mastery, but not innovation. Neither Gladwell's *Outliers* nor Shenk's *The Genius in All of Us* tell stories like Dantzig's, as such stories do not support their contention that we can all be outliers or geniuses.

Now that technology is changing rapidly and business is global with intense competition coming from everywhere, we have become very interested in innovation, and we will refer to some important studies in business later. For now, Steven Johnson's *Where Good Ideas Come From* is a good example of current understandings, identifying seven key elements in innovation. These include: *The adjacent possible*, for which he uses an image of a series of connected rooms, each with a door in each of its four walls. As you move from room to room, you continually have new possibilities, but you can never skip a room. Innovation can only be built on what is already established. *Liquid networks*, which provide support for innovation. *The slow hunch*, in which ideas may germinate for years before crystallizing. *The serendipity of accidental connection,* in which connections are made that could not have been anticipated. *Errors*, which can eventually lead to great ideas. *Exaptation*, the repurposing of already existing ideas in unforeseen ways. And finally *platforms*, on which innovations can be built.

And Tony Wagner, in his book, *Creating Innovators*, looks at how our educational system stifles young innovators and what we can do about it. Innovation is important for both the fulfillment of innovators and for a prosperous future, and it should be encouraged.

But innovation is not creativity.

Ordinary Creativity

It is interesting to see how approaches to creativity reflect the social ethos of the time. When individual achievement was valued, we were told that creativity comes from rare individuals of genius. In our current era of egalitarian values, we are told that we are all creative, and that creativity comes from collaboration.

Our current understandings of creativity? Creativity is the bringing into being of something new that was not previously obvious, and that exhibits beauty or utility. And beyond that? Most studies that purport to be about creativity are actually about mastery or innovation, while the best studies of creativity are biographies of artists, scientists, and other creatives. Of the few studies that actually address creativity, the earliest that is still commonly referred to is Graham Wallas's 1926 *The Art of Thought*, which presents what he calls "Stage Decomposition." Wallas sees creativity as a four-stage process: preparation, incubation, insight, and verification. There is much of value in Wallas's book, but no examples of art or science that we admire.

The most rewarding book on creativity is Arthur Koestler's 1964 *The Act of Creation*, which suggests that creative insights come from the shaking together by the unconscious mind of previously unconnected ideas. Koestler, a brilliant polymath, began his career as a literary and political figure, and ended it by writing a series of books on the history of science seen in cultural terms. *The Act of Creation* is rich with examples, and from time to time it is rediscovered by those studying creativity.

In addressing creativity, it is tempting to look at psychological studies. A very brief survey of the literature shows that before the 1970s, creativity was correlated to IQ. After the 70s, it no longer was. By then bipolar and other mood disorders were being studied, and creativity was connected to these disorders. There is some sense to this, as manics can obviously get

24

a lot done. Creativity is now also connected to schizophrenia-like symptoms such as hallucinations, hearing voices, having disorganized thoughts, and believing in magic. The claim is that these conditions cause the brains of creative people to be more open to incoming stimuli than those of noncreative people.

In the late 1970s direct measurements of brainwaves showed that creativity comes in two stages, inspiration and elaboration, each characterized by very different states of mind. One study found that while subjects were dreaming up stories, their brains were quiet, with the dominant activity being alpha waves. Then when the subjects were asked to develop their stories, the alpha waves dropped off and their brains became busier, revealing increased cortical arousal. The people who showed the biggest difference in brain activity between the inspiration and development stages produced the most creative stories. This change in activity was particularly noticeable on the right side of the brain. At one time some psychologists referred to creativity as a "right brain activity," and logical thinking as a "left brain activity," but these notions are no longer current. Later we will look at some recent developments in neuroscience that may help us to better understand creativity, but for now, the kind of research referred to above is of little help to those who aspire to be creative.

In the 1700s, craftsmen made marvelous mechanical birds that could walk about, sing, eat, and excrete. The feeling was that animals, and even humans, were machines, and these mechanical birds were evidence that we would soon be able to create life. In 1816, as electricity was being studied, Mary Shelley, then eighteen, composed the story that was to become *Frankenstein; or, The Modern Prometheus*, based on the notion that electricity could animate non-living matter. When telephone switchboards were developed, we were told that the brain is a switchboard, and when cybernetics was developed we were told that the brain is a feedback mechanism. Then when digital computers were developed, we were told that the brain is a digital computer and we would soon be able to make computers that would exhibit artificial intelligence. Now quantum computers are being developed and we are told that consciousness is a consequence of quantum computing done by the brain. Perhaps. But we must ask, has information like this ever helped a creative person? Knowing which clusters of neurons in the brain fire during creative activities is unlikely to help you or me write a book, make a painting, design a building, or make a movie.

In her book, *The Creating Brain*, neuropsychiatrist Nancy C. Andreasen notes that creative people have a fresh take on the world, ignore the rules, see things that others cannot, are open to ambiguity, reject absolutism, and inhabit a world without boundaries. In addition, Andreasen states that creative people tend to enjoy adventure, like to explore, dislike externally imposed rules, are indifferent to convention, are sensitive, are durable and are persistent in spite of repeated rebuffs, are intensely curious, have a singleness of vision, are dedicated to their work, and sometimes are mentally ill. Think for a minute; does this really tell us anything? It's very likely you can think of highly creative people who have the exact opposites of many of these characteristics. Debunkers of astrology point out how astrologers write their predictions in such a way that anyone can read anything into them. Do you sometimes get that feeling when you read about creativity?

Wallas, Koestler, Kuhn, and Andreasen do not look at creativity that is situated in specific cultural contexts nor do they focus on examples that changed the world.

Ordinary creativity is not Visionary Creativity.

Visionary Creativity

We referred before to Arthur Koestler's *The Act of Creation*. Two years earlier, in 1962, Thomas Kuhn published *The*

26

Structure of Scientific Revolutions. Kuhn, in seeking to explain how scientific ideas develop, introduced the now common term "paradigm shift" to refer to a change in a broad scientific mindset, and as a result of his book we now often use "paradigm" synonymously with "worldview." Prior to Kuhn, we had been told that science advances incrementally as new data accumulates and necessitates new theories to accommodate it. Kuhn shows that this is not the case. Science works within sets of assumptions that cannot be proven, but that seem obvious. But then these assumptions no longer seem obvious to a group of young scientists, who adopt a new paradigm in a paradigm shift. We will revisit these concepts later, but for now let's just say that a paradigm shift, which introduces a whole new way of experiencing the world, is an act of Visionary Creativity.

As we stated above and will be repeating throughout this book, Visionary Creativity is both embedded in its culture and recreates its culture anew.

Creative people, who we call "creatives" in this book are, as others have noted, those who bring into being something new of beauty or utility. Creatives may indeed be open to strange ideas and be able to shake together seemingly unrelated elements in their unconscious minds. And they may prepare for their work with long hours of study and practice. Finally, creatives may even be able to access parts of their brains that remain inaccessible to others. All of this is now being studied, yet all of it misses the most important attribute of *Visionary Creatives*, which is their immersion in their culture and their need to drive it forward into an unfolding future.

In *Outliers*, Malcolm Gladwell refers to a study which shows that once students have been admitted to a top music school—thus sorting out those with real talent—success is correlated with hours of practice. Those putting in over ten thousand hours gain positions in major orchestras. Besides the problem of cause and effect (in other words, does the ten thousand hours cause the success, or does motivation cause the ten thousand hours as well as the success), the major problem here is a confusion of mastery and ordinary creativity with Visionary Creativity. Playing in a major orchestra, of course, requires mastery and creativity, but it is not the same thing as being a composer who enters into the spirit of the time and redefines the course of music as is the case with every major composer. That requires Visionary Creativity.

We see something similar in architecture. Frank Lloyd Wright did not attend architecture school—there were very few in the country when he was young—and didn't even finish engineering school, but he was one of the more talented young architects in Chicago when he got a job with Louis Sullivan. However, there were several talented young architects in Chicago at the time intensely discussing architecture, including John Wellborn Root. Wright chose to work with the rebellious iconoclast, Sullivan, who was intent on embodying the American democratic spirit in his work, and Wright was going to take the same course for himself. (Think of Howard Roark in Ayn Rand's novel, *The Fountainhead*, choosing to work with Henry Cameron.) Root chose to work with Daniel Burnham (think Peter Keating choosing to work for Francon & Heyer) who was a masterful architect, but more intent on getting major commissions than changing the course of architecture. The hours were the same. The difference between Wright and Root (besides the fact that Wright outlived Root) was the choices they made regarding what they wanted to devote their lives to, a comfortable career or changing the world.

Academic psychology does make an effort to understand this kind of creativity by referring to "little-c and big-C creativity." The website of the American Psychological Association states: "Little-c creativity, which is often used as an indicator of mental health, includes everyday problem-solving and the ability to adapt to change. Big-C creativity, on the other hand, is far more rare. It occurs when a person solves a problem or creates an object that has a major impact on how other people think, feel and live their lives."

So they almost get it, but not quite. Visionary Creativity does not just have "a major impact on how other people think..." It creates the very world in which we all live! Steve Jobs did not just "have a major impact," he created a new world. As did Einstein and Dalí, as we saw above. As do all of the Visionary Creatives we discuss in this book.

The typical failing of those who study creativity is that they regard our selves and our world as fundamentally un-changing. Yes, they think new technologies bring about super-ficial changes, but at our cores we and the world remain the same. They believe that what we are as human beings, the val-ues by which we live, and the stage on which we act out our lives, are fixed realities for all people in all times and places, including the future. They mistakenly believe that what is merely the culture of our place and time is a universal reality. Friedrich Nietzsche, the late nineteenth century German philosopher and predictor of much of the moral structure of our modern world, writes:

Lack of a historical sense is the failing of all philosophers who, without being aware of it, take the man of the day, one who has arisen within certain religions or political events, as the fixed form for all of humanity.

As we will see throughout this book, we do not live in a universal reality, not even the one described by science. We live in cultures. Visionary Creatives are aware that the world in which they live is provisional, always changing. The under-lying motivation of Visionary Creatives is to make apparent to others through their work what is obvious to them, namely, that our world is no longer what it seems. Thus creativity and culture exist in a virtuous circle of destruction and generation in which created works acquire their meanings only in cultural contexts.

Abandoning Assumptions

One key to Visionary Creativity is the courage to reject established assumptions. Here are three examples. As we will discuss later, Einstein's relativity addresses the observation that the speed of light is always the same for all observers no matter their motion, and makes the constancy of the speed of light a fundamental part of his theory in violation of the principle of the addition of velocities. The Dutch physicist, Hendrik Lorentz, attempted to resolve the issue with what is called the Lorentz transformation that made assumptions about the dimensions of an object changing as it moves through space. In developing relativity, Einstein began with the Lorentz transformation, but changed one thing. He said that the speed of light is always constant and the addition of velocities does not apply because there is no fixed absolute space. Einstein was able to jettison an assumption that Lorentz held on to.

Another example involves John von Neumann. A towering genius born in Hungary who immigrated to America, Von Neumann was a polymath. He was a leading quantum theorist, he codified the architecture of the modern computer, pioneered game theory, worked on cellular automata, explored self-replicating machines, and he played a key role in creating the hydrogen bomb. While at a meeting he worked out on the fly an interpretation of quantum theory based on Hilbert space, which extends Euclidian space to infinite dimensions, so that the aging mathematician, David Hilbert, could understand the theory. Between 1905 and 1971, eight Hungarians won Nobel prizes, and there would have been at least two more if there were a Nobel Prize in mathematics. When asked why so many geniuses came from Hungary, Eugene Wigner, himself one of the Hungarian Nobel Prize winners, replied, "Hungary has produced only one genius. His name is John von Neumann."

Von Neumann also made major contributions to logic and wrote papers that hinted at the possibility that logic was built on a foundation of sand. But he did not make the leap, and it was left to his colleague at the Institute for Advanced Studies, Kurt Gödel, to show the inherent inconsistency in all of logic and mathematics. It would have been a short step for Neumann to reach the same conclusion earlier, but he did not take it.

For our third example of abandoning assumptions, let's look very briefly at Andy Warhol. Later we will refer to David Karp, founder of the social networking site, Tumblr, as a "mobile online digital native." Let's see how Andy Warhol was a "popular culture native." Later we will refer to Cezanne and to Picasso. By the 1960s and 70s we can see how the bowls of fruit in muted colors by Cezanne and Picasso would have looked antiquated to Andy Warhol. His world was one of flu-orescent-lit supermarkets, brightly colored packaging, images in magazines, and pop celebrities. Andy was immersed in that world, and continually documented it. And he not only aban-doned European assumptions about art, he also rejected the entire notion of high culture.

The fact that Andy Warhol began his career as a com-mercial illustrator doing images for advertising played a role in this. But equally important was the decade of the late 1960s through the late 1970s in which he did his pioneering work, which also influenced him, and which he did much to create. Before this period, there was a sharp distinction between pop-ular culture and high culture. In high school you listened to

Rock and Roll. In college you switched to jazz, and later to classical music. In junior high you read comic books. In high school you switched to Camus, and in college to the serious stuff like Dostoyevsky. Hollywood made popular culture movies. The Swedes, French, and Italians made high culture movies. But then the influential *New Yorker* movie critic, Pauline Kael, blurred the distinction and found serious intensions in popular American movies. The distinction between popular culture and high culture broke down. The emerging generation, as it grew up, continued to read comics, which became serious in the form of comix. Rock and Roll became Rock. And you could read Kurt Vonnegut as a kid and as an adult.

That was the world in which Warhol launched his career. He would not play by the rules of the past, and in his art he mixed the worlds of nightlife, the society pages, the drug culture, and his superstars, the strange orchids who gathered at his Factory and who are celebrated in Lou Reed's 1972 song, "Walk on the Wild Side." Andy's work included, besides paintings of soup cans, sculptures that looked just like the cartons in which Brillo pads were delivered to the grocery store, silk screens based on tabloid photos, and portraits of celebrities including Marilyn, Liz, Elvis, and Jackie. And he collected just about everything, going on endless shopping sprees.

Andy was a brilliant artist, but his success was as much due to the fact that he was a "popular culture native," living in the world of popular culture, not the previous world of "serious art." And he did as much as anyone to create that emerging world. Andy abandoned the assumption that art had to be "serious," and took us on a joy ride with his Pop Art and his antics, but more than that he brought us a new culture, one that broke down the barrier of a fortified high culture exclusivity.

And today? After all, Andy Warhol did much of his work a half a century ago, and although it still rings true for many of those who grew up with it, we need to ask, are we still in that world? Looking at the work of Jeff Koons, we might answer, yes. But what about much younger artists? Since 1923, the Scholastic Art and Writing Awards have recognized creative accomplishments of American teenagers. Previous winners have included Truman Capote, Sylvia Plath and Lena Dunham. And Andy Warhol. Seventeen-year-old Ellie Braun is a recent winner who is about to enter art school, and while Cezanne painted bowls of fruit and card players, Picasso painted guitars and art dealers, and Warhol painted soup cans and celebrities, Braun paints boys in girls' clothes. And cupcakes. Will Braun become the next Warhol? No way to tell, but someone like her, immersed in our time, will.

CREATIVITY IN CULTURAL CONTEXT

In which we see that culture stores our extended memories, and that Visionary Creativity is embedded in its culture and at the same time advances its culture. And we see that in any era numerous creative forms share similar underlying structures.

Perspective is nothing more than a rational demonstration applied to the consideration of how objects in front of the eye transmit their image to it.
~ Leonardo da Vinci

Culture as a Store of Ourselves

As we stated earlier, it is difficult for us to see our own culture or even recognize the very concept of culture; we tend to see our world as "real," rather than one of many possible systems of meanings. But over time and across the globe, not all people experience the world the same way. In acts of cognition, we process the impressions that come in through our senses, and the way we do this is different in different times and places. These differences define cultures.

We store much of ourselves in our culture, particularly in our arts. Recall the end of Ridley Scott's science fiction movie *Blade Runner*. In the movie, androids are created to work off-planet, are forbidden to come to earth, and are programmed to die in full health. Those who do come to earth are hunted by special police. The android Roy Batty, played by Rutger Hauer, as he is dying, says, "I've seen things you people wouldn't believe. Attack ships on fire off the shoulder of Orion. I've watched C-beams glitter in the dark near the Tannhauser Gate. All those moments will be lost in time, like tears in the rain. Time to die." He releases a white dove that carries away his experiences as he dies. The androids have no cultural forms, no art or literature, in which to store their memories.

Spirit of the Age

We said above that Visionary Creatives swim in the culture of their day and manifest in their work the spirit of their age. What do we mean by "spirit of the age?" Earlier we quoted the English Romantic poet, Percy Bysshe Shelley. Here is the context for that quote:

> It is impossible to read the compositions of the most celebrated writers of the present day without being startled with the electric life which burns within their words. They measure the circumference and sound the depths of human nature with a comprehensive and all penetrating spirit, and they are themselves perhaps the most sincerely astonished at its manifestations; for it is less their spirit than the spirit of the age. Poets are the hierophants of an unapprehended inspiration; the mirrors of the gigantic shadows which futurity casts upon the present; the words which express what they understand not; the trumpets which sing to battle, and feel not what they inspire; the influence which is moved not, but moves. Poets are the unacknowledged legislators of the world.

The great American architect, Frank Lloyd Wright, says, "Every great architect is—necessarily—a great poet. He must be a great original interpreter of his time, his day, his age." And the modern architect of glass and steel, Mies van der

36

Rohe, writes, "Architecture is the real battleground of the spirit.... Architecture depends on its time. It is the crystallization of its inner structure, the slow unfolding of its form."

While Shelly speaks about poetry and Wright and Mies speak about architecture, we can use their words to apply to all that we create. The true work of Visionary Creativity must express the spirit of its age, but it must also extend it; it must envision a future and carry us into it. The media theorist Marshall McLuhan refers to art as a distant early warning system.

Artists, when speaking about creativity, use terms like "spirit of the age." And throughout this book we will use not only that term, but also others such as "culture," "world," "worldview," and "paradigm" all somewhat interchangeably. When speaking about creativity, psychologists do not use such terms; they cannot measure the spirit of an age or a worldview, and therefore they cannot use such terms in academic papers. In this book we will rely on the insights of artists more than the studies of psychologists.

Imagine a stormy sky filled with clouds of ideas about who we are and how we should live, our relationships to higher powers, our notions of how the universe works, and the natures of our technologies, arts, and popular culture. These clouds churn, spiral apart and crash together as in a Baroque painting or a Beethoven symphony. Then they begin to condense, with eddies swirling in on themselves; they begin to take shape, and then suddenly they crystallize. That crystal—a work of art or architecture, a design, a novel, a musical composition, a scientific theory, a new technology, a new industry—gives us the opportunity to directly experience in form the spirit of the age out of which it crystallized.

So, in an era that sees humans in terms of neurons and brain scans, in an era that sees cultures in terms of resources and memes, we are talking about storms, Baroque paintings, and Beethoven symphonies. Here we take a stand with

Oswald Spengler who stated at the beginning of his monumental study of cultures, *The Decline of the West*:

The means whereby we identify dead forms is Mathematical Law. The means whereby we understand living forms is Metaphor.

What is it that we mean by metaphor? Ananda K. Coomaraswamy, the great interpreter of Indian culture for the West, here paraphrased by Joseph Campbell, states:

[Metaphor is] ... the representation of a reality on a certain level of reference by a corresponding reality on another: death by sleep, for example, ... the light of the sun as of consciousness; the darkness of caves or of the ocean depth, as of death, or of the womb; the waning and waxing moon as a sign celestial of death and rebirth; and the serpent's sloughing of its skin as an earthly sign with the same sense.

We are sometimes tempted to think of great creative works as isolated examples of brilliance. They often are, but they are usually created in cultural climates that produce works in other fields with which they share underlying structures. For example, we find the same emotionally charged layered complexity in the Baroque churches in Rome by the architect Francesco Borromini that we find in the musical compositions of the German composer Johann Sebastian Bach. Even brilliant creations exist in contexts. We will examine creativity in cultural context throughout this book, but let's briefly look at several familiar examples to illustrate our approach: Galileo's heliocentric solar system, Beethoven's Third Symphony, Vincent van Gogh's *The Starry Night*, and Frank Gehry's Guggenheim Museum in Bilbao. But before we do, a cautionary note. These examples exist within vast movements comprised of countless

38

creative works. Our isolation of these examples exaggerates their roles in the changes we describe and we could have chosen others. Our examples are touch points in cultural development.

Galileo's Heliocentric Solar System

Galileo Galilei (1564–1642) holds an important position in the development of Western science, having made contributions that led to classical physics.

In his *Dialogue Concerning the Two Chief World Systems* published in 1632, Galileo championed the Copernican theory that put the Sun in the center of the solar system and the planets in circular orbits around it. Copernicus had originally proposed this to resolve a problem with the earlier model that placed the Earth in the center of the universe. In that model, the planets moved around the Earth, thus continually changing their positions relative to the "fixed stars," that is the stars that are stars and not planets, and that keep their positions relative to each other. But since the planets move around the Sun and not the Earth, they occasionally appear to change directions relative to the fixed stars and go backwards. This had been addressed with what were called epicycles, in which each planet is assumed to trace a miniature orbit within its orbit around the Earth. That model was getting messy, and Copernicus made strides in resolving the problem.

Galileo's interests went beyond just mapping planetary orbits. He was interested in motion in general, and his thinking, culminating a half century later in Newton's clockwork universe with its laws of motion and gravity, came about in the context of a new kind of thinking that imagined space and time as abstract, uniform, and continuous, and also as freezable in a moment of time. But this notion of space and time was not unique to Galileo and Newton. It appeared in Renaissance perspective painting over two hundred years before Galileo published his book.

We identify the Renaissance with humanism, which includes the idea that knowledge comes from ourselves rather than from faith or authority. We observe with our senses, and we then use our rational minds to analyze our observations and render them into scientific laws. Galileo used his pulse and rhythmic singing in order to time balls rolling down inclined planes to make the observations that underlay his laws of motion and gravity.

In 1413 the architect Filippo Brunelleschi demonstrated a method of perspective in painting that allowed him to project the three-dimensional world onto a two dimensional picture plane. Twenty years later, another architect, Leon Battista Alberti, wrote *De pictura*, formalizing the process. Let's look at a perspective drawing by Leonardo da Vinci, a study for his 1481 *Adoration of the Magi*. There are different kinds of perspective, the simplest one being called single point perspective. In this approach parallel lines going away from us recede to a vanishing point, like railroad tracks converging in the distance, and this is the approach Leonardo used in this case. The vanishing point is located on what is called the horizon line, which is determined by the level of the observer's eyes. So a perspective drawing or painting is dependent on the position of the observer—change that position and the perspective changes. In the *Adoration*, Leonardo drew guidelines to create the perspective and left them visible in the drawing. He writes:

Perspective is nothing more than a rational demonstration applied to the consideration of how objects in front of the eye transmit their image to it, by means of a pyramid of lines. The Pyramid is the name I apply to the lines which, starting from the surface and edges of each object, converge from a distance and meet in a single point.

Perspective painting gives us a world of uniform space freezable at one moment in time, creating a stage that can be

40

occupied by objects and events. And it establishes *a point of view of a human observer* rather than of God, as had been the approach of the earlier medieval painters. From God's point of view, everything is equidistant, since God is everywhere, so there is no need for perspective. From the early 1400s to the late 1800s painters used perspective, and creativity unfolded on a stage of uniform space and time. This is the same humanist point of view that was central to Galileo's science. So, while Galileo's understanding of motion was remarkable, it was not isolated; it occurred within the broad context of a human observer and uniform space and time that had appeared two centuries earlier in art and was later to become foundational to the philosophy of Immanuel Kant.

Beethoven's Third Symphony

In 1802, in the depths of despair over his loss of hearing, Ludwig van Beethoven (1770–1827) composed a "suicide note" now called the Heiligenstadt Testament after the town where he was living at the time. He then decided on another strategy. He would conquer his despair and remake himself as Romantic Hero.

In 1805 he premiered his Third Symphony, the *Eroica*, a piece displaying operatic heights and depths, the first of a series of works of unprecedented scale combining structural rigor summing up the classical style that they would end, and emotional depth signaling the Romantic style that they would unleash. Thus he announced his artistic rebirth as Romantic Hero in recreating the expressive nature of instrumental music and of the role of the artist as creator. The music critic William Kinderman writes, "What Beethoven explores in the *Eroica* are universal aspects of heroism, centering in the idea of a confrontation with adversity leading to a renewal of creative possibilities."

We get a sense of how this notion of Romantic Hero

41

was seen in Beethoven's time from part of the oration at his funeral: "Just as the behemoth storms through the sea, so [Beethoven] swept through the frontier limits of his art. From the gurgling of the dove to the roaring of thunder, from the most ingenious weaving together of the idiosyncratic artist's material to the fearful extreme, when the cultivation passes over into the unruly caprice of nature's struggling forces, he has taken the measure of everything, comprehending it all."

The *Eroica* is ultimately joyous and triumphant, signaling Beethoven's turn away from suicide. Not so for Werther, the protagonist of Johann Wolfgang von Goethe's *The Sorrows of Young Werther*, revised in 1787. Werther loves a woman he can never have, and after much sensitive suffering, commits suicide. Werther was so admired by the German youth of the day that the authorities had to keep watch at bridges.

We feel Werther's longing in Caspar David Friedrich's 1818 painting, *Wanderer Above the Sea of Fog*, showing a young man standing on a mountain top, looking down at peaks pressing above the clouds. We feel the power of nature in Friedrich's painting of a ship crushed in an ice flow and the power of nostalgia in his painting of a cloister in ruins. And we feel the grandeur of nature in the paintings of storms by J. M. W. Turner in front of which we abandon the belief that we can ever know nature or ourselves through rationality.

Romanticism celebrated individual freedom as well as the uniqueness of the creative, and it challenged the Enlightenment rationalism that was based on the notion that the reasoned thinking that was proving so successful in science could be applied to human affairs. Romanticism held that reason was not adequate to account for the awesome powers of nature or the depths of the human emotions. And Romanticism objected to generalizing nature into laws. The

Romantic poet William Blake writes:

Now I fourfold vision see
And a fourfold vision is given to me
Tis fourfold in my supreme delight
And three fold in soft Beulahs night
And twofold Always. May God us keep
From Single vision & Newton's sleep!

So Beethoven's Romantic vision was a personal triumph, but it took place in the context of a larger movement, Romanticism, a celebration of the energies of the human psyche and the powers of nature.

Van Gogh's The Starry Night

In Vincent van Gogh's (1853–1890) most famous painting, *The Starry Night* of 1889, everything is filled with energy. The dark flame of a cypress tree licks a living sky ablaze with swirling stars, each a spiral nebula creating its own churning animated space. While *The Starry Night* is Van Gogh's most famous painting, we see this swirling energy throughout all of his work, including his 1889 *Wheatfield With Cypresses,* in which the wheat swirls like a roiling sea. The world is dynamic, electrified. But Van Gogh's vision did not take place in a vacuum; the world was becoming electrified.

In 1838 Samuel Morse sent the first message on his telegraph system using Morse code, and in 1866 the first transatlantic telegraph cable was laid, connecting Europe and America. In 1876 Alexander Graham Bell was granted a patent on the telephone, and in the 1890s radio was under development. An electrical net was being flung around the globe. Michael Faraday, a largely self educated son of a blacksmith's apprentice who had little mastery of higher mathematics, was seeing a world constituted of electromagnetic fields. He realized that moving a magnet near a wire would induce the flow of electricity through the wire, and flowing electricity through a wire would move a magnet, thus inventing the electric generator and the electric motor.

Place a piece of paper over a magnet and sprinkle iron filings onto the paper. The filings will arrange themselves in loops connecting the poles of the magnet, mapping the field that extends beyond the magnet into the space around it. And looking very much like the surface of a Van Gogh painting. For Faraday, the world was filled with fields. Following Faraday, James Clerk Maxwell, in one of the great acts of scientific unification, showed that electricity, magnetism, and light were all manifestations of the same phenomenon—the electromagnetic field—exhibiting in science an equivalence to the vision Van Gogh presents in his paintings.

Frank Gehry's Guggenheim Bilbao Museum

Frank Gehry (born 1929) designed the Guggenheim Museum in Bilbao, Spain, which opened in 1997. It has become one of the world's most recognized buildings with its exuberant walls of billowing titanium, announcing that architecture can once again put a city on the map. Modern architecture, continuing in the humanist tradition of the Renaissance, would typically begin with a grid, much like that in perspective painting. The grid established a frame of reference, a system within which walls and spaces could be deployed. There is no such grid in Gehry's Guggenheim. Gehry began with pieces of crumpled paper that were scanned into a computer. And the Guggenheim was built by workmen hanging on scaffolds holding laptop computers with GPS capabilities to determine where to place the sheets of titanium. Neither the inside nor the outside of the Guggenheim gives us any means of orientation, any frames of reference. What leads us to embrace Gehry's architecture that invokes post-modern literary theory

44

and fields of probability in quantum theory?

Later when we look at the twentieth century, we will see that one of its defining characteristics is the loss of any privileged point of view or fixed frame of reference. Early in the century we have Einstein's relativity with the loss of absolute space, Cubist painting with the loss of the point of view of the observer, and Joyce's novel, *Ulysses*, with the loss of an objective narrator. How do we navigate, how do we create, how do we live in a world like that? So, while we enjoy Bilbao's billowing walls, it also plunges us into a world for which the only frames of reference are itself, a world beyond James Joyce's *Ulysses* and into the world of his maddening novel, *Finnegans Wake*.

All of these—Galileo's heliocentric solar system, Beethoven's Third Symphony, Van Gogh's *The Starry Night*, and Frank Gehry's Guggenheim Museum—are great achievements, but they took place in the contexts of their cultures. And, as we will see when we revisit these four works, they destroyed old worlds as well as creating new ones.

CREATIVITY AND OUR CULTURE

In which we see that individuality and creativity are defining of our culture.

All right, then, I'll go to hell.
~ Huck Finn

Creativity and the West

We say in this book that the creative individual is central to our culture. We see this in demands that we create a unique Self, that we create original work, and that we have a creative economy. But before we look at these in some detail, let's ask, what do we mean by "our culture?" Beginning in Europe in the 1200s and coming to flower in the 1400s something occurred that had not happened before, the emergence of an individual with an inner moral center, and the opening of a vastness within which we could act out our creativity and our lives.

We might say that a culture begins by laying down its epic poems and its temple form, the epic poems delineating the moral structure of the culture, and the temple form the space in which members of the culture will live their lives, both figuratively and literally. Thus in ancient Egypt we see one's proscribed tasks in this life and the after life in the pyramid texts and later the *Book of the Dead*, and the limited path along which one could move indicated by the processional causeways to the pyramids and later through the Egyptian temples. In ancient Greece, we see in the *Iliad* and *Odyssey* the emergence of an individuality that remains subject to fate, and a tragic stand against the cosmos in the Greek temple. In ancient China we see an imperative to put one's Self in accord with the way of nature in the *Tao Te Ching* and in accord with society in the *Analects of Confucius*, and an openness to the flow of nature in the Chinese temple. And in the West?

The Arthurian Romances

We might see Western culture as crystalizing around the 1200s with the Arthurian Romances (the tales of King Arthur and the Knights of the Round Table) and the Gothic cathedrals. In the Arthurian Romances we see an emergence of the individual from the group and a requirement that this individual discover and follow their own path. As described by Joseph Campbell, in *The Quest for the Holy Grail*, the knights set out to view the Holy Grail, but "thought it would be a disgrace to go forth in a group, so each entered the forest at a point he, himself, chose where it was darkest and there was no path or way." If there is a path, it is where someone has gone, it is someone else's path, not yours. In the West, we are called on to act out of our own inner calling.

One of the most representative of the Arthurian figures is Percival. Though a formidable knight due to his purity, Percival is innocent of many of the ways of knighthood and acts out of the spontaneity of his own nature. In one of his quests he enters the castle of the wounded Fisher King, but fails to ask, "What ails you?" the question that would have healed the king, and is turned away from the castle. After years of effort he is able to return to the castle, ask the question, and heal the king.

We in the West are called to act out of our own inner sense of moral right and wrong, a notion that is at the core of much of Western literature to this day. We could look at hundreds of examples, but let's just mention America's fa-

48

vorite novel, Mark Twain's *The Adventures of Huckleberry Finn.* Huck believes that he will burn in hell for the sin of helping Miss Watson's slave, Jim, escape. Miss Watson never did anything to harm Huck, (although she had been given the job of "silizing"—civilizing—him). And he had heard the preacher speak against the sin of stealing a slave. But Huck finally says he does not care, he cannot help himself. He will assist Jim not only to escape, but also to steal his wife and child. "'All right, then, I'll go to hell'… It was awful thoughts, and awful words, but they was said." Of course we know that Huck is acting nobly out of his inner sense of morality, a truer guide than society's rules.

Gothic Cathedrals

Then the Gothic cathedrals. Beginning near Paris and spreading throughout Europe, eighty of these daring edifices were built primarily between 1150 and 1250 CE. Most of them are "Notre dame de …," which means "Our Lady of …," followed by the name of the town; thus Notre dame de Paris. They celebrated Mary, connecting the Europeans back to their pre-Christian great goddess, and in entering a cathedral one is entering the body of the goddess, the womb of the cosmos.

We all admire the structural elegance of the cathedrals, while it is a matter of taste whether we care for their rich decorativeness. The tallest is Notre dame de Beauvais at 157 feet to the vaults, the equivalence of an eighteen-story apartment building, an incredible feat of construction. But the Gothic cathedrals are also models of the cosmos in which the medieval Europeans lived. What do we mean by buildings as models of the cosmos? We mean that they present the deep principles—the symbolic meaning systems—that a culture understands to underlie the workings of its world, and that they are a means for members of that culture to put themselves in accord with their world. As Winston Churchill remarked, "We shape our buildings, and afterwards our buildings shape us."

The Gothic cathedrals provided a soaring experience, connecting the Earth with the heavens, and through an inter-penetration of inside and outside, connected the material and spiritual worlds. The stained glass windows allowed the luminous presence of God to flood into the interior, just as it flooded into a person's heart, while the flying buttresses carried the material forces of the stone vaults to the outside, just as our physical Selves exist in the world. Over the entrance portal to Chartres is a sculpture of Christ coming into the material world through the mandorla, the birth canal of the universe. Standing in the nave of a Gothic cathedral, we can sense that the descendants of its builders will be the ones to circle the globe and go out into space.

The Freedom to Create

Of course the freedom of the Western individual comes with stress and conflict, including the stress of the responsibilities for one's own life, and conflicts with one's family and community. Michelangelo wrote, "When I told my father that I wished to be an artist, he flew into a rage, saying that 'artists are laborers, no better than shoemakers.'" His father wanted him to become a man of letters. But with the Renaissance we have the emergence of the identity of the artist. On hearing that his sculpture of Mary holding the dead Christ, *La Pietà*, was being to attributed another artist, Michelangelo went out at night and carved on the sash across Mary's breast, "Michelangelus Bonarotis Florent Facibat" (Michelangelo Buonarroti, Florentine, made this). And yes, many, such as Galileo who spent the last years of his life under house arrest for asserting that the Earth moved around the Sun, were persecuted, but little by little, restrictions fell away and artists, writers, merchants, bankers, architects, and scientists could pursue things that interested them, even if their interests were

50

different from those of their parents and outside of the accepted orthodoxy.

The freedom to create, whether in art, literature, science, technology, or industry, may seem natural, and we may be tempted to think that cultures that did not host such creativity failed to do so because of their position in time. The necessary affluence or technology was not there. But that is simply not the case. Most cultures throughout history expended great efforts to repress the individual imagination. Look at an Egyptian mural from the time of the pyramids, then one from the time of Ramesses II, and finally one from the time of Cleopatra. To anyone other than an Egyptologist, they look quite similar. But Ramesses II lived over a thousand years after the time of the pyramids, and Cleopatra over a thousand years after Ramesses II. We do not expect our art to remain unchanged for twenty years, much less two thousand.

The Individual Today

And what about this individual in our literature today? The great American mystery writer, Raymond Chandler, writes in his essay on the detective story, "The Simple Art of Murder:"

> Down these mean streets a man must go who is not himself mean, who is neither tarnished nor afraid. The detective must be a complete man and a common man and yet an unusual man. He must be, to use a rather weathered phrase, a man of honor. He talks as the man of his age talks, that is, with rude wit, a lively sense of the grotesque, a disgust for sham, and a contempt for pettiness.

And then a thousand movies—*The Big Sleep, The Maltese Falcon, Shane, Dirty Harry, The Bourne Identity, Salt, Sin City, Jack Reacher*—in which the protagonist defies authority, acts with integrity out of inner authenticity, brings down a cor-

51

rupt system, and, for a time, sets things right.

Note that this is a Western vision. In the ancient Middle East, the task was to re-hear and obey the word of God. In ancient India, the task was to mold oneself into one's role and to identify with transcendence. In ancient China the task was to come into harmony with the flow of nature and serve the larger cause.

And in our emerging twenty-first century? The primacy of the individual remains embedded in our stories in many genres, including the science fiction adventure movie. When fully developed, this genre tells us that we must throw off a corrupt system in order to renew ourselves and our culture. It is interesting to see how many movies that may seem to be mindless sci-fi action flicks so closely follow this model. One, done particularly well, is *The Chronicles of Riddick* staring Vin Diesel. The race of Necromongers is moving across the universe, absorbing populations or destroying them. Vin Diesel's Riddick, one of the few survivors of a fiercely independent warrior-race called the Furyans, is drawn into the fray. He confronts the Purifier, one of the Necromongers sent after him. Speaking of his forced conversion, the Purifier, who is also a Furyan, says: "We all began... as something else. I've done unbelievable things in the name of a faith that was never my own."

Despite being a Furyan, the Purifier had not been strong enough to hold his own values and resist the Necromongers. How many of us make the decision not to resist in innumerable ways, large and small? The Purifier then steps out into the intense heat of Crematoria's twin suns, and as flames lick his body, says, "If only I could still feel the pain...." He crumbles to his knees and burns until white bone shows.

Turning away from the easy decision to join the herd requires giving up the comfortable life that the herd promises. Shamanism teaches us to burn away the flesh, leaving only purified white bones. Then we have already died, so we no longer fear death and we can be reborn. The Purifier is reborn into Riddick who will stop an unstoppable evil and, for a time, bring balance back to the universe. The victory against the hive in *Riddick* is not unlike that in the final episode of the television series *Star Trek: Voyager*, in which a parallel Captain Kathryn Janeway dies killing the Borg Queen, who with the statement, "Resistance is futile," had absorbed into her collective all she encountered.

In the ancient cultures of the Middle East where Job submits, Greece where Prometheus is bound to a rock, India where Arjuna performs according to his role, and China where Monkey is caged, one is discouraged from—even executed for—acting out of one's inner moral sense. Today for us that inner moral sense provides the theme of just about every action, science fiction, spy, and detective novel, movie, and television series, in which the hero bucks bureaucratic authority to set the world right.

And now a new genre has come to the fore, the cable network drama series. The modern incarnation of this genre began with *The Sopranos*, regarded by many as the best television series ever. Others in the genre include *Breaking Bad*, *Dexter*, *Mad Men*, *Walking Dead*, *Justified*, and *Game of Thrones*. Tony Soprano is a gangster who kills people with his bare hands. Walter White in *Breaking Bad* morphs from a mild mannered high school chemistry teacher into the mastermind of a meth empire who kills rival dealers. Dexter is a serial killer. And Don Draper in *Mad Men* is a cold, withdrawn, ruthless ad exec selling consumer products including cigarettes who remarks, "What you call 'love' was invented by guys like me… to sell nylons." Yet these are our new dramatic protagonists. They are complicated, idiosyncratic, and conflicted; "difficult" as indicated in the title of Brett Martin's book about them, *Difficult Men*. Yet there is something at the core of each of these characters that attracts us—a struggle to define and maintain an individual Self.

We often think of the West as being defined by its technological advances, and that characterization is correct. But why were those technological advances initially unique to the West? It is due to the release of individual creativity that had been suppressed in other cultures.

Creating an Original Self

In our culture we have the difficult task of creating an original Self. In his *Letters to a Young Poet*, Ranier Maria Rilke writes:

> *There is only one way: Go within. Search for the cause, find the impetus that bids you write. Put it to this test: Does it stretch out its roots in the deepest place of your heart? Can you avow that you would die if you were forbidden to write? Dig deep into yourself for a true answer. And if it should ring its assent, if you can confidently meet this serious question with a simple, "I must," then build your life upon it. It has become your necessity. Your life, in even the most mundane and least significant hour, must become a sign, a testimony to this urge.*

And James Joyce, in *Portrait of the Artist as a Young Man*, has Stephen Dedalus, his alter ego, say:

> *I will tell you what I will do and what I will not do. I will not serve that in which I no longer believe, whether it call itself my home, my fatherland, or my church: and I will try to express myself in some mode of life or art as freely as I can and as wholly as I can, using for my defense the only arms I allow myself to use—silence, exile and cunning.*

Ultimately this is a question of how we exist in our world.

The pioneer of modern dance, Martha Graham, writes:

There is only one of you in all time, this expression is unique. And if you block it, it will never exist through any other medium and it will be lost.

And more recently Steve Jobs, the cofounder of Apple, states in his Stanford commencement address:

You've got to find what you love. And that is as true for your work as it is for your lovers. Your work is going to fill a large part of your life, and the only way to be truly satisfied is to do what you believe is great work. And the only way to do great work is to love what you do. If you haven't found it yet, keep looking. Don't settle. As with all matters of the heart, you'll know when you find it. And, like any great relationship, it just gets better and better as the years roll on. So keep looking until you find it. Don't settle.

None of these passages could have been written outside the West. In other cultures you followed in your parents' occupation and you put yourself in accord with your culture. If you did not feel the resonance of your culture, you faked it. But in the West you are called to identify your own way and follow it. In our value system, failure to fulfill one's potential is a tragedy. Of course, to find one's unique way and successfully follow it is difficult, and many get lost.

While the failure to achieve Self-manifestation is a tragedy, the failure to even try leads to hollowness. We see the theme of hollowness in the literature of the 1920s and 30s as the collapse of the old order after the First Word War cut people adrift. Those not able to find their way are represented in this literature, including in T. S. Eliot's poem, *The Hollow Men*, Robert Musil's novel, *The Man Without Qualities*, and Bernardo

Bertolucci's later film, *The Conformist*, set in that period. Larry Darrell in Somerset Maugham's *The Razor's Edge* is traumatized by the War, but by being true to himself he is able to find inner peace, much to the consternation of those around him.

So, the first kind of creativity demanded by our culture is the creation of our Selves.

Creating Original Work

The next kind of creativity demanded by our culture is originality in our work. In our culture, the term "derivative" is almost always a pejorative, but not in other cultures. You have perhaps heard stories of the lack of creativity in Japan. This is not just a Western bias. Sony cofounder Akio Morita called for a "culture of creativity" in Japan, realizing that Japanese industry could not continue to prosper only by perfecting products invented elsewhere. Morita was disappointed that Sony's blockbuster product, the Walkman, was created not by his design or engineering departments, but by himself. In some cultures writers live in fear of saying something original. In our culture, writers live in fear of failing to properly footnote something and being accused of plagiarism.

Indeed, it is demanded of us that we not only create original work, but often even the style within which we work. William Blake writes, "I must Create a System. or be enslav'd by another Mans / I will not Reason & Compare: my business is to Create." So creativity is demanded by our culture, and is defining of the work we do.

A Creative Economy

Finally, creativity has become necessary for prosperity. In eighteenth-century mercantilism, a country gained economic advantage by exporting more than it imported. In the late nineteenth century, dominance was gained through the possession or control of natural resources—iron ore, coal, wheat, cotton. By the mid twentieth century, it was production facilitated by supportive infrastructure, a modern industrial plant, and skilled workers that led to economic prosperity. Japan rose to prominence during this period despite having little iron ore, coal, or oil. Now we are in the midst of another shift, and Japan is stagnating. In a talk about Asian universities, then president of Yale University, Richard Leven, suggests that the Japanese economy would not have stagnated over the past few decades if Google, Apple, Netscape, and Microsoft had been Japanese companies. In other words, if Japan had been able to innovate.

We are in the midst of a shift to creativity, sometimes called "the rise of the creative class." The most important ingredient in many products today is not the material, nor even the assembly, but creativity. How can this be? Think of a cutting-edge CPU computer chip that costs $400. What is that $400 paying for? Not the silicon in the chip; silicon is sand and costs pennies. What about the processing of the silicon? It does have to be spun into a cylinder of extreme purity and then cut into wafers. But in a few years that same chip will be too dated to be put in computers, and may instead be used to control refrigerators. Made with the same ultra pure silicon, it will then cost just a few dollars. A lot of the $400 for a chip when new goes to amortize the cost of the fabricating facility, but most of it is for the creativity of the engineers who designed it and the company that produced it.

Any of a hundred factories in China can manufacture an iPod, and pirated iPods are readily available, but only Apple could invent the iPod. The difference in what you pay for a real iPod over a pirated iPod is for Apple's creativity. And think of a song, a movie, or a book that you can download to your mobile device. Here there is nothing material. Whatever you are paying, you are paying for creativity, whether the creativity of the artists or that of the designers of the downloading infrastructure.

Let's look at Apple as an example of creativity in business. In 1996, when Steve Jobs returned to head Apple, the value of the company he had cofounded in 1976 and been forced out of in 1985 was about $3 billion and few people thought it would survive. When Jobs left his CEO role shortly before he died in 2011, Apple was worth about $340 billion and was the most valuable company on the planet. During the years of Jobs's leadership, the best description of his contribution to the company was a creative vision of what computer and communications devices can be. Apple under Jobs was not responsible for any major technological advances; it used the same components used by other electronics companies. And the items it sold, computers, MP3 players, smart phones, tablets, and software, were all made and sold by others before Apple introduced its unique versions. If you are a fan of Apple products you know why you prefer them—imagination, functionality, ease of use, design, elegance. Steve Jobs created $337 billion in value that was not there before through Visionary Creativity.

Deborah Wince-Smith, president of the Council on Competitiveness, contends that talent is the oil of the twenty-first century, and that innovation and creativity are the most important talents. So, from who we are as individuals, to how we approach our work, to the fundamentals of our economy, creativity is central to our lives today.

ART, DISCONTINUITY, AND NEUROPHYSIOLOGY

In which we look at art and see how it presents us with unanticipated experiences—"discontinuities"—that continually recode our neural connections, restructure our consciousness, and advance us into unfolding futures.

Art in its execution and direction is dependent on the time in which it lives, and artists are creatures of their epoch. The highest art will be that which in its conscious content presents the thousandfold problems of the day, the art which has been visibly shattered by the explosions of last week... The best and most extraordinary artists will be those who every hour snatch the tatters of their bodies out of the frenzied cataract of life, who, with bleeding hands and hearts, hold fast to the intelligence of their time.

~ Richard Huelsenbeck, First German Dada Manifesto

What is Art?

In a book about creativity, of course we will want to address art, and while we will not be able to fully say what art is, we can look at some of the things art might be able to tell us about Visionary Creativity.

Let's begin by noting that understanding beauty will do little to help us understand art. There are things that are beautiful that are not art, for example a sunset or an Arabian stallion. And many works of art are not beautiful, for example,

Francisco Goya's *Disasters of War*, or Munch's *The Scream*. Or Damien Hirst's *Physical Impossibility of Death in the Mind of Someone Living*, a shark in a tank of formaldehyde, which is just weird. So while some art is beautiful, beauty is not defining of art.

You stand in front of a painting, read a novel, watch a movie. What do you experience? Of course, the object itself, the craft and attention to detail. The layers of understanding that are embedded in the work. And something about the people in the culture of the artist and something about the human condition. There are many inspiring descriptions of the role of art—let's look at one given by William Faulkner in his 1950 Nobel Prize acceptance speech, which he titled, "I decline to accept the end of man."

> *I feel that this award was not made to me as a man, but to my work—a life's work in the agony and sweat of the human spirit, not for glory and least of all for profit, but to create out of the materials of the human spirit something which did not exist before....*
>
> *I believe that man will not merely endure: he will prevail. He is immortal, not because he alone among creatures has an inexhaustible voice, but because he has a soul, a spirit capable of compassion and sacrifice and endurance. The poet's, the writer's, duty is to write about these things. It is his privilege to help man endure by lifting his heart, by reminding him of the courage and honor and hope and pride and compassion and pity and sacrifice which have been the glory of his past. The poet's voice need not merely be the record of man, it can be one of the props, the pillars to help him endure and prevail.*

An entire book could be devoted to the concept of art implied by Faulkner's speech, but here we are interested in something else about art, how it alters our structures of consciousness, and in so doing, how it disrupts the dominant culture, changes the spirit of the times, brings to an end old worlds, and brings into existence new ones.

Discontinuity, Neuroscience, and Perception

All art is within traditions. An artist can uncritically work within a tradition, press its boundaries, challenge it, or deny it. But even in denying a tradition, an artist is still acknowledging it. An artist must first master the tradition within which he or she is going to work. The artist must know the histories, theories, techniques, personalities and masterpieces of the tradition. The gonzo journalist Hunter S. Thompson taught himself to write by typing out Faulkner's novels. The jazz trumpeter Miles Davis knew Charlie Parker's Bebop. The German-American architect Mies van der Rohe knew the free flowing spaces of Frank Lloyd Wright's open plan. We might say, echoing the literary critic Harold Bloom, that there are no works of art, but only relationships between works. Each movie, each novel, each painting, each piece of music, each building calls up to us myriad others that exist in relationship to them. This does not mean that an artist needs to be a historian or a theoretician; the way an artist knows is different. The artist knows from the inside, and may be annoyed by the scribblers who do not practice the crafts about which they write.

But an artist cannot simply work within their chosen tradition, they must extend it. Thompson enters into a deeper lunacy than Faulkner's; Miles extends Bird's forms into lyricism, and then Coltrane extends Miles's forms into complexity; and Mies translates Wright's open plan from organic materials to steel and glass. Imagine that an architect today were to design a truly excellent rectangular glass and steel skyscraper. All of the problems of the skyscraper are elegantly solved; it has an efficient core and a tight skin, it is well proportioned and carefully detailed. No one would pay any attention to this building; there would be no admiration of the elegant solutions. People would just say, "Mies already did that fifty years ago." The tradition must be extended. But that is not to say that the later work will be better than the earlier. Today we might prefer Miles to Coltrane, Wright to Mies, and certainly Faulkner to Thompson. But there is something in the nature of art that does not permit it to stand still.

Recall our description at the beginning of this book: *Visionary Creatives swim in the culture of their day and manifest in their work the spirit of the age. The things they create—in art, design, science, technology, business—embody that spirit, and at the same time are a little off center for us, somehow not what we anticipated, presenting a discontinuity that startles us, restructures our consciousness, and pulls us into the future.*

What do we mean by *discontinuity*? Let's start by flipping through the pages of an art history book. The most obvious thing we notice about art is that it changes. For example, in Italian painting we see a change from the Early Renaissance of Botticelli, to the High Renaissance of da Vinci, to the Baroque of Caravaggio. In modern painting we see a change from the drip paintings of Pollock to the soup cans of Warhol to the shark in formaldehyde of Hirst. What is the reason for these changes? We might at first be tempted to think that expanses of time would be the explanation, but Botticelli died in 1510 and Caravaggio in 1610 giving us a span of only a hundred years. And Pollock's drip period was between 1947 and 1950, while Hirst did his shark in 1991, a span of just over forty years. And we could look at the career of a single artist. In 1504, Michelangelo completed the *David* that we described at the beginning of this book, and which announced the movement from the Early Renaissance to the High Renaissance. In the 1520s he designed the Laurentian Library steps, totally out of proportion to the space into which they spill, and which are now considered defining of Mannerism, a style that breaks the rules. In the 1540s he designed the exterior of St. Peter's Basilica, which is Baroque in its play of concave and convex. And finally at the time of his death he was working on the Slaves, sculptures that are as modern as the figure in Edvard Munch's *The Scream*. From High Renaissance to Mannerism to Baroque and beyond, all in one lifetime. Something is going on here.

We might try to explain such changes by developments in the materials and techniques used by the artist, or changes in society, but so frequently? If these were utilitarian objects instead of paintings, we might expect changes if the uses of the objects had changed, but that is not the case with these examples. Since these changes are unrelated to function, we call the phenomena *non-functional stylistic dynamism*. And since we find this non-functional stylistic dynamism throughout all of the arts, let us for the moment assume it to be an essential quality of art, and see what role it plays in our experience of art.

Let's take a look at some of the latest findings in brain science. In his book, *How to Create a Mind*, Ray Kurzweil suggests that the brain operates through pattern recognition. The neocortex, the part of the brain responsible for hierarchical thinking, is made up of about 300 million pattern recognizing modules, each with about 100 neurons. Groups of these modules recognize specific patterns, which build up from something as simple as part of a letter of the alphabet to a person. And ultimately to all that we recognize. Once formed, the "wiring" in a given module is fairly stable, but the interconnections between modules are dynamic and plastic, and they continually change as we learn and have new experiences.

These modules communicate "upward" in a hierarchy to modules that handle ever higher levels of abstraction, but they also communicate "downward," so that if a module is set to recognize a certain pattern, it will sometimes "see" that pattern even if a signal is not really there, providing an explanation for why we often "see" what we anticipate rather than "what is there."

From the point of view of this book, we might say that the modules highest in the hierarchy are responsible for our worldviews, the structures within which our experience is organized. The lower down in the hierarchy of networks modules are, the easier it is for them to remake their interrelationships, allowing us to absorb new knowledge. However the networks higher up in the hierarchy are more difficult to change. It is these networks that are changed by the discontinuities we experience in art.

We usually think of perception as passive, with stimuli coming in through the senses, activating neurons, etc., but it is in fact highly active, playing a major role in forming our experience. The stimuli that come in through the senses are vague and indistinct. We do a lot of work, referred to in psychology as cognition, to make sense out of them, a process we can now see at work when neural firing not only goes up the hierarchy of modules in the neocortex sending information about what is "perceived," but also down the hierarchy, telling modules what they should assume they are perceiving or what to anticipate next. People native in different languages, people with different backgrounds, *people from different cultures*, do this differently. *People perceive the world the way they do because they grow up in cultures that mold their cognitive processes according to their culture.* From the relationship between Heaven and Earth to what will be on our breakfast table, we live in cultures, which means worlds of expectations. And by the time we reach adulthood, most of the situations we encounter are in fact what we expect them to be. When they are not, our cognitive processes work hard to cover over discrepancies, as we see in optical illusions when we put things right in front of our eyes and we do not see them. This is related to what is sometimes called "the social construction of reality."

Sometimes situations we encounter diverge so far from what we expect that we cannot fudge them. Things or situations for which we are not prepared, territories for which we have no cognitive maps. Imagine a person seeing an automobile for the first time, or a television, or a home computer. We might imagine that they would think, oh, a horseless carriage, or a radio with a miniature movie screen, or the home version of HAL. But that assumes that they are familiar with carriages, radios, movies, and computers. If they are not, they will have no prior concepts on which to hang what they encounter. There are reports that the Native Americans who saw Spanish ships in the Caribbean for the first time perceived them as clouds. We might have expected them to perceive giant canoes, but apparently the gap was too great. We call such a gap a *discontinuity*, the difference between what we anticipate and what we encounter, and we tend not to like it. However, there is one situation in which we are open to discontinuities: the art experience.

Discontinuities are fundamental to the art experience and occur in at least four forms: *internal discontinuities*, in which the work of art sets up expectations that it then violates, as in Haydn's *Surprise Symphony* with its burst of kettle drums after lulling us with a quiet passage, or Frank Lloyd Wright's Guggenheim Museum in which we enter under a low ceiling before the space explodes up into the rotunda; *stylistic discontinuities*, in which we might anticipate a Post-Impressionist painting, but encounter instead a Cubist painting; *formal discontinuities*, as when we go to a concert expecting to hear musicians play, and instead encounter the indeterminist modern musician John Cage fiddling with the knobs on a dozen radios; and finally, *contextual discontinuities*, in which we encounter a work of art outside of the environment in which we would expect it, as in the sophisticated late nineteenth and early twentieth century quilts by American women that were put in bedrooms rather than in art galleries, and then exhibited in the Whitney Museum in 1971.

Imagine going to the "Independents" exhibition of modern art in New York in 1917. *The Fountain*, a men's room urinal submitted by Marcel Duchamp, was hidden from view by a curtain, but if you had looked behind the curtain, you might have remarked, "You'd think the plumber would have gotten that out of here before the opening." In a reverse example of this in the late 1960s when wild things were happening in art, I walked past a painting in New York's Museum of Modern Art and came to a closed door. I paused and thought, "A bit extreme, but interesting. I'll accept this as art." Then I realized it was just a door.

Being open to discontinuities is difficult; it requires stripping ourselves of the protective armor of our preconceptions and leaving ourselves exposed to the unknown, which is why so many people are uneasy with art—they do not want to challenge themselves. And why we often experience art in quiet settings where we are protected from outside disturbances—museums, galleries, theaters, concert halls, libraries—that allow us to let down the guard of our preconceptions. The art experience is one in which we do not deny discontinuities, but rather remain open to them. As we become accustomed to a given style of art, it no longer produces a discontinuity; what we encounter becomes what we had anticipated. So, by continually changing, art keeps ahead of our anticipations.

Artists walk a fine line in the introduction of discontinuities. If they take them too far, their audiences will not be able to bridge the gap and the work will be rejected, perhaps to be rediscovered later and heralded as having been ahead of its time. We see this for example in the well-documented premiere of Igor Stravinsky's *The Rite of Spring*, which incited a riot. Music is very powerful at setting up expectations, and if these expectations are not met, we can feel extreme discomfort. In Stravinsky's case, it took audiences only one season to catch up. On the other hand, if the discontinuity is too slight, the artist will be criticized for being timid or no longer developing.

In an interview about his movie, *Apocalypse Now*, Francis Ford Coppola stated:

> *It was supposed to be sort of a war movie in their [the distributors] minds, and what they got was strange; it was surreal, it was long.... When it did come out... it was controversial; people didn't totally know what to make of it. Anyway, years later, I was sitting in a little hotel room with a little 17-inch television in London, and it came on, and I always liked the beginning of the picture, so I started watching it, and I wasn't planning to see the whole thing. But I watched the whole thing, and my reaction was, "Gee, this is nowhere near as far out or as unusual as we thought at the time." And you know, as often happens, art or work that everyone finds controversial, 15 years later... You know, I always like to say the abstract art of one period becomes the wallpaper a few years later.*

Note that this approach implies that different audiences and different individuals will have different art experiences. So, when people say, "That's not art to me," they may not be having an art experience—they may lack the contextual references. Or they may have already become jaded to that form and find the work derivative. Or they may have experienced a discontinuity, found it uncomfortable, and wanted to deny it.

This approach tells us that the defining quality of art is not in the art object, but in the art experience. If we look at the Duchamp urinal and say, "That's not art," we are right. The art is not in the urinal, but in our experience of it, as we will discuss later when we look at Duchamp in some depth. As we see throughout this book, this notion is fundamental to our understanding of creativity.

Art Changes Who We Are

What is the purpose of this discontinuity in the arts? Earlier we said that our perception works through preconceptions—we see the world that we anticipate—the modules in our neocortex are set up to look for patterns they already know and they try to fit things into those patterns even if they don't really fit.

Living in a world of expectations has its advantages. When stepping off a curb and hearing a hum or seeing a flicker, we do not want to engage in an analysis of what they might mean, we want to immediately step back. But it goes far beyond that; it is at the core of how we perceive the world and how we function in it. When we encounter anything—a door, a chair, another person—we do not scan it and do an analysis, we immediately impose a meaning on to it. We have a concept of a chair, what it means—we can sit on it—and we impose that meaning onto it, making it a chair for us. But what happens when the world changes, for example when chairs were first introduced into Japan, or when cars become electric and make very little noise? Or when identity is no longer attached to land, or wealth to natural resources, or education to Greek and Latin, or sex to roles, or information to print?

Earlier we said that the media guru, Marshall McLuhan, referred to the artist as an early warning system. Artists are constantly asking themselves, "What am I *really* experiencing?" Unlike the rest of us, they are not content to think they are experiencing what they have been told they should be experiencing. And not content to just have experiences, artists attempt to penetrate into the origins of their experiences. In so doing, they are in touch with changes in the world and themselves—to use our earlier terminology, changes in the spirit of the age and the structures of their consciousness—before the rest of us, and these changes become central to their art.

We are most aware of discontinuities in the arts, but they also occur in other fields, including science and business. When Einstein developed relativity and Larry Page and Sergey Brin developed Google, they were doing two things. First, they were advancing a scientific understanding of the workings of nature, or organizing all of the world's information and making it accessible to us. But second, they were restructuring our consciousness and making us more able to function in the emerging world that they were also reshaping. Artists are often aware that they are doing this because art criticism has been addressing this since the beginnings of modernism. But we have been told that scientists investigate nature and business people make money. That is why we have such poor understandings of science and business. We do not understand that scientists and business people, not just artists, can exercise Visionary Creativity. We do not realize that they can also be motivated to restructure our consciousness and move us forward into an unfolding future.

Larry and Sergey expressed this in a statement they released at the time of Google's initial stock offering, that Google had a vision, that this vision came first, before making money, and that if you did not agree with this approach, you shouldn't buy Google stock. They write: "Google is not a conventional company. We do not intend to become one. Throughout Google's evolution as a privately held company, we have managed Google differently. We have also emphasized an atmosphere of creativity and challenge, which has helped us provide unbiased, accurate and free access to information for those who rely on us around the world."

Thus the role of the creative is not just to help us *understand* an emerging world, but to present us with discontinuities that stretch and re-form our structures of consciousness to enable us to live in, be part of, *experience* a new world. We might say that an essay can change *what* we know, but we need discontinuities to change *how* we know, and thereby even who we are. That is why art is so difficult, and why so many people are intimidated by it. And a failure to realize that the same can be true of science and business is why, as we stated above, science and business are so thoroughly misunderstood.

In the last part of this book we will look at becoming a Visionary Creative, but we already have a hint of what is to come. The Visionary Creative lives in an emerging new world, and asks, *"What am I experiencing?"* instead of "What have I been told I am experiencing?" From that questioning comes the new in art, science, technology, and business.

CREATIVITY AS DESTRUCTION

In which we see that creativity implies destruction; the old must be swept away to make space for the new. We look at destruction in business, art, and science. And we revisit our examples of Visionary Creativity in cultural context and see how each also destroyed an older world.

The major advances in civilization are processes that all but wreck the societies in which they occur.
~ A. N. Whitehead, English mathematician and philosopher

Death is very likely the single best invention of Life. It is Life's change agent. It clears out the old to make way for the new. Right now the new is you, but someday not too long from now, you will gradually become the old and be cleared away. Sorry to be so dramatic, but it is quite true.
~ Steve Jobs, cofounder and former CEO of Apple, speaking six years before his death

Destruction

Creativity does not come free of cost; it comes with destruction, as we see in the Indian myths of Shiva, the destroyer of the world, following Brahma the creator and Vishnu the preserver, in eternal cycles. J. Robert Oppenheimer, the American physicist who was the director of the Manhattan Project, had read the *Bhagavad Gita* in the original Sanskrit, and as he witnessed the first nuclear bomb test in 1945, the phrase "Now I am become Death, the destroyer of worlds," from the epic poem, leapt into his mind. In India the cycles of time are seen as real processes in the world, but also as metaphorical of processes in ourselves in which we seek to obliterate ego and negative attachments in order to allow new growth.

Besides obvious self-preservation, our aversion to destruction comes in part from a misconception of nature that we have come to think of as peaceful, stable, subject to gradual change. It's not. Our universe began with a "Big Bang," an event of inconceivable violence. Just a few decades ago galaxies were thought to form in a slow condensation of gasses and dust. We now know that the process is violent with massive black holes at the cores of galaxies swallowing billions of suns and emitting the light of trillions of suns. Galaxies grow through collisions that shred structures and toss about stars. And stars are nothing less than continuously exploding hydrogen bombs. Stars are furnaces creating the heavier elements, and when they explode as supernovae, they give off more light than entire galaxies, blowing those elements into the void to become material for the formation of new stars and solar systems with heavy element planets.

The formation of our planet was also violent. Our Moon may have been blown out of the Earth in a collision with an object the size of Mars four and a half billion years ago, melting the Earth. If life had begun before the collision, it had to begin again. Then four billion years ago there was a reign of destruction from asteroids that melted the surface of the Earth, again eliminating any possible life, and 200 million years after that, single celled organisms that are our ancestors appeared. Sixty-five million years ago, an asteroid ten miles in diameter struck the Earth, wiping out the large dinosaurs in hours, one of five mass extinction events in the past half-billion years. The Earth has suffered eras of violent volcanoes and of ice ages, the most recent having occurred just ten thousand years ago, creating glaciers up to several miles deep, grinding all beneath them as they advanced. Even the evolution of life itself has been violent, for example with the release of the deadly toxin, oxygen. Until recently, ecologists spoke of "climax forests" that were thought to occur when the succession of different species of trees stopped and a final, balanced forest appeared. They no longer speak of such climax forests, recognizing that there is no such thing as balance, that change is continuous. Life lives on life, and even modern humans, as they spread out of Africa, exterminated all other hominid species everywhere they went. So destruction is as inherent to nature as is creation. And, as we will see in looking at business, art, and science below, in the human realm, creation happens within the context of destruction.

Business

In business, destruction is a key to innovation and progress as we see in "creative destruction" and "disruptive innovation."

As described by the Austrian economist Joseph Schumpeter, creative destruction is the process whereby businesses and even entire industries are swept away to make room for innovation by entrepreneurs as they generate new growth. Digital technologies provide us with numerous examples: digital photography has destroyed the film industry; digital music has destroyed the record store and the CD; online news is fast eroding newspapers; ebooks are threatening printed books; digital downloads and streaming is threatening cable television; and cell phones are threatening the use of landlines, stand-alone cameras, watches, and now even computers. Free market economies permit creative destruction and thrive as new industries are born; planned economies thwart it by protecting outmoded industries, thereby suppressing the rise of new industries, and they stagnate.

A related concept in business is "disruptive innovation," a term coined by Harvard Business School professor Clayton Christensen, who contrasts sustaining innovations with disruptive innovations. The electric typewriter was a sustaining innovation. It improved an existing technology, it did not change a business structure that included secretaries and typing pools, and it allowed most existing typewriter manufacturers to prosper. The word processor, on the other hand, was a disruptive innovation. It allowed executives to do their own typing and allowed documents to be stored and transmitted digitally by email, thus totally changing the nature of business documents and business communications. Most of the typewriter companies went out of business and typing pools disappeared. A disruptive innovation totally transforms a field and thereby destroys companies. We might have expected typewriter companies to find new lives making computer printers, but they didn't. We will see why when we look at computers below. Disruptive innovations work in a very particular fashion. A technology will dominate. A cheaper technology that does something related comes along; but at first it is not very capable and therefore is not a threat. But then the cheaper technology accelerates in capability until it overtakes the dominant technology, which promptly disappears, since nobody wants to pay more for something that does less.

In an oversimplified example, IBM mainframe computers at one time dominated. Smaller computers called minis (minis were about the size of three washing machines), including ones made by DEC, came along. Universities and research organizations, which did not need the power of mainframes, bought minis, which were not able to do what mainframes did, and IBM did not take them seriously. But minis gained in capability, and eventually presented a serious challenge to mainframes. Then workstations, single-user computers that were basically super PCs with powerful graphics capabilities, came along. DEC ignored them, since they could not match the capability of minis, but scientists and engineers liked having their own computers on their desks. Eventually workstations approached minis in capability at a much lower price and without the need for a dedicated computer room and staff. DEC disappeared. Workstations were much more powerful than PCs, so Sun, Apollo, and Silicon Graphics, which made workstations, ignored PCs. But lots of PCs were being sold, and Intel, which made the CPU chips for PCs, could afford to do the research and development to make their chips more and more powerful, and when the PC you bought at the office supply store became almost as powerful as a workstation but a lot cheaper, Sun, Apollo, and Silicon Graphics disappeared.

With the benefit of hindsight, you would think that IBM could have made competitive minis, DEC could have pioneered the workstation, and Silicon Graphics could have made add-on graphics cards for PCs that would have boosted their power to workstation levels. Each could have owned the subsequent technology and its market, had they made the right moves. They didn't, and we used to say they were dumb. Christensen's brilliance was to closely study innovations in several industries (although not the one presented above) to understand exactly what happened. What he found was that those in the companies that were destroyed were not dumb, they were doing the only thing they could do. While it is possible for a company to move to a new, disruptive, technology, it is very difficult. Heads of companies in Silicon Valley read Christensen's papers and books and vowed that it would not happen to them, but again and again they were powerless to stop it.

Yes, DEC could have made workstations, etc., but the new products had much smaller profit margins than their core businesses, and they had customers clamoring for the next generation of their highly profitable core products. It would not have made sense to divert their resources to infant businesses with tiny profit margins in fields where their employees had little ability or interest to make products their high paying customers did not want.

But wait. Couldn't better planning by these corporations, or government planning, or government providing the right incentives have prevented the "inefficiencies" of this kind of destruction? The answer is no. Governments and monopolies can extend the lives of companies by blocking new technologies, but then we all suffer. There have been enough planned, top-down economies for us to know that they only lead to stagnation.

Art

We see in the arts many parallels to disruptive innovation in business, for example the destruction of Beaux Arts architecture. In late nineteenth and early twentieth century America a style of architecture called the Beaux Arts, named after the school in Paris where many architects of the day studied, was the style of choice for monumental buildings that communicated solidity and a rootedness in Europe.

Let's look at Beaux Arts architecture and the modern architecture that replaced it in a bit of detail to see how a style in art can be more than a fashion, how it can embody a culture's understanding of itself, and how it can be destroyed when that understanding changes. In New York City, Beaux Arts buildings still standing include the Metropolitan Museum of Art, Grand Central Station, and the Public Library. At the turn of the last century, the style was so dominant and used for so many important buildings, that the emerging modernism of Frank Lloyd Wright and some European architects hardly seemed a threat. The substance and depth of the Beaux Arts, the refinement of its spaces, and its system of ornament rooted in twenty-five hundred years of Western history could hardly have been considered vulnerable. But by 1941 the young progressives who had come to Washington for Roosevelt's New Deal were outraged by the new Beaux Arts styled National Gallery of Art that was constructed on the Mall. How, they asked, could something so dated be built in this modern era? After the National Gallery there were no more important Beaux Arts buildings.

This was more than a change in fashion; something fundamental had happened. The Beaux Arts vocabulary with its columns, arches, and domes was descended from the Renaissance, which was, in turn, derived from Rome, which had Greek influences. Our use of this vocabulary implied that Americans of the late nineteenth and early twentieth centuries were cultural descendants of Leonardo and Petrarch, Cicero and Ovid, and Plato and Aristotle.

But by the turn of the twentieth century we no longer regarded ourselves as classical Europe's cultural descendants. We partook of a new universal humanity, and an architecture that spoke in a universal, not a European, vocabulary was called for. Reason and scientific knowledge, not history, were now the defining human qualities and the means through which we would know the world, our society, and ourselves. Early twentieth century architects had no use for the past, they would build a new world based on science and engineering. Architectural history was banned from architecture schools, Beaux Arts teachers were swept from the schools, the Beaux Arts style was ridiculed, and its greatest American example, Penn Station in New York City, was demolished. Art destroys as surely as it creates.

Science

Throughout this book we look at science as much as the arts in our discussions of creativity. We should stop here for a moment and consider science as creativity. Of course we credit many scientists with being creative, but does not art come from the human imagination, while science comes from observations of what is actually out there in reality? Not exactly.

Let's look again at a book we mentioned earlier, Thomas Kuhn's *The Structure of Scientific Revolutions*. Kuhn shows that there are two kinds of science, *normal science* and *revolutionary science*. (We will see in a moment how these parallel what we call ordinary creativity and Visionary Creativity.) Normal science proceeds through the rigorous methods of experimentation, verification, and falsification with which we are familiar. But normal science always works within models called *paradigms*. Those paradigms are established and overthrown by revolutionary science.

In some ways, what Kuhn means by paradigms is similar to what we have been calling worldviews. So, for example, classical physicists worked within the Newtonian paradigm of uniform space and time while using normal science to systematically advance their understandings. Einstein's relativity, which was a new paradigm, completely upset the Newtonian understandings, something we will discuss in a later chapter. The change from Newton's to Einstein's physics did not come about through the processes of normal science, it was an example of revolutionary science. Such a change, called a *paradigm shift*, takes place through intuitive leaps achieved by scientists who are Visionary Creatives immersed in the cultures of their times who see that the world has changed and who are disturbed that others do not also see this. Scientific Visionary Creatives bring forth their works to make these changes visible to others. So the ultimate source of Visionary Creativity in science is the same as it is for other realms including the arts.

A paradigm is a worldview and includes a set of underlying assumptions that we cannot prove, but which seem so obviously self-evident that we accept them. The example we all know from high school math is the assumption that parallel lines never meet, an assumption that held for almost two millennia until non-Euclidian geometry showed that, yes, this is true for flat surfaces, but what about curved surfaces such as the earth where lines of longitude meet at the poles?

The mechanistic Newtonian paradigm gave way first to that of Maxwell's fields, then to that of Einstein's relativity, and then to that of quantum theory, in each case due to the collapse of old assumptions and the adaptation of new ones as much as to new observations.

Most readers of Kuhn's book misunderstand it, thinking that Kuhn says paradigms shift when accumulated anomalies—things that don't fit the prevailing paradigm—finally cause a paradigm to fall. But that is not what Kuhn says. He points out that anomalies are often there at the beginning when a new paradigm is proposed. So, if it is not fully supported by rock solid evidence, why is a paradigm accepted? And why do paradigms shift? Kuhn does not say, but the answer is that old paradigms are destroyed and new ones created when the work of scientists who are Visionary Creatives resonates with other scientists. The new work is accepted not just because the arguments for it are convincing, but because it feels right, or more specifically, feels right to a new generation of young scientists. Max Planck, the German theoretical physicist who originated quantum theory, wrote: "A new scientific truth does not triumph by convincing its opponents and making them see the light, but rather because its opponents eventually die, and a new generation grows up that is familiar with it." Scientific theories are not absolute and eternal; rather they rest on assumptions, on what Kuhn calls paradigms, and these paradigms are culturally rooted and are generated by Visionary Creatives. So science, like art, is built on the culture of its day, and scientists, like artists, swim in their culture and at the same time remake their culture anew. Thus changes in culture destroy old scientific paradigms as surely as they destroy old styles in the arts.

Despite continued evidence that science changes in revolutionary leaps through paradigm shifts, we are continually told that various disciplines in science today are "settled." Whenever you hear that something is "settled science," you can be sure that it will soon be overturned.

Revisiting Our Examples and Finding Destruction

Earlier we looked at examples of creativity in cultural context: Galileo's heliocentric solar system, Beethoven's Third Symphony, Van Gogh's *The Starry Night*, and Frank Gehry's Guggenheim Bilbao Museum. Let's look at them again, this time focusing on what they destroyed.

Galileo's Heliocentric Solar System

Imagine you are a giant space creature situated outside of our solar system, seeing it as Earth's inhabitants imagined it. First you see the pre-Copernican model with the Earth at the center and all of the planets as well as the Sun circling it. Then after the Copernican-Galilean revolution, you see the Sun at the center and the Earth as just one of the planets circling it. But actually, if you were seeing the solar system as Earth's inhabitants imagined it, the pre-Copernican image would not be as we just described it. By imagining an abstract uniform space in which the solar system is situated, with either the Earth or the Sun at its center, you are already in a Copernican-Galilean-Newtonian universe. For medieval Europe before Copernicus, the Earth was not just in the center of the solar system, it was the unmoving center of the cosmos, of existence.

It is not easy for us to imagine this, since it is so far from our notions, but that is the point. It was different, just as the ancient Chinese notion of space having five directions, north, east, south, west, and center, was different. We would respond, wait a minute, "center" is not a direction, it is an arbitrary point of reference from which you perceive directions. Yes, for us, but not for the Chinese, and not for the pre-Copernican Europeans. Center was a fixed place and therefore a direction you could move toward just as you could move toward each of the cardinal directions. For the ancient Chinese, the location of the Forbidden City was not arbitrary; it was the permanent fixed center of existence, just as the Earth was for the pre-Copernicans.

How can a "center" not be fixed, the ancient Chinese and pre-Copernicans might ask? If it is not fixed, if a center can be anywhere, then it is not a center. But after Copernicus, that center was gone. It did not evolve and it was not improved, it was destroyed, and with it entire symbolic and value systems, including an understanding of who we are as human beings and what our place is in the cosmos. With Copernicus and Galileo we no longer understood our place in relation to the center, and the question became, in relation to what? Where were we?

It is important to realize that this destruction came not just from empirical observation, but from the imaginations of Visionary Creatives. Galileo's solar system did not just respond to observations, it was the product of a new vision. As Arthur Koestler points out in his book, *The Sleepwalkers*, and Kuhn in his *Structure of Scientific Revolutions*, science does not progress by the accumulation of observations, but rather by changes in cultural orientation. And today we no longer hold Galileo's position. He believed that the Sun is in the center of the universe and is unmoving. We do not believe that the Sun is the center of the universe, nor that it is unmoving. And he believed that the planets move in circular orbits, while

Johannes Kepler, his contemporary, had already shown that they move in elliptical orbits.

Recall that we said earlier that Copernicus had proposed his heliocentric model to resolve a problem with the existing model that placed the Earth in the center of the Solar System. Since the Earth is not in the center, the planets occasionally appear to change directions and go backwards against the fixed stars in the night sky. But the Copernican-Galilean model did not make things much better, because while the Earth and the planets do revolve around the Sun, they do so in ellipses, not circles, with the Sun at one foci of the ellipses. And their motions are not uniform, but vary, speeding up as they come closer to the Sun, and slowing down as they move away. Galileo had seen Johannes Kepler's writings suggesting elliptical orbits and varying speeds that cleared up the problem, but he dismissed them. He liked circles. Galileo wrote: "The great book of nature is written in the language of mathematics, and its characters are triangles, circles, and other geometrical figures, without which it is humanly impossible to understand a single word of it." Thus he privileged mathematics over observation, and believed that the purpose of experiment is to identify the mathematical forms he believed to underlie nature.

Newton, who was born the same year Galileo died, made a leap of abstraction, and generalized the principles formulated by Galileo and Kepler to understand the order of the physical universe as a whole through his laws of motion and gravity. He used the same laws to explain both the path of a cannonball we fire on the Earth, and the orbits of the Moon falling around the Earth and the planets falling around the Sun. Think for a moment of the implications of this; the same laws that govern the paths of cannonballs on Earth govern the paths of the Moon and the planets. This meant that there were no longer two realms, earthly and heavenly, but only one. This idea was huge and it gave Newton superhero cultural status.

Newton's assumption of his axioms of space, time, and causality, like Galileo's assumption of circles, was a creative act. Galileo's assumptions were set in the static world of the Renaissance; Newton's in the dynamic world of the Baroque, which saw a similar dynamism in the arts. Since we began this book with a reference to Michelangelo's *David*, let's contrast his *David* to one by the Baroque sculptor and architect, Gianlorenzo Bernini. Michelangelo's *David* is static, poised in a contemplative moment before his encounter with Goliath. Bernini's *David* is dynamic, caught in the midst of flinging his stone. And while Michelangelo's *David* is self-contained, Bernini's engages the space around it. Looking at the position of his sling and the direction of his intent gaze, we can triangulate and locate the presumed position of Goliath.

Newton's assumptions destroyed Galileo's just as Galileo's had destroyed those of the pre-Copernicans, and Einstein's assumptions would eventually destroy Newton's. And in each case it was not just astronomy that changed, it was the stage on which we lived our lives and exercised our creativity.

Beethoven's Third Symphony

Earlier we looked at Beethoven's Third Symphony, *the Eroica*, in the context of Romanticism. It was a plunge into the turmoil of the emotions, after which there was no turning back to Viennese classicism. What was going on here?

Let's step way, way back and look at the Gothic cathedrals we discussed earlier. They were part of a progression of styles from the dark, heavy vaults of the Romanesque in about 1000 CE, to the soaring Gothic vaults in the 1200s, to the classicism of the Renaissance in the 1400s and 1500s, to the dynamism of the Baroque in the 1600s, and finally to the highly ornate churches of the Rococo in the early 1700s. Then it was over.

The European temple form had played itself out. There was nothing beyond the Rococo. Now what?

There are two choices in creative endeavors at a time like this: to go backwards or to go forward. Going backwards is called Neoclassicism. In effect it says, the principles that have governed us up to this point have worked well, and we are in trouble now only because we have abandoned them. To continue on this course can only lead to chaos. We should return to proven principles.

The argument for going forward is that the past is over, we are entering a new world and we need a new vision. But how will we find our way in this new world? Romanticism contends that we should be led by visionary artists who look deep into their creative psyches, since the artist's psyche will correspond to the "psyche," or spirit of the age, of the emerging world.

Mozart had broken free of the Baroque complexity of Bach's music of "too many notes" to occupy simultaneously the world of Fragonard, whose Rococo paintings depicted frivolous aristocrats, and the intellectual salons of the Enlightenment. His 1791 opera, *The Magic Flute*, has Enlightenment themes borrowed from Freemasonry and gives victory to Sarastro, standing for the new world of rationality, over the Queen of the Night, standing for the old world of superstition. The music has a brilliant clarity embodying the Enlightenment project of extending rationality beyond the understanding of nature to the understanding and betterment of the human condition, and it is accessible to the new "ordinary person."

Just fourteen years after the *Magic Flute*, Beethoven's *Eroica* shattered that world. With the optimism of the French Revolution collapsing into the Terror, and then Napoleon's betrayal of the Revolution by declaring himself Emperor, the confidence of the Enlightenment was tempered by a sense that there were forces beyond human rationality. Mozart's and Haydn's classicism had used principles of proportion and rationality; the parts are to each other as they are to the fully comprehendible whole. But the Viennese symphony of Mozart and Haydn was over, shattered by Beethoven's Romanticism. Beginning with his *Eroica* and culminating in his late string quartets, Beethoven uses classical structures only to violate them. One way to put it is to say that classical composition fits emotions to the structure, while Romantic composition fits the structure to the emotions. Romantic music used emotional expression to describe the deeper truths of human feelings and of nature, rejecting rationalism for the sublime. The Romantic poet William Blake, deriding two great Enlightenment thinkers, writes:

> *Mock on, mock on, Voltaire, Rousseau;*
> *Mock on, mock on; 'tis all in vain!*

The sublime, the aesthetic of Romanticism, holds that reason is not adequate to describe the overwhelming grandeur of the cosmos, the irresistible power of nature, the depth of the human psyche. Emotion and awe overpower rationality, and grand sweeps of nature confound human attempts at understanding. The sublime presents the power we feel in the paintings of Caspar David Friedrich and J. M. W. Turner that we referred to earlier, and it presented a totally new notion of how we should relate to and live in the world. In architecture the clarity of Neoclassicism is challenged by Piranesi's engravings of his *Carceri d'invenzione*, or Imaginary Prisons, first published in 1750 and republished in a reworked state in 1761. His prisons are vast spaces in which humans are overwhelmed. The column, against whose verticality and proportions we had measured ourselves since the Greeks, is gone, signaling the end of the humanist world, while vast arches reaching back into receding labyrinthine spaces presents an opening into the abyss of the unconscious that would usher in a new age.

The Enlightenment had extended Renaissance humanism and created a world built on science and reason. Romanticism in general and Beethoven's *Eroica* in particular destroyed that world, opening us to the vastness of nature and the depths of the human psyche.

Van Gogh's The Starry Night

Earlier we looked at Vincent van Gogh's 1889 painting, *The Starry Night*, in the context of the then new electric communications technologies. A new world of shimmering electromagnetic fields, of energy, of flux, was emerging.

Newton had given us a mechanistic world of matter. Energy was emergent, a consequence of the motion of matter. Today we are more likely to see the world as energy, and matter as disturbances in an energy field. Newton's world was one of discrete objects located in a uniform space and time, governed by the laws of physics. Not all were happy with that world; recall that we earlier quoted William Blake's reference to Newton's "Single vision."

What was an aesthetic inclination for the Romantics became the science of the late nineteenth century. Just as Newton's physics and perspective painting had shattered the holism of the medieval world, so Faraday's and Maxwell's electromagnetic fields shattered the mechanistic clockwork world to bring us one where matter is vortices in energy fields. Van Gogh's *The Starry Night* introduced not just a new style, but a new way for us to be in the world in which we would directly feel the energies flowing through the world and ourselves. Van Gogh had experienced this flow in his religious ecstasies, and struggled to make paintings that would open all of us to his experiences. His *The Starry Night* destroys the Newtonian world as much as it opens up the modern world.

Frank Gehry's Guggenheim Bilbao Museum
Earlier we looked at the 1997 Guggenheim Museum in Bilbao
Spain by Frank Gehry, recognizable by its billowing titanium
walls, in the context of its culture. Now let's look at the world
it destroyed. In 1958 the Seagram Building, designed by Mies
van der Rohe, opened on Park Avenue in New York. The stark
glass and bronze uniform grid of its façade came to epitomize
the glass skyscrapers that were to eventually dominate cities
around the world. It was a time represented by Sloan Wilson's
1955 novel *The Man in the Gray Flannel Suit*, looking at conformity in the executive suite; by William H. White's 1956 *The
Organization Man*, looking at the absorption of business executives into the organization; and by the advertising agencies
of the early 1960s presented in the television series, *Mad Men*.

Mies's concern is to represent his world. There is no
judgment. Mies does not say that the past was, or the future
will be, better. This is the time and place, the industrial United
States at mid twentieth century with its corporate bureaucra-
cies, in which we live. He says, "Architecture is the will of an
epoch translated into space."

There were many steel frame buildings built in New York
decades before the Seagram Building, including the Chrysler
Building of 1930 designed by William van Alen, which is today regarded by many as the most beautiful building in the
city. Yet not thirty years later a series of glass skyscrapers, including Seagram, sprang up in the New York skyline, defiant,
perhaps sterile, challenging the Chrysler Building, which is
clad in patterned hand-laid brick and has Art Deco elevator
cabs inlayed with exotic woods. The spire of the Chrysler
Building represented a hierarchal corporation headed by an
individual, Walter Chrysler, just as Henry Ford headed Ford
and Alfred Sloan headed General Motors. The Seagram
Building, despite housing the offices of Seagram's head,
Edgar Bronfman, is not hierarchical, but a uniform grid, de-

stroying the early twentieth century hierarchical world of captains of industry and replacing it with the buttoned down mid-century world of the "organization man," technocrats like Robert McNamara's Wiz Kids who reshaped Ford and later the Pentagon, both problematically.

Then, just four years later, Eero Saarinen's TWA Flight Center at New York's Kennedy Airport, evoking a bird in flight, announced the coming cultural upheavals of the sixties and a breaking away from conformity. And forty years after TWA the billowing titanium walls of Gehry's Bilbao completed the destruction of the old world of corporate hierarchies and organization men, and ushered us into a post-modern world. The culture of Silicon Valley was to supplant that of IBM, and the executives in the Seagram Building in gray flannel suits and buttoned down shirts were replaced by the tech entrepreneurs of Silicon Valley in jeans and T-shirts. The world of the grid had been destroyed and we were plunged into a world of flux, from postmodernism in literary theory, to flickering fields of probability in quantum physics, to characters in movies existing in overlapping layers of reality. And today? Younger architects question the arbitrariness of Gehry's approach of beginning his designs with crumpled paper. They are using genomic processes in which rule-based systems generate complex outcomes that we will look at in our discussion of the twenty-first century. Gehry's Bilbao destroyed the world of the organization man, just as its world will in turn be destroyed in our emerging networked genomic era.

Picasso and Matisse: Creativity as Struggle

The notion of creativity as destructive is a consequence of creativity as struggle, sometimes historic struggle. We see an example of such struggle in the competition between Henri Matisse and Pablo Picasso to be the leading modern artist of their day, a struggle that was not just about styles, but also about visions of the then emerging twentieth century.

In the early 1900s, Pablo Picasso (1881–1973) was an ambitious young artist in the Paris scene, but he was quiet, biding his time. He saw his opportunity when Matisse exhibited *Le Bonheur de Vivre* (the joy of life) in 1906. *Le Bonheur* was a large painting, eight feet across, the kind of size an artist uses when asserting that a painting is of major importance. It depicts nude figures dancing, lounging, and making out in a glade. The lines are sensuous and the colors, muted reds, oranges, yellows, and greens, are meant to convey emotion rather than depict nature. Matisse had staked his ground. Picasso responded by asking, what if the joy of life is only skin deep, and beneath it lies a primitive savagery? And what if I can use this notion to wrest from Matisse the role of the leading modern artist? If Matisse would champion erotic joy, Picasso would cut open a vein of suppressed ugly primal energy that threatened the foundations of European civilization, positioning Matisse as representing bourgeois comfort and himself as a rebel plunging into the dangerous unknowns of the modernist future.

In 1907 Picasso painted *Les Demoiselles d'Avignon* (the young ladies of Avignon), a large painting portraying five nude prostitutes at a brothel in Barcelona. Perspective was gone, and the angular forms of the figures opened the way to Cubism. With its primitive masks, angular figures, and incompliant, aggressive female sexuality, *Les Demoiselles* was such a violent challenge to the self-image of European civilization that for many years Picasso showed it to only a few people.

In an essay titled "Reflections on Matisse," the art critic Hilton Kramer writes:

After the impact of Les Demoiselles d'Avignon, *however, Matisse was never again mistaken for an avant-garde incendiary. With the bizarre painting that appalled and electrified the cognoscenti, which understood that* Les Demoiselles *was at once a response to Matisse's* Le bonheur de vivre *(1905-1906) and an assault upon the tradition from which it derived, Picasso effectively appropriated the role of avant-garde wild beast—a role that, as far as public opinion was concerned, he was never to relinquish.*

Picasso continued this theme in many paintings and studies of figures in torment, and revisited it in his 1937 monumental protest to war, *Guernica*. The early twentieth century world chess champion, Emanuel Lasker, remarked, "Life is struggle, and chess is struggle." And, we might add, so is creativity.

So yes, creativity ushers in new worlds that we cannot even imagine until they arrive. But creativity also comes with destruction. Joseph Campbell says:

Life lives on life. This is the sense of the symbol of the Ouroboros, the serpent biting its tail. Everything that lives, lives on the death of something else. Your own body will be food for something else. Anyone who denies this, anyone who holds back, is out of order. Death is an act of giving.

ENEMIES OF CREATIVITY

In the previous chapter we saw that by bringing in the new, creativity sweeps away the old. Here we see how the old resists. This resistance has a long tradition.

To restrict the artist is a crime. It is to murder germinating life.
~ Egon Schiele, Austrian fin de siècle
Expressionist painter

The Man in the White Suit

We might wonder why anyone would be an enemy of creativity; is not creativity universally admired? But of course it is not. Earlier we quoted Shelley's essay, "A Defence of Poetry," which ends with the line, "Poets are the unacknowledged legislators of the world." We could take this as a charming notion, but suppose we take it seriously. Legislators write laws, and laws can change things. Those embedded in the status quo usually do not want things changed. In addition, in the previous section we saw the destructive potential of creativity, and we should expect that there will be those who object to having their worlds destroyed.

   In the 1951 British movie, *The Man in the White Suit*, a satirical comedy, Alec Guinness (a brilliant actor with a long career, best know now as Obi-Wan Kenobi) plays Sidney Stratton, a young research chemist who develops a super strong fiber which is made into a suit for him that has to be white, since not only does the fiber repel dirt and never wear out, it won't absorb dye. It is also luminous because it is somewhat radioactive.

Stratton is lauded as a genius until both textile mill owners and union leaders realize that once consumers have purchased one of every kind of garment, they will never need another; demand will dry up and the industry will collapse. They turn on Stratton and his invention, and in the climactic scene, chase him through the streets at night, his glowing white suit enabling them to track him. But when they grab him, his suit comes to pieces. There was a flaw in his chemistry. The mob is triumphant and Stratton is left standing in his underwear. But as he walks off looking at his research notes, he spots something and exclaims, "I see!" He is intent on reproducing his fiber, this time without the flaw.

Our first thought about *The Man in the White Suit* is that it presents conflicting interests. The mill owners wish to protect their investments and the workers their jobs, while Stanton wishes to advance his career as an up-and-coming chemist. But this is not quite right. The mill owners could have made plenty of money in a new economy of durable fabric by turning to changes in fashions. The workers could have bargained for generous buy-outs and tuition for their children to attend fashion school. And Stanton does his career no good by upsetting everyone. No, there are other motivations here. The owners seek to protect their privilege while they are too lazy to exercise the imaginativeness, inventiveness, and risk-taking of their grandfathers who created their industry, and the workers seek to protect a static way of life. And Stanton? He is driven not by his career, but by creativity.

A hundred stories come to mind of inventions repressed or ignored, often by companies that could have owned the future. In 1973, eleven years before the introduction of the Apple Macintosh computer, researchers at the Xerox Palo Alto Research Center, working with ideas pioneered by Doug Engelbart, developed the

Xerox Alto computer, incorporating a graphical user interface and a mouse (now used for Mac and Windows computers), able to handle video, and linked by a local area network to high speed laser printers, which they also developed. Other computers at the time required telephone book-sized manuals next to them to remind users of the obscure commands they had to type on the keyboard to make anything happen. Xerox did not know what to do with the Alto and eventually had to bring in executives from the auto industry to kill it. Apple and eventually Microsoft did know what to do with this technology, and are now two of the largest companies on the planet. At the time of this writing, Xerox ranks 131st.

A Creative Realm

Suppose we say that there is a creative realm that exerts an influence on our world. Recall the painters and novelists who have reported that they became vehicles for their works to complete themselves. We are again in the realm of metaphor, thinking in ways not allowed in academia. Let's look at this notion in the work of one important Visionary Creative.

Next to Frank Lloyd Wright, Louis Kahn (1901–1974) is the most important American architect. Kahn's work was undistinguished until he was sixty when his designed a laboratory that brought him major recognition, and he went on to do a handful of buildings regarded as among the most important of the twentieth century, including the Kimbell Art Museum in Fort Worth, Texas, and the Salk Institute in La Jolla, California. What brought about this change in Kahn's work?

Kahn began his transformation by attacking a fundamental problem of modern architecture, its lack of spiritual depth. He asked, what is it that we as architects most deeply value, and how does our modern architecture celebrate that? For the most part he found the answers to be nothing, and it didn't. Kahn called this spiritual depth he was looking for "Order." And it was not just our architecture that was lacking Order, it was modern culture. Twentieth century architecture and twentieth century culture needed to become rooted but not in a historical past. Rather it needed to become rooted in existence itself.

By Order Kahn did not mean "orderly," but rather the principle underlying all things. Kahn writes:

> *Silence, the Unmeasurable, desire to be, desire to express, the source of new need, meets Light, the Measurable, giver of all presence, by will, by law at a threshold which is inspiration, the sanctuary of art, the Treasury of Shadow.*

Silence is the realm of potential, the source of all things, and the Visionary Creative reaches into this realm to bring things into Light where they then manifest in our material world.

Kahn was not unique in this vision. The architect Louis Sullivan presents a drawing of a seed split open to show the germ. Under it he writes:

> *The germ is the real thing; the seat of identity. Within its delicate mechanism lies the will to power: the function which is to seek and eventually to find its full expression in form.*

And Frank Lloyd Wright writes:

> *Deeper than the truths of Philosophy or the laws of morality is the sense of honor. What is honor? Not the rules of a code—but the nature of honor. What would be the honor of a brick? That in the brick which makes the brick a brick.*

What Kahn calls "Form," Sullivan calls "function" and Wright calls "honor" is an existence will—that which makes the thing what it is. Thus Order is the way something exists with integrity, clarity, and rootedness, fully expressing its inner

94

nature. And again of course, none of this can be expressed in academic terms.

The Creative and the Bureaucrat

Joseph Campbell, one of the major cultural figures of the twentieth century, worked with the idea that myth, religion, literature, and art are repositories of the workings of our deep psychology and of the cosmos, as well as a means of participating in our world. His most influential book, *The Hero With a Thousand Faces*, provided the themes for George Lucas's *Star Wars* movies, and at the end of his long career Campbell participated in a series of interviews with journalist Bill Moyers that were presented on public television in a series titled *The Power of Myth*. In the series Campbell repeated one of his favorite phrases, "Follow your bliss." The common understanding of this phrase is that if you listen, you will hear an inner calling, and if you follow that calling, you will find a kind of fulfillment that you cannot find in any other way. There is seemingly nothing controversial here—it is what wise people have counseled forever, and what just about every commencement speaker advises new graduates. Earlier we saw Rilke's, "There is only one way: Go within. Search for the cause, find the impetus that bids you write." And we saw similar admonitions from Joyce, Graham, and Jobs. And we could have cited a hundred more.

But *The Power of Myth* series became immensely popular. Too many people were exposed to Campbell's "dangerous ideas," and his remark was not taken well—the cultural left and right piled on. Unfortunately, Campbell had died at age eighty-three just before the series was aired, so he was unable to defend himself from what were in many cases vicious attacks. To exaggerate just a bit, some on the right feared that those who followed their bliss would take drugs and drop out, while some on the left feared that if everyone followed their bliss, they would all become Wall Street bankers and get rich. Both right and left feared that people would be doing what they themselves thought best, rather than doing the socially productive work proscribed by the right, or the (different) socially productive work proscribed by the left. Both apparently prefer a system in which an outside authority determines one's life course.

What are the origins of this fear of people acting for themselves? Campbell sees it going all the way back to our earliest cultures in the opposition between the shaman and the priest. Shamans, he says, are independent of their societies and are in touch with a spirit realm. Priests are agents of institutions who gain their powers from ordination, not from their own experiences. They repress shamans.

We see a similar tension in the opposition between the creative and the bureaucrat everywhere today, including in Dilbert's daily cartoon conflicts with his manager. The abilities of creatives are native to themselves, as are Dilbert's and those of shamans. Either they have mastery, talent, insight, and creativity or they do not. They gain nothing from the title of a position. Managers may or may not have mastery, talent, insight, or creativity, but it often does not matter. Their authority comes from their organizations and their powers are those listed in their job descriptions. We are all familiar with poor managers, and hopefully with some great managers.

We see the effort to repress individuality and impose groupthink everywhere, beginning in kindergarten where children are assigned group projects and extending into colleges where political correctness discourages independent thought. Everywhere we are told that we need community, collaboration, cooperation, consensus, compromise. Susan Cain, in her book, *Quiet: The Power of Introverts in a World That Can't Stop Talking*, writes that solitude is now out of fashion and that our culture is in thrall to what she calls the New

Groupthink. We are told that creativity comes from the group, that collaboration is in, and that lone geniuses are out.

Imagine two college applicants. One has spent a summer in Peru with a volunteer group helping to bring water to a village. The other spent a summer reading Russian novels. To which will the admissions committee respond more favorably? Working in Peru our applicant might have learned the values of community and collaboration. Reading the novels of Tolstoy, Dostoyevsky, Turgenev, and Gogol, our other applicant might have gained insights into the human condition, the depths of the human psyche, the torments of the soul, and the surreal nature of our world. Both activities are worthy, and both realms of learning are valuable. The question is, in what balance?

We are constantly pushed toward our social responsibilities, toward group participation, toward collaboration while being asked to subsume our individual Selves and focus on the common good. All of this is laudable, and the solutions to some of our problems may well come from such collaboration. Indeed we can find countless studies that show that community, collaboration, and consensus can improve workplace productivity. But can they improve Visionary Creativity? The studies don't say.

We are now told that true creativity happens only in groups, and when individuals think they are creating alone, they are actually using the work of groups. But might there also be such a thing as individual creativity? And might not some of our problems respond to that kind of creativity? We could look at a hundred examples, but for now here are two. Working by himself after hours from his Hewlett-Packard job, Steve Wozniak designed the first Apple computer, the Apple I, sold mostly to hobbyists, and then the Apple II, one of the first commercially successful personal computers and the machine that launched Apple, the company Wozniak cofounded with Steve Jobs. Wozniak writes:

Most inventors and engineers I've met are like me ... they live in their heads. They're almost like artists. In fact, the very best of them are artists. And artists work best alone... I'm going to give you some advice that might be hard to take. That advice is: Work alone... Not on a committee. Not on a team.

And Max Planck, a pioneer of quantum theory, writes:

New scientific ideas never spring from a communal body, however organized, but rather from the head of an individually inspired researcher who struggles with his problems in lonely thought and unites all his thought on one single point which is his whole world for the moment.

Of course creatives are dependent on others. Wozniak teamed with Jobs, and Planck was one of a group of physicists who developed quantum theory. Both Shakespeare's language and his stories are built on what came before; we all know that. And we have been saying throughout this book that creativity takes place in the context of its culture and builds on or rejects what has come before. The issue is where the emphasis is put and why. In other times, we celebrated the individual creator while now it's the commons. And obviously much creativity does require collaboration, as we can see by looking at the credits at the ends of movies and television shows, so let's look at what is happening here. The past several decades of movies have seen periods of remarkable creativity, each dominated by different groups of directors: the early 1960s by Fellini, Godard, Bergman, Antonioni, and others; the late 1960s and the 1970s by Coppola, Kubrick, Scorsese, Altman, Lucas, and others. But more recently movies have become bloated with special effects (especially explosions) and weighed down by clichéd stories, and they are no longer our dominant art form. As budgets have increased and as investors have demanded higher returns, studio executives have been unable to refrain from sticking their fingers into the creative process (collaborations of "community, consensus, compromise"), and their meddling has often brought mediocrity.

There are dozens of instances of ineptitude on the parts of Hollywood studio executives that wrecked movies and cost investors hundreds of millions of dollars. And one in which studio executives failed to get their way at every turn. Talking about the making of *The Godfather*, its director and co-screenwriter, Francis Ford Coppola says:

> *The Godfather was a very unappreciated movie when we were making it. They were very unhappy with it. They didn't like the cast. They didn't like the way I was shooting it. I was always on the verge of getting fired. So it was an extremely nightmarish experience. I had two little kids, and the third one was born during that. We lived in a little apartment, and I was basically frightened that they didn't like it. They had as much as said that, so when it was all over I wasn't at all confident that it was going to be successful, and that I'd ever get another job.*

Coppola was not Paramount's first choice to direct the movie, and was given the job only after two others turned it down. Paramount was perpetually on the verge of firing him, and kept a "shadow director" on the set to step in should they be successful in doing so. Paramount fought Coppola on casting Brando as Don Vito Corleone, declaring, "Marlon Brando will never appear in this motion picture." They wanted Danny Thomas. The attempted interventions were endless, and Coppola expended as much energy fending off studio executives as he did crafting his movie. Paramount even attempted to introduce a "violence coach" into the production to make the movie more sensational, and was successful in destroying the recording of the original musical score, now regarded as one of the most memorable in movie history. A degraded copy had to be used.

The outcome of all this? *The Godfather* won three Academy Awards and is generally regarded as one of the greatest movies of all time. And the studio's concern about a return on its modest investment? It still holds records as one of the top grossing movies of all time.

Despite the fact that some movies, like *The Godfather*, have been able to slip by studio executives, the studios have been able to assure the mediocrity of many recent movies, and a new genre has now come to the fore, the long-form drama broadcast on cable television and distributed by such companies as Netflix, leading some to refer to the current period as television's Third Golden Age. The genre is the signature American art form of the first decades of the twenty-first century. Earlier we mentioned Brett Martin's book *Difficult Men* that chronicles the making of *The Sopranos*, conceived by David Chase and regarded by many as the best television series ever; *The Wire*, created by David Simon and Ed Burns; *Mad Men*, created by Matthew Weiner and Jon Hamm; *Six Feet Under*, created by Alan Ball; and *Deadwood*, created by David Milch; among others. One after another these shows exploded into our living rooms, shocking us with their depth of drama, grittiness of character, violence, and language. And with the brilliance of their writing, acting, and directing. And they continue to pour forth, with *Justified*, *The Walking Dead*, *Game of Thrones*, *Manhattan*, *Boardwalk Empire*, *Hell on Wheels*, *House of Cards*, and *The Nick* among recent examples. It would not be hyperbole to call these dramas Shakespearian in their storytelling, dramatic power, and conflicts of family and clan. And in their language. *Justified*, created by Graham Yost, takes place in the hill country of eastern Kentucky where many of the residents are still close to their English

100

ancestry, and its dialogue, as is that in the series *Deadwood*, is noticeably Shakespearian. What underlies the emergence of this new genre and why are the shows so often excellent?

Of course the ability to develop characters and plots over numerous episodes over several seasons is a factor, but of most importance is that the cable studio executives came to accept a new breed of creative called a "show runner." The book *Crafty Screenwriting* defines a show runner as: "the person responsible for all creative aspects of the show, and responsible only to the network (and production company, if it's not his production company). The boss. Usually a writer." The *Los Angeles Times* columnist, Scott Collins, describes show runners as a combination of artists and operations managers who have immense responsibilities for every aspect of their shows.

Obviously show runners work with huge teams; just look at the credits at the end of one of their shows. So yes, they are involved in collaborations. But these are not collaborations of "community, consensus, compromise," but rather collaborations taking place in the context of vision and leadership. David Chase had a vision of Tony Soprano. He writes:

I want to tell a story about this particular man. I want to tell the story about the reality of being a mobster—or what I perceive to be the reality of life in organized crime. They aren't shooting each other every day. They sit around eating baked ziti and betting and figuring out who owes who money. Occasionally, violence breaks out—more often than it does in the banking world, perhaps.

The reason *The Sopranos* turned out as it did is that Chase was able to tell his story his way, not the way studio executives thought it should be mangled. And we should notice something that distinguishes the movie directors we listed above.

101

They all rebelled against the studio system and asserted their independence to make their movies in their own ways. Coppola even left Los Angeles for San Francisco in an attempt to distance himself from the restrictions of the studios and the unions.

Now take this lesson and apply it to an electronics firm developing a new smart phone or an automobile company developing a new car. Allowing designers and engineers to create smart phones and cars can lead to great smart phones and cars. No guarantee, but it is more likely. Allowing management to interfere with the process is more likely to lead to mediocre smart phones and cars.

Despite all we are told about community, collaboration, cooperation, consensus, and compromise, not only is most creativity done by lone individuals, but it tends to happen only after such individuals have had time alone to think. J. K. Rowling began her Harry Potter novels while teaching English at night and being alone writing during the day, and later being able to sit in quiet pubs with her baby to think and write. Einstein famously worked as a clerk in the Swiss patent office, deliberately avoiding a promotion so that he would have time to think. And Newton developed his theories of calculus, optics, and gravity while spending two years in isolation at his home in Woolsthorpe, a hamlet in Lincolnshire because Trinity College, where he was a teaching assistant, was closed due to the Great Plague. We suspect that Rowling, Einstein, and Newton were not involved in group brainstorming sessions.

Even when work is done in teams, great designs are more likely to result when the teams have strong leaders. To design the Macintosh computer at Apple, Jobs removed his team from the corporate headquarters to a building across the street where he ran up a pirate flag. Shortly after the release of the Macintosh, which had a graphical user interface now found on all computers, tablets, and smart phones, Apple's new

CEO, who had been recruited from Pepsi, fired Jobs for "insufficient consensus and compromise," and Jobs spent the next eleven years in the wilderness before being brought back to lead Apple from near bankruptcy to being the most valuable company on the planet. Part of his strategy on returning was to release the creative talents of Apple's chief designer, Jony Ive, whose ideas had been bottled up in his studio.

While we are enriched at every level of our lives and of our society by the creations of individuals, our educational, corporate, and political institutions seek to suppress that kind of creativity and promote the commons—the good of the whole—usually as decided by self-appointed elites.

Who Owns Your Creativity?

But the problem is even more chilling. Not only does the bureaucracy want its roles to dominate, it even wants to control individual creativity, as we see in the contrast between Ayn Rand's Objectivism and Michael J. Sandel's Communitarianism.

Objectivism holds that the purpose of one's life is the pursuit of one's own rational self-interest, and that the social system should enable that pursuit through *laissez-faire* capitalism. But this is not exactly what we see in Rand's perpetually best-selling novel, *Atlas Shrugged*. In it we meet Hank Rearden, creator of Rearden Metal. Rearden Metal is a marvelous alloy with the potential to change the world. The government attacks Rearden Metal as unproven and dangerous even while seeking to force Rearden to surrender his secrets and the control of his company in hopes the government can use both to prop up itself and an economy it has driven into a ditch. While Rand's philosophy promotes self-interest, her novel suggests something else. If Hank Rearden were seeking only to maximize his own self-interests, he would forget the hassles of making Rearden Metal, make junk steel, and get very rich.

But he doesn't do that; there is something else driving him, something not addressed in Objectivism that we will get back to in a moment.

Michael J. Sandel is a professor of philosophy at Harvard University, where his course on justice regularly attracts over a thousand students. In it he asks, "What's the right thing to do?" Sandel confesses that the course is structured to lead to his own values, which are Communitarian. Sandel's brand of Communitarianism contends that we are not independent individuals, but rather we are embedded in communities of families, institutions, nations, etc. Once establishing that we are so embedded, he contends that these communities have obligations to us, and we likewise have obligations to them. According to Sandel, our obligations to our communities are so profound that we do not have ownership of what we produce and earn, but must share it, with the manner of sharing to be determined by the community. Since most social systems have long accepted taxes, there is nothing out of the ordinary in his position regarding what we produce and earn. But Sandel goes further, and implies that the community also owns our creativity, and that the community should decide how our creativity may be deployed. A half century after Rand's *Atlas Shrugged*, Sandel has provided the political philosophy to justify the government that torments Rearden and undermines its country.

So, who is right, Rand or Sandel? Who should own your creativity? I have to confess to a negative reaction to Sandel's position. It is wrapped in a seemingly benign philosophy that is presented not only in a course at Harvard, but in a PBS television series and a book, all titled *Justice: What's the Right Thing to Do?"* Who could be against justice? Who wants to do the wrong thing? But what if those deciding the correct disposition of our creativity are not as wise and benign as Sandel? The Soviet ballet dancers, Rudolf Nureyev and Mikhail

Baryshnikov, were treated like princes by their commons, showered with material goods denied others, and privileged with audiences that understood ballet and appreciated their artistry. They both defected to the West, feeling that artistic freedom was more important than what was granted by their commons. The true power behind their commons did not appreciate this defiance, and the Soviet dictator, Nikita Khrushchev, ordered that Nureyev be brutally killed.

Visionary Creatives are in touch with the energies of the cosmos. We are deluded if we think it benefits us to attempt to tell them, and by extension the cosmos, what to do. I suggest that we should have the faith to leave people to "follow their bliss," and to believe that in so doing we will end up with a better distribution of leaders, nurturers, producers, actives, scholars, mystics, somnambulists, and creatives, and that each will be more likely to produce what we need than if we put that determination in the hands of "philosophers of justice."

But I also think that Rand's Objectivism is wanting. There is more to human beings than "rational self-interest." What if neither Sandel nor Rand is right, what if in a vibrant, dynamic, life-affirming world, in the world of the people who built the Gothic cathedrals and created the Arthurian Romances and imagined Huck Finn, in the world of Galileo and Newton and Einstein, in the world of Van Gogh and Picasso and Duchamp, in the world of Joyce and Fitzgerald and Rowling, in that world, which is our world, *our creativity owns us*. The New York School painter and printmaker, Philip Guston, stated: "When you're in the studio painting, there are a lot of people in there with you—your teachers, friends, painters from history, critics... and one by one if you're really painting, they walk out. And if you're *really* painting YOU walk out."

In *The Future and its Enemies: The Growing Conflict Over Creativity, Enterprise, and Progress*, the cultural writer, Virginia Postrel, describes a conflict between two approaches to progress, "stasism" and "dynamism." Stasists fall into two categories: reactionaries who fear an unknown future and value stability, and technocrats who value the future but only if it conforms to their plans, who fear chaos, and who wish to control and regulate the future. Both abhor an open future and an open society.

Dynamists embrace the messy progress that takes place in the context of exploration, change, and creativity that brings us individual choice, an open future, and an open society. In other words, they embrace Visionary Creativity.

We should not tell our creativity what futures to make for us. If we do, we will get only narrow limited worlds that our rational minds can cobble together, and not the expansive worlds offered to us by the cosmos. Creatives are conduits for the flow of creative energy from the cosmos into manifestation, and stifling them can only limit what the cosmos brings us.

If we were to make an animated film of a caterpillar morphing into a butterfly, we might show wings emerging from the caterpillar's back, etc. But that is not what happens. What happens is that the caterpillar encases itself in a cocoon and then dissolves into a mush from which the butterfly forms. What an incredible act of faith to let go like that. How does the caterpillar know something will come out of the mush? In like manner, while there is no guarantee, our creativity can take us to luminous futures, to butterflies, but only if we let go and allow it to do so.

PART TWO:
■ BECOMING A VISIONARY CREATIVE

YOU BECOMING A
VISIONARY CREATIVE

In which we look at how you might become a Visionary Creative and we examine Nietzsche's parable of the camel, the lion, and the child.

I will tell you of the three metamorphoses of the spirit: how the spirit becomes a camel; the camel, a lion; and the lion then a child.
   ~ Friedrich Nietzsche

The Three Metamorphoses of the Spirit

How might you prepare yourself to become a Visionary Creative? Of course it will depend on your field of interest—do you wish to become a composer, a physicist, an architect, a filmmaker? But let's assume that we do not know, so our approach will have to be general.

We might begin by looking at studies by psychologists and educators who address creativity, but as we mentioned at the beginning of this book, most such studies seek to assure us that we are all creative and even that we can all be geniuses. And while studies by neurophysiologists might present us with interesting insights, they are of little practical use for the creative.

Recall our description at the beginning of this book: *Visionary Creatives feel that our world is no longer what we have thought it to be and that a new world is struggling to be born. They wonder what is wrong with others that they do not also feel this and their motivation becomes to produce work that will help others feel what they feel. Their audiences may initially reject their work, but after they have encountered it, they will be changed, and they will be in a new world in a new way.*

Few psychologists, educators, or neurophysiologists would be able to make any sense of the preceding description, and most institutions, granting agencies, and schools, even if they can sometimes recognize it, find it difficult to support. But Friedrich Nietzsche recognized it and promoted it. So let's start with Nietzsche's "The Three Metamorphoses of the Spirit" from his *Thus Spoke Zarathustra*. Nietzsche writes:

> *I will tell you of the three metamorphoses of the spirit: how the spirit becomes a camel; the camel, a lion; and the lion then a child...*
>
> *"What is difficult?" asks the spirit "So that I can take it upon me and celebrate my strength," as it kneels down like a camel willing to accept its burden...*
>
> *All of the most difficult things the spirit that would be burdened much takes upon itself: and like the burdened camel it then speeds into the desert. But, in the loneliest desert, the second metamorphosis occurs: here the spirit becomes a lion who wants his own freedom and to be master of the desert.*
>
> *Here he wants to make an enemy of his last god; he wants to battle the great dragon for ultimate victory.*
>
> *What is the great dragon who the spirit no longer wishes to call Lord and God? "Thou Shalt," is the dragon's name. But the spirit of the Lion says, "I Will."*
>
> *"Thou Shalt," lies in his path, covered in scales of shimmering gold, and on every scale is written, "Thou Shalt." "All Values have already been established, and I am the personification of All Established Values, there should be no more."*
>
> *My Brother, what need is there for a Lion Spirit? Is it not enough, the beast of burden, who is obedient and reverent?" To Create Freedom, and declare "No" to conventional*

obligation, this the lion can do.

To create new values, the lion is not capable of this. But to create the freedom to create the new, this is within the lion's Power...

But tell me, Brother, what can the child do, which even the Lion could not? Why must the Lion still become a child?

A Child is innocence and forgetting, a new beginning, a game, a wheel rolling out of its own center, a first movement, a "Yes."

"Yes", to the game of Creation, my Brothers, yes to saying "Yes" to life: the Spirit wants its own Will and the one who had been lost to the world now conquers the world...

That was a long excerpt, but worth quoting, as it describes the path you will be taking in becoming a Visionary Creative. First as a camel you master your culture and the traditions and techniques of your discipline. Then as a lion you confront the traditions you have mastered, which take the form of a dragon named Thou Shalt, and if they do not ring true for you, you challenge them and if necessary, destroy them. You must reject everything you have been told about the world, and then live in—fully experience—the world as it (now) is.

Earlier we described how Michelangelo, in contributing to the creation of humanism, helped destroy the medieval notion of what a human being is, and how Mark Zuckerberg helped destroy the private humanist Self. As you find your own way, you will be surprised how quickly you see flaws in the approaches of even the figures you most respect. As a child, a wheel rolling out of its own center, you put forward your own work and overthrow theirs.

Art in particular and creativity in general imply originality, the bringing of something new into being. Yet, paradoxically, art and creativity almost always occur within existing traditions, making possible the discontinuities we discussed above. Recall

111

that we earlier said, echoing the literary critic Harold Bloom, that there are no works of creativity, only relationships between works. Each painting, each musical composition, each scientific theory, each chunk of software code, calls up for us myriads of others and exists in relationship to them. So you begin by mastering existing traditions. We see that many who break rules to forge new forms were fully the masters of the traditions they smashed. Beethoven had mastered the Viennese symphony of Haydn and Mozart before he launched Romanticism. Picasso had mastered classical painting by the time he dropped out of the academy at sixteen. Thelonious Monk worked with the jazz greats of his day, from Dizzy Gillespie to Miles Davis, in the creation of bebop before entering into his own world. Robert Venturi outraged the architectural world with his attacks on orthodox modernism in his book, *Complexity and Contradiction in Architecture*, but in the book he shows that he understands the modern masters more deeply than do his critics. However, keep in mind that you will know your discipline as a practitioner, not as an academic or a historian.

We swim in seas of traditions: of our culture, of an art form, of preceding works of art. Art is almost always discussed and even experienced with an awareness of its rootedness in nested Russian dolls of tradition, from recent work related to the one under consideration, to the history of the particular form, to our cultural condition today, to the context of the work's culture, and sometimes even to the history of art going all the way back to the caves.

Education

A Framework

Let's see how Nietzsche's parable might apply to you. If your education was cohesive—if your task as a camel was successful—it will have given you a framework into which you can weave what you will do for the rest of your life. What you weave into your framework should strengthen it, enrich it, fill it out. A framework situates you so that you are not buffeted about by every new thing that comes along. And it may be that you challenge and rework your framework. It should be flexible. But if your education was a series of randomly thrown together unrelated happenings, you will have no coherent place to hang your ongoing experience. You will accumulate your learning and even your life haphazardly and it will never make sense.

If your education was not cohesive, if it failed to provide you with such a framework, you might begin to construct one for yourself. We will see an example of how this can be done below when we look at Joseph Campbell's self-education.

Schools

The most important thing a school can do is to have a cohesive point of view that helps you form a framework, but this is rare today. Despite this failure, schools have an inordinate influence on our lives, far beyond what they should have. For example in order to teach musical composition today one must obtain a PhD, and that might take until your late thirties. Some would not have made it. Chopin died at thirty-nine, Gershwin at thirty-eight, Bizet at thirty-seven, Mozart at thirty-five, and Schubert at thirty-one. And Kurt Cobain, Brian Jones, Jimi Hendrix, Janis Joplin, Jim Morrison, and Amy Winehouse are among the dozens of Rock stars who died at the age of twenty-seven. Just think what they could have accomplished if they had lived long enough to have finished graduate school. We could make the same observation regarding writing. Sylvia Plath and Emily Brontë died at thirty, Stephen Crane and Percy Bysshe Shelley at twenty-nine, and John Keats at twenty-five. Arthur Rimbaud died at thirty-seven, but stopped writing at twenty-one, leaving Europe with

113

the remark, "True life is elsewhere," to become a gunrunner. And none of them had a PhD.

In physics, George Gamow observes that Newton came up with his law of gravity at twenty-three, Einstein with his theory of relativity at twenty-six; and Niels Bohr his theory of the atom at twenty-seven. Gamow adds that he published his work on the transformations of the atomic nucleus at twenty-four. Today's physicists would not have completed their PhDs at such ages, and are not permitted to make such contributions. And today physics is a group effort. Fundamental breakthroughs (paradigm shifts that destroy old approaches and introduce new ones) by individuals are no longer welcome—they are too threatening to established physics.

It may have been an intuitive sense that the longer one stays in college and delays entering the fray, the less successful one will be, that led many tech entrepreneurs, most famously Bill Gates, Steve Jobs, Larry Ellison, Michael Dell, Mark Zuckerberg, and Jack Dorsey, founders of Microsoft, Apple, Oracle, Dell, Facebook, and Twitter, to drop out of college, and Sergey Brin and Larry Page, founders of Google, to drop out of graduate school. More recently, David Karp, founder of the social networking site, Tumblr, whom we looked at earlier, didn't drop out of college, as he didn't even go to college; he didn't even finish high school, having dropped out of prestigious Bronx Science. His mother saw how bored he was in school and how absorbed he was at night in front of his computer. Seeing that his passion was computers, she encouraged him to drop out of school.

In an earlier generation, Edwin Land, the developer of the Polaroid instant camera, dropped out of Harvard and would sneak into laboratories at Columbia University at night to do his initial research. Michael Ellsberg, author of *The Education of Millionaires*, writes, "If a young person happens to retain enough creative spirit to start a business upon grad-

114

uation, she does so in spite of her schooling, not because of it." Perhaps they were all motivated by the spirit of Alexander, who led armies at the age of sixteen, and who modeled his life on that of Achilles. Steve Jobs remarked, "None of us has any idea how long we're going to be here, nor do I, but my feeling is I've got to accomplish a lot of these things while I am young."

It is not necessarily that schools are teaching the wrong things, but that they crowd out the opportunity for something else: actually doing what one aspires to do.

Teachers

Your teachers—real people who influence you, or composites that you create for yourself—bring to you an objectivity and clarity that you initially do not have. The best teachers have a point of view, are in command of their tradition, help you enter into your discipline in your own way, and believe that you have the potential to surpass them and do all they can to help you do so. Eventually you will internalize your teachers. In school, you bring your work to the studio. Your classmates admire it. Your teachers work with you, take it apart, analyze your intentions, identify your strategies, find weaknesses, and help you move forward with a deeper understanding. Then you enter your discipline and you are no longer with your teachers but you can still hear their voices. Eventually that fades and you hear your own voice. You take your work apart, analyze your intentions, identify your strategies, find weaknesses, and move forward with a deeper understanding on your own.

The great modern architect, Louis Kahn would ask, " 'How am I doing, Corbusier, how am I doing Gothic architecture, how am I doing Greek architecture.' You see, Corbusier was my teacher, and Paul Cret was my teacher. I have learned not to do as they did, not to imitate, but to sense their spirit." Kahn studied with and worked for the Beaux Arts master, Paul Philippe Cret, but he never studied with or worked for Le Corbusier, he simply adopted him as a teacher. And he revered the great eras in architecture and considered them also to be his teachers.

Colleagues

With rare exceptions, excelling in your discipline comes from being taught by, mentored by, advised by, getting feedback from, working with, and competing with those who excel. And then from you yourself providing such support for others. An extra edge comes from the intensity of a competitive atmosphere, being continually pushed to do better. And your first audience may be the colleagues with whom you have competed.

During second-wave feminism artists and critics pondered the fact that there have been no great women artists. Why? Possible answers included the notion that women lacked a "creativity gene," that there were great women artists but the art establishment refused to recognize them, and that there is no such thing as a great artist. All of these explanations were problematical. Then Linda Nochlin published an essay, "Why Have There Been No Great Women Artists?" In it she shows that great art flows out of interactions between the best artists, interactions that had been denied to women.

There are advantages to being part of a movement with a group of colleagues early in your career. Claude Monet emerged from the Impressionists, Henri Matisse from the Fauves, Salvador Dalí from the Surrealists, Andy Warhol from the Pop artists. A movement provides a launching pad and the other members of the movement are your initial source of support. Being part of a group can also help you gain recognition. If you do something new on your own, the reaction might be, "Don't they know that's not what we're doing

116

right now?" But if a half a dozen people are doing something new, the reaction might be, "There appears to be something new happening. We better check it out."

Take Control of Your Education

Most colleges no longer have any vision of their purposes. They have abandoned agreed-on bodies of material, or canons, with which you should be familiar, and as we mention above, they have also abandoned cohesive points of view around which you could organize the material they present. So you are on your own. How might you go about putting together your own personal canon and point of view? Let's look at the example of the mythologist, Joseph Campbell. Campbell studied medieval literature at Columbia University and in 1927 went to Paris and then Munich to continue his studies. But while in Europe he also became interested in the current cultural scene, discovering, among others, the psychologists Freud and Jung, the painters Picasso and Klee, and the novelists Joyce and Mann, figures not yet widely known in this country. He returned to the states with a broader vision for the direction of his studies, but Columbia informed him that there was no place in academia for his vision.

The stock market had crashed, so Campbell went to Woodstock in New York where he was able to rent a cabin for fifty dollars a year. Buying books on credit, he lined his shelves with the world's literature and read nine hours a day for five years, often pursuing threads backwards. He read Spengler, who mentions Nietzsche, so he read Nietzsche, which took him back to Schopenhauer, and then back to Kant. Then he returned to Joyce, whom he had read while in Paris, and saw that Joyce was addressing the same issues as was Schopenhauer. Then Jung again, seeing the parallels between his thinking and that of Spengler. He read carefully, underlining, putting notes in the margins, absorbing material,

117

putting together the ideas he would later present in his major works, *The Hero With a Thousand Faces* and *The Masks of God*, which are rich with references to the philosophies, literatures, myths, arts, and religions of many cultures, ideas that underlie our approach to mythology to this day.

Campbell arrived at an organizing insight that pulled together what he had mastered and provided him a framework within which to add new material. Campbell's insight was that what we call the philosophies, literatures, myths, arts, and religions of the world's cultures are not separate disciplines, but are, for each culture, a supra-psychology—metaphors for its experiencings of the Self, the world, and the cosmos, and the "opening through which the inexhaustible energies of the cosmos pour into human cultural manifestation."

Of course you will not follow Campbell's path, and you will not arrive at his organizing insight; your organizing insight might not even come from books. It is up to you to find your own path and your own organizing insight for today. Just realize that school will not find them for you, although if you are lucky, you may encounter one or more teachers who can help you.

YOUR WORK

In which we urge you to be in the world, ask if you are a hedgehog or a fox, and look at the arc of your work.

riverrun, past Eve and Adam's, from swerve of shore to bend of bay, brings us by a commodius vicus of recirculation back to Howth Castle and Environs.
   ~ Opening line of Finnegans Wake by James Joyce

Be in the World

As a creative you may be tempted to live in your own world, creating imaginary paintings, novels, movies, buildings, and even cities—all in your mind. In his novel *Invisible Cities*, Italo Calvino imagines the wondrous cities that Marco Polo encountered in his travels and described to Kublai Kahn.

Leaving there and proceeding for three days toward the east, you reach Diomira, a city with sixty silver domes, bronze statues of all the gods, streets paved with lead, a crystal theater, a golden cock that crows each morning on a tower.

Novelists can work alone and a few may not even care if their work reaches an audience, but for the most part, creatives must work with others and must reach an audience. We could discuss what happens if a novel is written and nobody reads it. Certainly, there must be great novels and paintings that no one other than the writer or painter ever saw; we can surmise as much because we know of examples that came to light but might not have. Before he died, having already destroyed ninety percent of his work, the novelist Franz Kafka wrote, "My last request: Everything I leave behind me… in the way of diaries, manuscripts, letters (my own and others') sketches and so on, be burned unread." They weren't, but they might have been, and if they had been burned we would not have *The Trial*, *The Castle*, or *Amerika*. T. E. Lawrence, known as Lawrence of Arabia, titled his book about his participation in the Arab revolt during the First World War *The Seven Pillars of Wisdom* as an homage to a book, now lost, that he had written about seven ancient cities. Emily Dickinson, now regarded as a major American poet, published just a handful of her poems during her life, and even these were changed by editors. It was only after her death in 1886 that her younger sister found her poems, and still no one would publish them as she had originally written them—they were too unconventional in structure—until 1955. They might easily never have been found, or never published as written.

However these are exceptions. Your created work is not an independent, self-existing entity, but part of a larger system that includes, besides the work, yourself, all those working with you, your audience, the referents in your work, and ultimately the entire culture. Later we will see Marcel Duchamp's contribution to this understanding of art. Your work exists in terms of the effect it has on an audience. Indian aesthetic theory has a highly sophisticated sense of this, addressing an audience's experience during an encounter with a work and then the mental states that resonate after that encounter. Aesthetics should not be understood in terms of characteristics of works of art, but as features of relationships.

Despite this need to reach an audience, your work must always have an internal integrity. You should not work backwards, starting with what you think your audience wants. Work done that way is often marketing, not creating. Your work has to grow from inside you, but that inside has to be in touch with the world. The Romantic notion of the artist as lone genius, misunderstood, defiantly creating in the face of an uncaring world does have some validity. You must be true to yourself and your work, and we appreciate Frank Lloyd Wright's motto, "Truth Against the World." The social critic Paul Goodman once said, "I do not write for audiences today. I write for Socrates and Plato and Spinoza." But in looking at the major figures in the arts, we see the importance of reaching audiences.

A Hedgehog or a Fox

As your career unfolds, you should know if you are a hedgehog or a fox. The distinction comes from a 1953 essay by the cultural critic Isaiah Berlin, who borrowed it from the ancient Greek poet Archilochus who wrote, "The fox knows many things, but the hedgehog knows one big thing." Berlin stated that hedgehogs view the world through the lens of a single defining idea, and they include Plato, Dante, Pascal, Dostoevsky, Nietzsche, Ibsen, and Proust. Foxes address many ideas, and they include Aristotle, Shakespeare, Molière, Goethe, Pushkin, and Joyce.

Norman Mailer (1923–2007) intended to become the major literary figure of his time. Since the position was held by Ernest Hemingway, he challenged Hemingway to a fight, but Hemingway never responded. Mailer began his career with his novel of the Second World War, *The Naked and the Dead*. He eventually wrote novels about Hollywood, the Cold War, the CIA, Ancient Egypt, Christ, and God. His subjects kept getting larger. His nonfiction covered jazz, race, sex, bull fighting, protest politics, Picasso, feminism, boxing, the landing on the Moon, the assassination of John F. Kennedy, and Marilyn Monroe. Besides writing, Mailer, who had studied aeronautical engineering at Harvard, made movies, produced a play, created an organization to monitor the CIA, ran for mayor of New York, stabbed one of his six wives, and sponsored the release from prison of a murderer who murdered again. Mailer was a Fox.

John Updike (1932–2009) also intended to become a writer. He was fortunate to get a job with *The New Yorker*, but at the age of twenty-five he left New York and his job to move to a small Massachusetts town where he lived for the rest of his life. Updike wrote over thirty novels and hundreds of short stories, essays, and reviews, but central to his work were five novels that chronicled the life of Harry "Rabbit" Angstrom over the course of several decades, from young adulthood to his death. While Mailer was depicting the lives of sociopathic killers, drug addicts, sexual competitors, jazz musicians, beats, movie stars, politicians, and astronauts, Updike entered the American protestant psyche to depict work, religion, sex, and death in the lives of middle class people like himself.

When he was nineteen, Updike had already decided to depict life in the America of his time. He wrote to his parents, "We do not need men like Proust and Joyce; men like this are a luxury, an added fillip that an abundant culture can produce only after the more basic literary need has been filled." And, "This age needs rather men like Shakespeare, or Milton, or Pope; men who are filled with the strength of their cultures and do not transcend the limits of their age, but, working within the times, bring what is peculiar to the moment to glory. We need great artists who are willing to accept restrictions, and who love their environments with such vitality that they can produce an epic out of the Protestant ethic."

Updike knew that to be a writer he would have to read and write, and to make the challenge interesting, he decided to make his living from his writing. Every day he went upstairs in his house to his rooms with a huge chair for reading and desk for writing. At seventy-five, in reply to questions sent to him by the novelist Nicholas Delbanco, Updike summed up his journey: "I set out to make a living with my pen, in privacy, in the commercial literary world as it then existed, and am grateful that I managed. It's been a privilege and a pleasure; and it goes without saying that I've been lucky." Updike was a hedgehog.

Albert Einstein is associated with several major developments in physics, including the nature of light, quantum theory, and establishing for physicists the reality of the atom, but his most important contributions were special and general relativity. He essentially had one great idea, that the geometry of space and time is not the Cartesian grid that we learned in school, but rather is curved, dynamic—shaped and even created by matter. All of contemporary cosmology unfolds from that idea. Einstein was a hedgehog.

Richard Feynman is one of the more important scientists of the late twentieth century. He is best known in physics for his work in developing quantum electrodynamics, bringing together quantum theory and relativity, and for his Feynman diagrams, a means of visually representing the behavior of subatomic particles. But Feynman also worked on the Manhattan Project where he led a team of human computers, did work in superfluity, proposed nanotechnology in a famous paper titled "There's Plenty of Room at the Bottom," conceived of quantum computing, and contributed to the idea of quarks. His recorded lectures on physics are still widely listened to. He gained popular attention for his role in investigating the Space Shuttle Challenger explosion. Feynman mixed an interest in theory and experiment, and would have accomplished more if he had not insisted on re-deriving from the beginning everything he worked on. There was no central organizing idea behind his work, and Feynman was a fox.

Find creatives who interest you, immerse yourself in their work and their biographies, and then find your own identity and live it. You may be a hedgehog, you may be a fox, or you may be a something else.

The Arc of Your Work

Look at the work of creatives you admire. More often than not, you will find in their earliest work the themes that play out over their careers.

James Joyce published three novels. *A Portrait of the Artist as a Young Man* established his approach of focusing on interior monologue and a character's psychic reality, stated his aesthetic theory, and set the outlines of what he intended to accomplish. Then as we described earlier, in *Ulysses*, he summed up the novel form and the key themes of Western culture. There are eighteen chapters, each covering roughly one hour of the day, and each employing its own literary style. Each chapter also relates to an episode in Homer's *The Odyssey* and to a color, art or science, and bodily organ. His final work, *Finnegans Wake*, begins "riverrun, past Eve and Adam's, from swerve of shore to bend of bay, brings us by a commodius vicus of recirculation back to Howth Castle and Environs." And ends, "A way a lone a last a loved a long the," which leads back to the opening. Joyce uses Vico's historical cycles to plunge into the depths of the mythic structures of the psyche and point to the future of art. Three works, a perfect arc, all laid out in the first.

In 1896 Frank Lloyd Wright built a windmill he called Romeo and Juliet that was rooted into the ground and extended upward with interlocking forms. In 1901, he built the Ward Willits House that had open spaces extending around a chimney core. And in 1904 he built Unity Temple that had a major space, a minor space, and an entrance in between, and had an interior space surrounded by balconies and open to a skylight in the middle. His later work moved to greater abstraction and exuberance, culminating in The Illinois, his project for a mile high tower that referred back to Romeo and Juliet; Fallingwater that referred back to the Ward Willits House; and the Guggenheim Museum that referred back to Unity Temple. All within the organizing principles he had laid down in his early buildings.

The modern painter Piet Mondrian began with landscapes, then moved to trees, the branches of which become more and more abstractly vertical and horizontal. After he encountered Frank Lloyd Wright's work, he began his paintings of vertical and horizontal black lines on white backgrounds with fills of primary colors exploring life and death. And one without black, *Broadway Boogie Woogie*. Look again at the early landscapes and trees and you will see in them premonitions of his later paintings.

Elvis Presley began his career at Sun Records with recordings of established rhythm and blues and country and western songs, giving them an accelerated pace and a beat that came to be known as Rock and Roll, in such songs as *That's All Right*, *Blue Moon of Kentucky*, and *Mystery Train*. These songs were his best work. After he left Sun for RCA, he burst onto the national stage as a Dionysian figure threatening to bring down the culture with such hits as *Blue Suede Shoes* and *Hound Dog*. Then came ballads, movies, drugs, and Las Vegas in white leather jumpsuits. But before the end he recorded *From Elvis in Memphis*, containing images of loneliness reaching back to the themes of the Sun recordings and showing how they led to the country and western, soul, pop, and rhythm and blues that were extended on what he started.

Some died before they were able to complete the arc of their work. Mozart died before he could usher the West out of the Enlightenment into the Romantic, burdening Beethoven with the task, and while Buddy Holly created a Rock and Roll of pure joy, he died before he could usher in the maturity of Rock, leaving the task in the ultimately capable hands of the Beatles, the Rolling Stones, Jefferson Airplane, and other groups.

So make sure you get your initial work right. And live long enough.

HOW DO WE JUDGE
CREATIVE WORKS?

In which we see that creative works are experienced in context, so that our judgment of them changes over time. Then we look at several figures about whom our opinions have changed.

Talent hits a target hit by no one else, but genius hits a target seen by no one else.
~ Arthur Schopenhauer, German philosopher

Genius

How do we define genius? How do we identify a work of genius? Many books on the subject start with a vague notion that everyone is a potential genius, and then present a lot of wishful thinking. Too often genius, talent, or other traits that psychologists seek to measure are covers for their political agendas for what they wish us all to be: contemplative, insightful, tolerant, collaborative. Of course genius involves a combination of brilliance and the production of things we judge to be important, but now we have the problem that what we judge to be important changes over time.

Changing Judgments

We might hope that our work will be judged on its own merit, for the brilliant insights it conveys. It won't be. It will be judged in the context of its culture, and culture is in constant flux, so the judgment of our work will also be in flux.

The changing reactions by the film critic, Roger Ebert, to Federico Fellini's 1960 film, *La Dolce Vita* ("the sweet life") presents an example of this. The film stars Marcello Mastroianni as Marcello, a handsome but weary soul seeking escape from the ennui of empty nights and lonely dawns, who aspires to do serious writing, but is caught up covering Rome's nightlife for tabloids as he hangs out at clubs on the Via Veneto. In the course of a week he has one hollow experience after another as he sleeps with a bored society woman, deals with his fiancée's suicide attempt, wades in the Trevi Fountain with a buxom actress played by Anita Ekberg, witnesses religious hysteria, attends a party at the crumbling estate of a crumbling aristocratic family, and spends a night with his father with whom he is unable to establish any communication. He meets an old acquaintance who invites him to a party filled with writers and artists and Marcello thinks he has found a home, but then the acquaintance commits suicide. The movie systematically shows Marcello being failed by love, passion, celebrity, family, religion, and the life of the mind. Or them being failed by him. The movie ends with Marcello emerging from a decadent party at a beach house to see fishermen dragging the decaying corpse of a giant fish onto the beach. An angelic girl whom he met earlier waves to him but he does not recognize her and turns away, unable to make contact with the powers of potential renewal. A sad story, but a great movie capturing a certain exuberance and occupying a place on many top ten lists.

La Dolce Vita portrayed the Rome of its time and awakened America to a new kind of movie, reaching our shores around the same time as Antonioni's structurally subversive *L'Avventura*, Ingmar Bergman's psychoanalytic *Wild Strawberries*, and Jean-Luc Godard's re-envisioning of film noir, *Breathless*. All happening at a time when Hollywood was bringing us such idiotic fare as *Under the Yum Yum Tree* with Jack Lemmon.

How do we react to *La Dolce Vita*, how do we evaluate it? On one level, we can admire its cinematography, story telling, portrayals of characters, cityscapes of Rome, impeccable clothing. But then you might ask, what is *my* reaction to this movie? And that will depend on who you are. Are you a man or a woman? How old were you when you first saw it? Did you first see it in 1960 when it arrived in the United States and it seemed to portray a living world, or recently when it portrayed a world half a century in the past? A work of art is changed by changing times. Ebert writes:

When I saw La Dolce Vita in 1960, I was an adolescent for whom "the sweet life'" represented everything I dreamed of: sin, exotic European glamour, the weary romance of the cynical newspaperman. When I saw it again, around 1970, I was living in a version of Marcello's world; Chicago's North Avenue was not the Via Veneto, but at 3 a.m. the denizens were just as colorful, and I was about Marcello's age.

When I saw the movie around 1980, Marcello was the same age, but I was 10 years older, had stopped drinking, and saw him not as a role model but as a victim, condemned to an endless search for happiness that could never be found, not that way. By 1991, when I analyzed the film a frame at a time at the University of Colorado, Marcello seemed younger still, and while I had once admired and then criticized him, now I pitied and loved him. And when I saw the movie right after Mastroianni died, I thought that Fellini and Marcello had taken a moment of discovery and made it immortal. There may be no such thing as the sweet life. But it is necessary to find that out for yourself.

Our evaluations of creators are in constant flux, as are our evaluations of their works. If you go to the library and thumb through books and magazines from the past hundred years on art, architecture, philosophy, or culture, you will find many people and works prominently featured about whom we care little today and some we never heard of. And the people we care about today are constantly shifting in their respective pantheons; in the near future, some we now lionize will be all but forgotten. Let's look at a few examples of shifting judgment.

We mention several times in this book Isaac Newton's notion of space as absolute, as an abstract potential that can be occupied by objects and independent of those objects. Newton's great rival, Gottfried Leibniz, rejected this approach, stating: "As for my own opinion, I have said more than once, that I hold space to be something merely relative, as time is, that I hold it to be an order of coexistences, as time is an order of successions." Newton remains the single greatest scientist of all time, but today relativity and quantum physics are closer to the approach of Leibniz than that of Newton.

The Flemish painter, Rubens, was popular with collectors throughout Europe. Rembrandt, born thirty years after Rubens in another part of what is now Holland, was also recognized as a major artistic talent, but several of his commissions were refused by clients and his guild eventually forbade him to sell paintings. Today we appreciate Rubens for his place in history, but if we wish to stand quietly for some time in front of a painting, it will most likely be a Rembrandt.

Until the mid twentieth century, Bernini was the defining architect of the Italian Baroque, while Borromini, the architect of just two small churches, was regarded as proof that the Baroque had gone off the deep end. Bitter at the success of rivals he thought his inferiors, Borromini committed suicide. Today many prefer Borromini to Bernini.

Thomas Edison was a prolific inventor with over a thousand patents to his name. His chief rival was the electrical engineer Nikola Tesla. The two clashed, Tesla advocating alternating current, Edison direct current for the transmission of electricity. Tesla was right. Tesla had an intuitive feel for electrical fields and it became his ambition to transmit information and even electricity without wires. His ideas contributed to the development of radio, remote control, radar, and computer science. Thirty years ago, Tesla was all but forgotten. While we should not take anything away from Edison, today we recognize that we are living in a world envisioned by Tesla.

Sigmund Freud ushered in the twentieth century with his discovery of the unconscious. Freud saw an animal drive that he called the id originating from the genitals and pressing upward. Carl Jung had a far deeper concept of the unconscious than did Freud, describing it not just in terms of animal instincts, but as containing our cultural history and the images and symbols that we find in the world's arts. For decades Jung was rejected as a mystic, but not anymore. Today Jung's ideas exert a greater influence in the arts and in culture than do Freud's. Following are some more examples of the vicissitudes of history.

Twain, Melville, and Fitzgerald

In many reckonings the three most important American novels are Mark Twain's *The Adventures of Huckleberry Finn*, Herman Melville's *Moby-Dick*, and F. Scott Fitzgerald's *The Great Gatsby*.

Of these, only *Huckleberry Finn* was popular form its first publication and has remained so to this day. It was initially criticized for its coarseness and is sometimes criticized today for its racial language, but for the most part it is loved. Ernest Hemingway says, "All modern American literature comes from one book by Mark Twain called *Huckleberry Finn*."

Twain suffered the slings and arrows of the prudes of his day, but for the most part was very well received as a writer from the time of his short story, "The Celebrated Jumping Frog of Calaveras County" to the time of his death. Not so Melville and Fitzgerald.

Herman Melville's early life was one of adventure, including jumping ship in the Pacific to live among the South Sea Islanders. His early book, *Typee*, which became an overnight bestseller, was based on these experiences.

More successful books followed, and Melville envisioned a literary career. He befriended Nathaniel Hawthorne and spent years working on *Moby-Dick*, which he hoped would win him major literary status. The book was ignored, failing to sell out its initial printing of three thousand copies in thirty years. Melville fell on hard times, and was forgotten by the time he died.

> *Call me Ishmael. Some years ago—never mind how long precisely—having little or no money in my purse, and nothing particular to interest me on shore, I thought I would sail about a little and see the watery part of the world.*

The book is variously interpreted as representing American democracy, vengeance, the wildness of nature, the cruelty of whaling, and obsession. Recall that Natty Bumppo in James Fenimore Cooper's Leatherstocking Tales (which include *The Last of the Mohicans*) moves effortlessly through Eastern forests, and Huck and Jim drift down the Mississippi through episodes of the American character. *Moby-Dick* can be seen as continuing that image of the American psyche adrift with its panoply of characters now afloat on a whaling ship.

Thirty years after Melville's death, several critics, including D. H. Lawrence in his *Studies in Classic American Literature*, began to bring attention to *Moby-Dick*, and it is now regarded as one of the most important American novels.

F. Scott Fitzgerald burst into the literary scene as a defining figure of the Jazz Age at a time before television and even before the heyday of movies, when short stories in popular magazines were the dominant literary genre. His short stories brought him fame and an income and he sought literary stature through his novels with limited success. To support himself and pay for treatment for his wife's schizophrenia, he churned out short stories, borrowed money, and even turned to writing for Hollywood. As we mentioned at the beginning of this book, he was part of the Lost Generation meeting in Parisian salons that also included Ernest Hemingway, Ezra Pound, T. S. Eliot, Sherwood Anderson, John Dos Passos, John Steinbeck, and Cole Porter as celebrated in Woody Allen's movie, *Midnight in Paris*. Fitzgerald died of a heart attack, broke and an alcoholic, at the age of forty-four. His obituaries described his literary fame as something from a by-gone era. The novel he cared for the most, *The Great Gatsby*, had received mixed reviews on its publication, several reviewers saying that it was a period piece that would soon be forgotten. In the late 1930s, when wanting to buy a copy of the book to give a friend, he would be told in bookstores that it was out of stock, and that the author was dead.

Then a few years after Fitzgerald's death literary figures began to look at the book again. It was taken more seriously, and in a few years it was selling 50,000 copies a year. Today it sells 500,000 copies a year, a figure that spikes when a new movie version comes out.

America offers the promise that we can make and remake ourselves. Gatsby, who is from a modest background, briefly meets and falls in love with Daisy who is from a wealthy family, at a party just before he departs for Europe during the First World War. He feels that he will have to be wealthy to win her, and on his return from the War delves into various criminal activities and remakes himself as fabulously wealthy, but the Daisy he is seeking is a memory bearing little relation to the vacuous woman, now married and a mother, that he pursues. All ends poorly. A simple story, but unmatched in American literature in the telling.

Hedy Lamarr
Billed as the most beautiful woman in the world by the great stage director Max Reinhardt, Viennese-born actress Hedy Lamarr began her career by appearing nude portraying sexual passion in the German film, *Ecstasy*. Later she moved to Hollywood where she became a leading lady working opposite Clark Gable, Jimmy Stewart, and Charles Boyer, among many others, which necessitated more modesty. Desiring to help America during the Second World War, she worked in her living room with avant-garde musician turned Hollywood composer, George Antheil, designing advanced electronically controlled weapons.

Their efforts were focused on guidance systems and proximity fuses, looking for ways to detonate a weapon at a given distance from its target, and ways to defeat an enemy's attempt to jam the guidance and detonation signals. Their designs are the forerunners of today's smart bombs, as well as playing a role in cell phones, Bluetooth devices, GPS guidance instruments, and other devices.

Lamarr and Antheil were more suited to their task than one might have imagined. Both were very smart, Lamarr had been married to a wealthy Austrian munitions manufacturer and had sat in on some of his negotiations with his clients, and Antheil had built complex mechanisms for his machine age concerts. In 1942 they received a patent for their radio-controlled spread spectrum torpedo-guidance system, but not recognition. At the time the military did not take Lamarr seriously, but in 1997 when she was eighty-two, she was honored for her work by the Electronic Frontier Foundation.

Antheil's honor was posthumous. In 2003 Lamarr was featured as a leading woman of science in a series of Boeing commercials and her work was chronicled in a 2011 book. But it is hard to be taken seriously in the field of high tech weaponry when you are the most beautiful woman in the world.

Claude Shannon

Few have heard of Claude Shannon, although we live in a world he created. In 1948 Shannon, a reclusive thirty-six year old mathematician, electrical engineer, and tinkerer working at AT&T's Bell Labs in New York's West Village, published an article titled "A Mathematical Theory of Communication." The article was modest in its intent; Shannon wanted to quantify the amount of information that could be sent through a given channel, but to do so he had to define information. By the time he was done, his short paper had created what we now know as information theory. What Shannon realized was that the information in a message can be quantified by the number of 0s and 1s required to transmit it, and has nothing to do with its content. We now call these 0s and 1s bits, a term coined by Shannon in his paper.

This paper was preceded some years earlier by Shannon's MIT master's thesis in electrical engineering. In the 1840s the English mathematician and philosopher, George Boole, developed what is now called Boolean logic, which formalizes a set of rules in which, for example, we might say that if A and B are true, then we get C. If A is true and B is not true, then we get D, etc. In his 1937 master's thesis, titled "A Symbolic Analysis of Relay and Switching Circuits," Shannon showed that these rules could be built into electric circuits, enabling the logic operations to be automated, thus laying the foundation for all electronics including modern computers. His thesis did not gain any special attention when he wrote it, but it is now recognized as the most important master's thesis of all time. With these two papers, Shannon had created the modern technological world. Besides being the basis of computer science and everything we do on the Internet, his information theory is now being used to recreate all of science: physics, chemistry, biology, psychology, etc., as we will briefly discuss later.

In other words, Shannon developed the science on which our entire digital age is built and on which all of science is being rebuilt. Neil Sloane, editor of Shannon's papers, stated that, "He's one of the great men of the century. Without him, none of the things we know today would exist. The whole digital revolution started with him."

In his book, *Microcosm,* George Gilder observes that in the macrocosm (the realm of big industrial machines), when devices become more powerful, they become larger, more likely to break down, more expensive, and more energy consuming. But in the microcosm (the realm of the computer chip), when devices become more powerful, they become smaller, less likely to break down, less expensive, and less energy consuming. And Gilder observes that our entire economy is moving from macrocosm to microcosm, from matter and energy to information, that is, to the world conceived by Shannon.

Also in 1948, in the same building in which Shannon worked, a group of Bell Lab scientists developed the transistor, later to be miniaturized and placed by the billions on single chips in our computers. Three of these scientists received the Nobel Prize. Shannon did not receive a Nobel Prize; there is no Nobel Prize in information theory or computer science or even in mathematics. Shannon is one of the most important scientists of the twentieth century, indeed one of the most important Visionary Creatives of all time, but it is hard to get recognition in a field that no one knows about because you just invented it. Few people have heard of Claude Shannon.

Hugh Everett III

John Archibald Wheeler was a towering figure in physics, having worked with both Einstein and Niels Bohr. He coined the terms "black hole," "worm hole," "quantum foam," and "it from bit," and we quote him several times in this book. He is also known for his prominent students, including physicist Richard Feynman and quantum computing pioneer David Deutsch. And Hugh Everett III, who only belatedly received some recognition.

At the age of twelve, Everett was writing fan letters to Einstein, and later he became a physics student at Princeton studying under Wheeler. In 1956 he completed a paper titled "Wave Mechanics Without Probability", proposing a radically different approach to quantum theory. Everett was bothered by Niels Bohr's proposal that particles are waves of probability until we look at them and then they "collapse" from a "superposition" into a "classical state" and become particles. What did this mean? How did this collapse come about? Everett asked, what if we assume that the "particles" remain waves of probability and never collapse into particles? Then all quantum possibilities would play out in a multitude of universes. In other words, when a particle has to make a choice, it makes all choices, and the universe divides, one for each choice, as in, "When the particle comes to a fork in the road, it takes it."

In describing Wheeler, one of his colleagues writes: "Somewhere among those polite facades [of Princeton] there was a tiger loose... who had the courage to look at any crazy problem." But Everett's idea was too crazy even for Wheeler. Wheeler showed it to Niels Bohr, who was his mentor, but Bohr hated it. Rather than backing his student, Wheeler pressed Everett to modify his PhD thesis so that it became essentially meaningless. Wheeler did arrange for Everett to meet with Bohr, but Bohr was unable to understand what

137

Everett was talking about, and one of Bohr's acolytes said that Everett was "undescribably stupid and could not understand the simplest things in quantum mechanics." In disgust, Everett left physics and joined the Pentagon doing weapons systems analysis and later founded several companies. He became overweight, drank, smoked, and died at the age of fifty-one. After Everett's death, Wheeler formally renounced his theory.

Go to a large gathering of physicists today and ask for a show of hands on which interpretation of quantum theory attendees agree with. Everett's many worlds theory, also known as the parallel universes theory, will often win. The physicist, Max Tegmark, refers to it as one of the most important discoveries of all time, comparable to Newton's theory of gravity and Einstein's theory of relativity. But few have heard of Everett.

Billy Lee Riley and Carl Perkins

Much of what we call Rock and Roll began in the 1950s at Sam Phillips' Sun Records in Memphis, Tennessee. Sun began the careers of Jerry Lee Lewis, Carl Perkins, Johnny Cash, Elvis Presley, and Roy Orbison among others.

Sun was tiny and lacked the resources to properly promote its artists, and Phillips famously sold Elvis Presley's contract to RCA to keep his company going. One Sun artist, Billy Lee Riley, a Rockabilly pioneer, had a modest hit with "Flyin' Saucers Rock and Roll." He then did "Red Hot," a song that had the potential to break out, but Phillips pulled his promotional efforts to focus on Jerry Lee Lewis's "Great Balls Of Fire." Lewis became a major star. Riley, after a few more recordings at Sun with no promotion, went to Los Angeles to become a backup musician for major performers, and then quit music to move back to Arkansas where he had been born to start a construction business. In the late 1970s he was rediscovered and went back to performing. In 1992 he was rediscovered again, this time by Bob Dylan, who had been a fan since the 1950s. He began performing again, this time until his death in 2009, but he was never a major star.

Carl Perkins was always an important figure in Rock and Roll and the defining figure in Rockabilly as well as working with many leading musicians. In 1956 he participated with Elvis Presley, Jerry Lee Lewis, and Johnny Cash in an impromptu jam session at the Sun studios that is now known as the "Million Dollar Quartet." Later in his career he worked with the Beatles, Paul McCartney, George Harrison, and Bob Dylan among others. But there was a missed step at the beginning. Perkins wrote and recorded *Blue Suede Shoes*, released it in 1956, and it spent sixteen weeks on the Cashbox list. But his promotional tour and television appearances were cut short by an automobile accident. Elvis Presley had done a cover of the song and was available for television appearances. Perkins remained a respected and influential musician. Elvis became the King.

If someone were listing major creative figures, would Twain, Melville, Fitzgerald, Lamarr, Shannon, Everett, Riley, and Perkins be on the list? Certainly Twain at any point in his career and through today. Fitzgerald during his early career, then forgotten, and now widely read. In their own times, perhaps Lamarr and Perkins would have been recognized, but not as major figures. Today, Melville and Shannon would certainly be. Everett is all but forgotten, while Lamarr is remembered today only by movie buffs, and Riley and Perkins only by Rock and Roll buffs. Fitzgerald is regarded as one of our greatest novelists. Many have talent. A few ignite themselves and burn as supernovas, and sometimes we notice. Some are discouraged and never fully ignite. Some are extinguished. And some all but disappear, perhaps to reappear at another time.

From Fame to Obscurity to Fame in the Movies
From the era of the Great Depression through the 1950s, movies were the dominant entertainment form. Glamorous

stars graced the silver screen and defined the possibilities of good and evil, masculinity and femininity, responsibility to family, response to adversity, courage in war, solving mysteries, winning the West, struggling for one's art, triumph and defeat. And elegant dress. Glamour did exist in the lives of some stars, but much of it was manufactured by movie studios as a part of the dreams they sold.

By the 1960s the studio system was in decline, movies had been diminished by television, and tastes had turned to a new kind of realism. Through the 60s and 70s, many of the older stars who were still alive, including Cary Grant, Fred Astaire, William Powell, Ginger Rogers, Vivien Leigh, Myrna Loy, and Barbara Stanwyck, got occasional television roles, lived on their savings and investments, attended parties, and began to forget a bygone era. Movies had been created to last just a few weeks. The thousands of prints made for distribution to theaters were destroyed at the end of a run, and the originals were stored in vaults, or just forgotten in dusty storerooms. Most of the movies made in the 1920s have long ago dissolved in their film canisters, and some made later fared little better. Those shot in Technicolor can be recreated if the three black and white originals, from which the color prints were made, survived, but some of the first movies shot in Eastmancolor quickly faded. The studios and the stars understood they were working with an ephemeral art, although Vivien Leigh believed that *Gone With the Wind* was important enough to survive for perhaps five years.

In the 1960s a few larger cities had revival houses that featured some of the old movies. Otherwise, aside from the few that aired on late night television, most were forgotten. Then in the 1970s videotapes for home use sparked an interest in old movies while the proliferation of cable television channels enabled the creation of networks dedicated to old movies. Movies that had almost disappeared became re-imprinted into the cultural imagination, and stars who had been all but forgotten became towering artists who occupied a new pantheon from which they again defined the possibilities of good and evil, masculinity and femininity, responsibility to family, response to adversity, courage in war, the struggle for one's art, triumph and defeat. And elegant dress.

As we said above, we might hope that our work will be judged on its own merit, for the brilliant insights it conveys. It won't be. It will be judged in the context of its culture, and culture is in constant flux, so the judgment of our work will also be in flux.

So we will not attempt to define genius and just say that *Visionary Creatives swim in the culture of their day and manifest in their work the spirit of their age. The things they create—in art, design, science, technology, business—embody that spirit, and at the same time are a little off center for us, somehow not what we anticipated, thus pulling us into the future.*

JOY

In which we look at what Visionary Creativity means
for the Visionary Creative. We start with the idea of
happiness and find it lacking. We propose instead that
we should seek joy, and that joy comes from accomplishment at something about which one is passionate. We describe joy for the Visionary Creative as an
experience of the spirit of the age, of the energies of
the universe pouring into the world, and the creation
of works that reproduce that experience for others.

> *Wings, wings to fly above life! Wings to fly above the grave
> and death! That is what we want, and I am beginning to un-
> derstand that we can get them.*
> ~ *Vincent van Gogh in a letter to his brother, Theo*

Happiness

Through most of this book we have been looking at works
by Visionary Creatives from the point of view of those who
experience those works. What about those who create them?

Earlier we asked, what qualities do we admire in others
and aspire to in ourselves? Before focusing on creativity, we
mentioned wealth, political power, and beauty. Of course each
of these would be worthy of a book in itself, as would many
other qualities we might have mentioned, for example courage
and wisdom. But there is one quality we omitted that is important and that we should now address: happiness. Recall the

second line of our country's founding document, the Declaration of Independence:

> *We hold these truths to be self-evident, that all men are cre-*
> *ated equal, that they are endowed by their Creator with cer-*
> *tain unalienable Rights, that among these are Life, Liberty*
> *and the pursuit of Happiness.*

What is it about happiness that got it this prominent placement? Today happiness is usually defined as a feeling of contentment, satisfaction, wellbeing, pleasure; a positive emotional state. So, did our country's founders rebel against the British, putting at risk their lives, their fortunes, and their sacred honor for the right to pursue the feelings you get when you eat chocolate, play the harpsichord, or see your child take its first steps? Or perhaps they had a different meaning for the word happiness than we do today, and of course they did. By happiness, our country's founders meant flourishing, thriving, identifying one's individual interests and potentials and realizing them.

Difficult Lives

But before we explore further what is meant by happiness today, let's look briefly at several historical figures.

Pope

Alexander Pope (1688-1744) was deformed, including having a severe hunchback, and grew to only four feet six inches due to tuberculosis of the bone, a condition that also caused difficulty breathing, fevers, inflamed eyes, and frequent abdominal pain. He also suffered from being Catholic in England at a time when it was illegal for Catholics to attend a university, teach, vote, hold public office, or live within ten miles of

London. Pope briefly attended illegal Catholic schools and then was self-taught.

While Pope never married, he had many female friends and a lover. He was a poet, satirist, and wit who was also known for his translations of Homer. His satirical verses included the mock-heroic narrative poem, *The Rape of the Lock*. And since we refer to Newton in this book, we should quote Pope's epitaph for him:

Nature and Nature's laws lay hid in night:
God said, "Let Newton be!" and all was light.

Pope is the third most frequently quoted writer in *The Oxford Dictionary of Quotations* after Shakespeare and Tennyson. He died the greatest poet of his age.

Was Pope happy?

Beethoven

Ludwig van Beethoven (1770-1827) grew up with an abusive alcoholic father and while he loved his brother, he would never address him by the name he shared with their father. In 1796 he began to lose his hearing from causes variously attributed to syphilis, lead poisoning, typhus, and an autoimmune disorder. In the spring of 1811 he became seriously ill, suffering headaches and fevers. In 1813 his brother became seriously ill and Beethoven spent all of his money caring for him and his family. Between 1815 and 1817 Beethoven was again ill. His brother died in 1815 and Beethoven embarked on an ugly and ill-conceived legal effort to gain custody of his brother's nine-year-old son from his mother. He was not successful until 1820, and after six years of Beethoven's guardianship, the boy shot himself in the head. He survived and a year later joined the army.

Beethoven had difficult relationships with women, and

fell into despair when he realized he could never be with his Immortal Beloved, the one woman he loved, and whose identity remains in dispute. In 1825 Beethoven was bedridden with illness for a month. In 1826 he was again ill and nearly died. Beethoven's deafness caused havoc with his personal life, and made performing almost impossible and conducting a constant humiliation, leading him to contemplate suicide on more than one occasion. Between 1796 and his death in 1827 he produced some of the most profound music ever conceived. He composed his Ninth Symphony and his late string quartets, among other works, while almost totally deaf. Beethoven died a towering figure in music, the most famous and influential composer of all time.

Was Beethoven happy?

Nietzsche

Friedrich Nietzsche (1844–1900) was a German philosopher and critic of the religion, morality, and culture of his day. At the age of twenty-four he was appointed to the Chair of Classical Philology at the University of Basel, the youngest person to receive such an appointment, but resigned in 1879 due to ill health, probably growing out of injuries and infections acquired during military service. Later, when he sought a new teaching position, he was told that his writing had made an appointment impossible.

He was initially a friend and philosophical supporter of the composer, Richard Wagner, but became alienated by Wagner's championing of "German culture," which Nietzsche thought a contradiction in terms, leaving him with few friends. His one romantic interest was Lou Salomé, a brilliant Russian-born psychoanalyst and author, with whom he spent a summer. She claims he proposed marriage, but that she turned him down.

He traveled constantly, looking for climates that would help his health while he wrote a series of books that gained little recognition during his lifetime. Nietzsche's health problems included severe headaches and failing eyesight to the point that he had to have others read to him. Eventually, before disease destroyed his brain at the age of forty-four, he was barely able to drag himself to his desk to write for a few minutes a day his books of saying yes to life, books that have become some of the most influential throughout our culture.

Was Nietzsche happy?

Van Gogh

One could imagine few people as tormented as Vincent van Gogh (1853–1890). One of his first jobs was working for an art dealer who fired him due to his contempt for commercialism in art, an attitude not appreciated by the dealer or his customers. He fell in love with his landlady's daughter, and when she rejected him, he became despondent, turning to religion. He studied for the ministry, but flunked the exam. He tried another denomination, and flunked again. He got a temporary position ministering to coal miners, and chose to live with them, but the church dismissed him for the inappropriateness of this behavior, and he returned home. His father inquired about having him committed to an asylum.

Van Gogh always drew, and at the suggestion of his brother, Theo, he took up art in earnest. He fell in love again, was refused, responded by holding his hand in a flame, and again fell out with his father. He took up with an alcoholic prostitute who had two children, and then another she claimed was by him. He left them, and she eventually committed suicide. He returned to stay with his parents, and took up with a neighbor's daughter, but their marriage was opposed by both of their families, and she took strychnine. Then Van Gogh's father had a heart attack and died.

He moved to Antwerp to work on his art, spent most of

the money Theo sent him on art supplies, and lived on coffee and cigarettes. His teeth became loose and he was ill for months at a time. Then he moved in with Theo in Paris and continued to paint, but disagreed with Theo about the importance of the artists Theo represented, including Monet, Degas, and Pissarro, making Theo's life unbearable. Ill from drinking and smoking, he moved to Arles. He found the place miserable and the people there did not think much of him either, but the bright light and the landscape animated his paintings and he produced important work.

He developed relationships with other artists, including Gauguin, but that relationship deteriorated, causing him great anxiety. He cut his ear off. He spent a month in the hospital suffering from hallucinations and delusions that he was being poisoned, perhaps as a consequence of drinking absinthe. Around this time, he wrote, "Sometimes moods of indescribable anguish, sometimes moments when the veil of time and fatality of circumstances seemed to be torn apart for an instant."

He left Arles and entered an asylum in Saint-Rémy-de-Provence where he produced his most important paintings, including *The Starry Night*. His work was exhibited in Paris where the symbolist poet and critic, Albert Aurier, described him as a genius, and Toulouse-Lautrec, Signac, Monet, and others praised his work. On July 27, 1890 he walked into a field and shot himself in the chest, then walked back into town. Two days later he died. He was thirty-seven. Theo was at his side, and reported his last words as "La tristesse durera toujours." (The sadness will last forever.) Theo, who had supported his brother and never stopped believing in him and his art, died six months later. They are buried side by side.

Van Gogh experienced the world as a religious vision of swirling energies, presciently seeing the modern stage on which we would all eventually live. He attempted to convey that experience in his paintings, which are today among the

148

world's most recognizable and most valued works of art. Was Van Gogh happy?

Solzhenitsyn

The Russian writer Aleksandr Solzhenitsyn (1918-2008) studied mathematics, philosophy, literature, and history. During the Second World War he served as a commander in the Red Army and was twice decorated. In 1945 he was arrested for writing derogatory comments about Stalin and spent eleven years in slave labor camps. During that time he began to compose books in condensed code on scraps of paper about his experiences and the character of the Soviet system, and he envisioned bringing integrity back to Russian culture through his writing. When he practically died of cancer in the slave camps, he rallied himself with his vision of saving Russia. Of that time he writes, "during all the years until 1961, not only was I convinced I should never see a single line of mine in print in my lifetime, but, also, I scarcely dared allow any of my close acquaintances to read anything I had written because I feared this would become known."

In 1962 his *One Day in the Life of Ivan Denisovich* was published and became an instant hit and was studied in schools in the Soviet Union. Then in 1969 he was expelled from the Soviet Union of Writers, meaning he could not be published. In 1970 he was awarded the Nobel Prize in Literature, but was not permitted to attend the ceremony to receive the prize. From 1958 to 1968 he composed *The Gulag Archipelago* on the Soviet prison camp system. It was published in the West in 1973 but not in the Soviet Union until 1989. It eventually sold over thirty million copies in thirty-five languages.

In 1974 Solzhenitsyn was arrested, deported from the Soviet Union and stripped of his Soviet citizenship. The Soviets then began a large-scale operation to discredit him and his family, infiltrating his staff, publishing books hostile to him in the names of those close to him, and threatening him. When Solzhenitsyn moved to Vermont in the United States, he had to live in a compound surrounded by barbed wire.

While Solzhenitsyn appreciated American freedoms, he was highly critical of much of American culture and decried what he saw as the weakness, ugliness, and spiritual vapidity of the moral fiber of the West, stating that, "the human soul longs for things higher, warmer, and purer than those offered by today's mass living habits... by TV stupor and by intolerable music."

In 1990, his Soviet citizenship was restored, and, in 1994, he returned to Russia. He died in 2008 at the age of 89. Russian and world leaders paid tribute following his death.

Solzhenitsyn's books documented the horrors of communism and did much to bring it down. But he was not satisfied that Russia should become a liberal democracy, advocating for the restoration of the Russian monarchy and the reestablishment of the key role of the Russian Orthodox Church, both necessary, he thought, to save the Russian soul.

Was Solzhenitsyn happy?

The Somnambulist

There is an extensive literature addressing happiness. Books, journals, university departments, institutes. One book on happiness, which we will take as representative, is *Before Happiness* by positive psychology advocate, Shawn Achor, which presents five steps to help you raise your levels of positive genius: select the reality that will lead to positive growth, chart the best route to accomplish your goals, use success accelerants, suppress interference, and transfer your positive reality to others. Of course there is often some value to what the field has to offer in terms of individuals achieving a satisfying life and workplaces being productive. But unfortunately, while some of this literature might be inspiring, like most of the social sciences, it must be taken with a strong dose of skepticism. Cause and effect often cannot be determined. And we ask, where is biography? In reading biographies of artists or business leaders, we typically sees references to their lives, training, work, obsessions, successes, failures, or to competing businesses, social treads, new technologies. Not so in books from social scientists, in which one is more likely to encounter something like: "Fostering social cohesion in the team by introducing after work beer parties increased productivity by nineteen percent," than about the determined vision of a business leader.

Recall our brief definition of happiness—a feeling of contentment, satisfaction, wellbeing, pleasure; a positive emotional state. This stuff is actually taken seriously. An article in an otherwise serious science magazine stated:

> *Feeling good has also been shown to improve people's creativity and ability to solve problems. In one experiment, subjects were shown a video of comedy bloopers to lighten their mood, before being presented with a practical problem involving a box of matches, a box of tacks and a candle. … experimenters found that people who had viewed the comedy clips were more likely to solve the problem…*

How unfortunate that Pope, Beethoven, Nietzsche, Van Gogh, and Solzhenitsyn did not know about this and about the five steps to achieve positive genius.

Tools are being developed to measure happiness in individuals and in communities, and we now have a measure of a country's gross national happiness (GNH) as an alternative to gross domestic product (GDP). Given that GDP includes all economic activity, so that a hurricane can increase the GDP, one can see how an alternative that would give positive or negative weight to various activities would be tempting. But one can also see how various biases could affect the choice of which activities to assign positive and negative values to. For example if one's bias is communitarian, one might assign a negative value to working in isolation to write a novel. Sure enough, a ranking put out by a British group places the United States 150th in happiness among the world's countries, with Vanuatu, Columbia, Costa Rica, and Dominica as the top four. Dominica also has the word's highest murder rate, leading one to wonder exactly what are the group's criteria. And happiness is now being used to promote social policies. If people are unhappy, we are justified in promoting policies that will eliminate the causes of that unhappiness. Never mind that happiness appears to be an innate quality in people and, except in extremes, not a response to external circumstances.

In an era of government regulation of ever more of our lives, legislators, regulators, and policy pundits need criteria to measure the effects of what they are doing. One approach has been cost-benefit. If we close a paper mill, what will be the benefits in terms of a cleaner environment verses the cost in terms of lost jobs and more expensive paper? Now a new criterion is being considered: happiness. How will a proposed policy increase or decrease happiness? The term "hedonics" is used to give the effort a sense of seriousness, but that doesn't make it any less frightening.

The question is, of course, what kind of world do those conducting these happiness studies and proposing hedonic policies want for us? Apparently a world rich with social support, but also a static world without risk, a world that shuns the unknown. And one without creativity? It appears so. Their happy person? An apathetic creature with no passion or commitment, unable to dream, who just earns a living, keeps warm, and uses compact fluorescent light bulbs? A somnambulant conformist couch potato? Apparently.

At least some are skeptical of happiness. The actor

Hugh Laurie says: "I equate happiness with contentment, and contentment with complacency, and complacency with impending disaster."

The Visionary Creative and Joy

The cultural and political commentator, Arthur Brooks, presents an alternative concept of happiness, describing it as coming from "earned success:"

> *Earned success involves the ability to create value honestly—*
> *not by inheriting a fortune, not by picking up a welfare check.*
> *It doesn't mean making money in and of itself. Earned suc-*
> *cess is the creation of value in our lives or in the lives of oth-*
> *ers. Earned success is the stuff of entrepreneurs who seek*
> *value through innovation, hard work and passion. Earned*
> *success is what parents feel when their children do wonderful*
> *things, what social innovators feel when they change lives, what*
> *artists feel when they create something of beauty.*

And the *New York Times* columnist, David Brooks, in
commenting on commencement addresses, writes:

> *The graduates are also told to pursue happiness and joy. But,*
> *of course, when you read a biography of someone you admire,*
> *it's rarely the things that made them happy that compel your*
> *admiration. It's the things they did to court unhappiness—*
> *the things they did that were arduous and miserable, which*
> *sometimes cost them friends and aroused hatred. It's excel-*
> *lence, not happiness, that we admire most.*

Since the term "happiness" has been hijacked by the advocates of hedonic somnambulism, let's use the term "joy."
Joy comes from earned success at something about which one

153

is passionate. Joy comes from achieving insight. Joy comes from accomplishment. *Joy comes from unleashing inner drives so frightening to policy makers and academics that they do not even want to acknowledge their existence.*

Achieving joy means first identifying one's temperament and one's deepest interest—one's passion. Recall the types of people we listed at the beginning of this book: leader, nurturer, producer, active, scholar, mystic, somnambulist. A leader might find joy heading a corporation or taking a university department to another level. A nurturer might find joy in seeing a child grow up healthy and go on to flourish, or teaching and opening up opportunities for others. A producer might find joy in organizing the manufacturing process for a new mobile communications device or making a violin. An active might find joy in climbing a mountain or fighting a fire. A scholar might find joy in pursuing a scientific insight or researching a book. A mystic might find joy in meditation or experiencing oneness. A somnambulist might find happiness in achieving a feeling of wellbeing. For the creative, joy comes from bringing into being something new that was not previously obvious and that exhibits beauty or utility. And joy for a Visionary Creative? Let's look a bit further.

If you ask someone in "creativity studies" about how someone might become creative, you might get a response that includes terms like "outside the box" and "overcoming preconceptions." And terms like "balance" and "harmony." And if you look at the lives of creatives, you will find many that are balanced and harmonious. For example, the American poets, Wallace Stevens, William Carlos Williams, and T. S. Eliot (in the case of Eliot, American-British) lived balanced lives and were, respectively, an insurance executive, a doctor, and a banker as well as being poets. But the lives of many others were not balanced and harmonious. The French novelist, Honoré de Balzac, would awaken at midnight, drink dozens of cups of black coffee, and work for fifteen hours straight. The French Symbolist poets, who believed that the truth of things lies beneath the surface and can only be described symbolically, included Charles Baudelaire, Paul-Marie Verlaine, and Arthur Rimbaud. Their poetry was remarkable. Their lives were tumultuous, and included poverty, indebtedness, imprisonment, alcoholism, drug addiction, syphilis, violence, and early deaths. And little happiness, but perhaps some joy.

We see the notion of sacrifice for one's art more recently in a story told by Jerry Seinfeld whose sitcom, *Seinfeld*, is on most lists of the best television series of all time. When the series ended, Seinfeld was worth several hundred million dollars. What to do next? In his mid forties, he had no interest in retiring, so he returned to his roots, doing stand-up comedy in small clubs. His efforts were recorded in a documentary movie titled *Comedian*. In it a young comic complains to Seinfeld about not having a normal life. No wife, no kids, no house, no money. Seinfeld becomes annoyed and responds:

I have to tell you a story. Glenn Miller's orchestra, they were doing a gig somewhere and they can't land where they were supposed to land because it was snowing, so they have to land in this field and walk to the gig. And they are dressed, and have to carry their instruments. So they are walking to where they are supposed to perform and it's wet and slushy, and in the distance they see this little house, and there are lights on and there's smoke coming out of the chimney. So they walk up and look in the window and they see this family: a guy and his wife, she's beautiful, and two kids and they are all sitting around this table. They're smiling and laughing and eating. There's a fire in the fireplace. These guys are standing outside in their suits and they're wet and they're shivering. They're holding their instruments. They're watching this incredible Normal Rockwell scene.

155

And one guy turns to the other and goes, "How do people live like that?"

That's what it's about. Love of the craft! The band much rather struggle doing what they love the most than be "comfortable" in a place they hate. Chasing your dreams, or letting your dreams chase you. That's what it's about!

Once one identifies one's passion, the next step is to enter the fray; participate, have dreams, desires, and goals, and strive to achieve them. One might not be successful, but if one earns success at something about which one is passionate, one will find joy. And if one never enters the fray, one can still be supportive of those who do.

For Visionary Creatives, joy comes from swimming in their culture, interacting with those on the cutting edge who are redefining reality, arguing with them, collaborating with them, experiencing their creations. And producing works that manifest the spirit of their age and making apparent to others what is obvious to them: that our world is no longer what it had been. Works that propel our world into an unfolding future.

Recognition for the Visionary Creative can be tenuous, and at times in the absence of recognition, satisfaction may have to come in the perfection of one's craft, acknowledgments from those in one's field who know, and internal dialogues with past masters, as when the architect Louis Kahn would ask, "How am I doing, Le Corbusier?" If Visionary Creatives are fortunate, they will be recognized and rewarded materially, but in some cases their greatest satisfaction might have to be that those who know appreciate what they have accomplished.

So, were Pope, Beethoven, Nietzsche, Van Gogh, and Solzhenitsyn happy? Would they have thought the question inane? As they seldom experienced feelings of contentment, wellbeing, or positive emotional states, no, they were not happy. But they were able to pursue their passions, and were able to swim in the spirit of the age and create works that changed the world. And at times they received recognition for what they accomplished. They were joyful.

The Flow of Energy

There is a notion that mental illness or a difficult life can contribute to creative output, and that may, in some cases, be true, but let's be clear, we are not saying that was the case with these figures. Our point is that they were able to achieve joy in producing great works despite not being happy under the prevalent definitions of happiness. Others achieved joy in producing great works equal to those of these creatives while leading long lives free of mental illness and great suffering, including Shakespeare, Haydn, Picasso, and Twain. (Although Picasso made the lives of many around him miserable.) Of these, Shakespeare died the youngest at fifty-two and Picasso the oldest at ninety-one. Franz Joseph Haydn in particular was happy and cheerful, living to the age of seventy-seven. He was called Papa Haydn, not because of his age—he received the appellation when he was in his thirties—but because he took care of those who worked with and under him. He had a sense of humor in both his life and his music, and he loved practical jokes. He was a loyal friend and mentor to Mozart, and he was tolerant of Beethoven despite Beethoven's bad behavior toward him. He is the father of the symphony and of the string quartet and he was a leading figure, along with Mozart, in classical era Viennese music. At the time of his death he was one of the most celebrated composers in Europe. So no, we are not equating suffering with creativity; rather we are attempting to describe something other than happiness that one might aspire to, something that values creativity.

Certainly no one would want to suffer what Pope, Beethoven, Nietzsche, Van Gogh, and Solzhenitsyn suffered.

Especially what Van Gogh suffered; what an unhappy life in every respect. But let's imagine we could ask each of them if he would trade his life for one of feelings of contentment, satisfaction, wellbeing, pleasure; a positive emotional state. We know how Nietzsche would answer. We suspect Van Gogh might answer the same way, following the admonition to participate joyfully in the sorrows of the world and declaring himself with William Blake:

As I was walking among the fires of Hell,
delighted with the enjoyments of Genius;
which to Angels look like torment and insanity.

Doctor Who is a long running British television science fiction series about a Time Lord, Doctor Who, who travels through time in a phone booth. In an episode titled "Vincent and the Doctor," regarded as one of the best in the series, the Doctor and his companion, Amy, travel to Provence in the south of France in 1890 to enlist Van Gogh's aid in fighting a space monster. They form an affection for Van Gogh and in an attempt to relieve him of his despair, take him to our present to see an exhibit of his work in Paris. Van Gogh is overwhelmed by the enthusiastic reception for his paintings. Then, within earshot of Van Gogh, Doctor Who asks the exhibit's curator, "Where do you think Van Gogh rates in the history of art?" The curator, played with British solemnity by Bill Nighy, replies, "Well, big question. But to me, Van Gogh is the finest painter of them all. Certainly the most popular great painter of all time, the most beloved. His command of color the most magnificent. He transformed the pain of his tormented life into ecstatic beauty. Pain is easy to portray, but to use your passion and pain to portray the ecstasy and joy and magnificence of our world—no one had ever done it before. Perhaps no one ever will do it again. To my mind that

158

strange wild man who roamed the fields of Provence was not only the world's greatest artist, but also one of the greatest men who ever lived."

Van Gogh never heard words like that, and of course it would have been wonderful if he had. But did he need to? He wrote to his brother, Theo, "Wings, wings to fly above life! Wings to fly above the grave and death! That is what we want, and I am beginning to understand that we can get them." We see from Van Gogh's letters that his greatest despair was not his misfortunes, but his inability to fully convey in his paintings the luminous world he experienced. As much as we admire what he accomplished, he wanted to accomplish so much more.

Sometimes artists realize they will not receive the world's recognition in their lifetimes. The Austrian painter, Egon Schiele, died of the Spanish flu at the age of twenty-eight in 1918. He spent the last three days of his life drawing his dead wife, also a victim of the flu, who had been six months pregnant. He could not afford a coffin. The twisting tormented figures in Schiele's drawings and paintings captured the unconscious of *fin de siecle* Vienna as well as his own suffering. Although encouraged by the older and established painter, Gustav Klimt, Schiele was an outcast and had even been arrested for pornography. But as befits an artist, he had unlimited self-confidence, writing to his mother, "All beautiful and noble qualities have been united in me... I shall be the fruit which will leave eternal vitality behind even after its decay. How great must be your joy, therefore, to have given birth to me." And then at the end he wrote, "The war is over—and I must go. My paintings will be shown in all the museums."

Why do artists do what they do? Why, for example, does Francis Ford Coppola make his next movie? The question points at human motivation, and shows the inadequacies of the measures we usually use. Money? Coppola has as much money as he needs, and he now makes movies that might not make money. Fame? He has that. Posterity? Yes, there is a satisfaction to leaving a coherent body of work, but there is something else at work here. Joseph Campbell states, "People say that we're all looking for meaning in our lives. I don't think that is the case. I think that what we're seeking is an experience of being alive, the rapture of being alive." Let's look at a notion from the Spanish philosopher, José Ortega y Gasset regarding the energies of the cosmos that pour into us.

[T]he political or cultural aspects of history are... the mere surface of history; that in preference to, and deeper than these, the reality of history lies in biological power, in pure vitality, in what is in man of cosmic energy, not identical with, but related to, the energy which agitates the sea, fecundates the beast, causes the tree to flower and the star to shine.

So perhaps Coppola makes movies to feel the rapture of being alive, to feel the flow of the energy of the cosmos. What does that feel like? We could turn to psychological studies to find out, such as those presented by Mihaly Csíkszentmihályi in his book, *Flow: The Psychology of Optimal Experience.* According to Csíkszentmihályi, flow is a mental state in which one is completely absorbed in what one is doing, fully involved, and enjoying the activity to the point where everything else is shut out. One is in the zone, in the groove, on a roll. For Csíkszentmihályi, flow has six characteristics: intensely focused concentration, merging of action and awareness, loss of self-consciousness, sense of control over the situation, loss of a sense of time, and finding the activity intrinsically rewarding. And flow can involve a feeling of rapture, although in some cases one is so absorbed in the activity that one is not even in touch with one's emotions.

Surely the creative figures in this book were often in

states of flow while doing their work. But many people are also in states of flow when assembling model airplanes or playing video games. Csíkszentmihályi does not make a distinction between deep creative processes and trivial recreation. It is interesting that Csíkszentmihályi's studies of flow are regarded as so important to the understanding of creativity, and that they are among the few examples we have of studies of what creatives experience. But they are far from the mark.

So, to more deeply understand the experience of the Visionary Creative, let's turn to the arts. In *The Immoralist,* a novel by the French Noble Prize winner, André Gide, Michel, a scholar profoundly out of touch with himself, travels to Tunisia on his honeymoon. While there he has a cathartic experience with tuberculosis and as he recovers, he discovers a life-force welling up within him, a need to let "the layers of acquired knowledge peel away from the mind like a cosmetic and reveal, in patches, the naked flesh beneath, the authentic being hidden there." He plunges deeper and deeper into the North African desert where he experiences this life-force burning in him like the hot sand, his outer journey paralleling his inner journey: "I did not understand the forbearance of this African earth, submerged for days at a time and now awakening from winter, drunk with water, bursting with new juices; it laughed in this springtime frenzy whose echo, whose image I perceived within myself." Michel does some things we do not admire, and it is not clear if all will turn out well for him. The energies of the universe are not always in tune with our values.

Today we are less likely to read Gide, so let's look at a movie that portrays this same experience of a life-force welling up, *Wolf,* directed by Mike Nichols and staring Jack Nicholson. Nicholson plays Will Randall, a mild mannered chief editor at a book publishing firm who is being undermined by a colleague and is about to be pushed out of the firm during a corporate takeover. He does not have the will to defend himself, and is resigned to his fate. Driving in the country at night, Randall hits a wolf. When he goes to look at it, it leaps up, bites him, and runs off. Of course it was a were-wolf, and over the next few days, Randall's senses sharpen; he can smell where people have been, he can hear conspiratorial conversations anywhere in the building. He mounts a coun-terattack against those seeking to oust him. The movie has its twists and turns, but ends with Randall defeating his adver-saries, and with his love interest, now also a werewolf, leaping into the forest. The movie is urging us not to find a werewolf to bite us so that we can enter the forest, but to engage our lives with fierceness, focus, and joy while feeling the energies of the universe flow through us.

What were the joys of Van Gogh and others who had horrendous lives, as well as of Picasso and others who had largely pleasant lives? What did they experience? Throughout this book we have been referring to the idea of the spirit of the age, including in quotes from Frank Lloyd Wright and Mies van der Rohe. We mentioned Ortega's notion of the energies of the cosmos flowing into the world. And we men-tioned Joseph Campbell's remark that, "Myth is the secret opening through which the inexhaustible energies of the cos-mos pour into human cultural manifestation." When Wright and Mies refer to architecture, and Campbell refers to myth, we would substitute all of life, and it is through engagement in the arts, sciences, technology, business, that the Visionary Creative directly *experiences* this spirit of the age, these inex-haustible energies that others can only attempt to understand. And in response to this spirit and this energy the Visionary Creative produces works that are conduits for their flow into our world and at the same time are vehicles for the remaking of our world. That is the joy of the Visionary Creative, of Van Gogh as well as Picasso. What greater satisfaction, what greater joy for a creative could there be?

162

PART THREE:
■ CREATING THE FUTURE

HOW THEY CREATED
THE 20TH CENTURY

In which we ask, what is the world in which Visionary Creatives are working today? Before looking at the emerging twenty-first century and the stage it will unfold for our lives and creativity, we briefly examine the twentieth century. Throughout society and in the sciences we are experiencing a loss of fixed frames of reference. We end with Marcel Duchamp, a bridge between two centuries.

Sanity is only that which is within the frame of reference of conventional thought.
  ~ Erich Fromm, German-American psychologist and philosopher

... our meaning is now the meaning that is no meaning; for no fixed term of reference can be drawn.
  ~ Joseph Campbell, mythologist

The Loss of Fixed Frames of Reference

We have been saying throughout this book that Visionary Creativity takes place in cultural contexts: Visionary Creatives swim in the culture of our day. The things they create—in art, design, science, technology, business—embody that culture and at the same time pull us into the future. How should we describe the culture, the stage, of our twenty-first century?

Let's begin by looking back at the twentieth century, which began by giving us fixed frames of reference against which to orient ourselves, and ended by withdrawing all such references, plunging us into a world of insecurity. And we will see how we attempted to orient ourselves without such references. While the nineteenth century brought vast social, scientific, and technological changes, for the most part those changes were rooted in firm cultural, social, and scientific foundations. Those foundations crumbled during the twentieth century.

Social Upheavals

Let's very briefly mention some of the cultural and social upheavals that beset the twentieth century. The twentieth century began with the Victorian conviction of human perfectibility and the view of Western civilization as the culmination of world history. That conviction and view took a hit with the First World War, led by aging statesmen and generals who wiped out their progeny. Europe entered the war dominated by Empires, some of which saw themselves as descendants of the Roman Empire. After the war, most of the empires were gone, replaced by unstable regimes, and by a decade after the Second World War, a quarter of a billion people had died in wars, epidemics, concentration camps, revolutions, famines, and outright exterminations. Not strong arguing points for claiming to be the culmination of world history.

Then religion. Christianity had positioned Westerners as the favored children of the ruler of all creation. But the authority of Christianity faded under rapid advances in science and contacts with other religions that sometimes revealed theologies of great sophistication. With the commandments of a Middle Eastern deity no longer accepted as literal, commentators feared moral relativism. At the same time, the social or-

166

der was changing with the authority of status fading in the face of democracy and entrepreneurial accomplishment, and with women moving toward parity with men.

Changes in our understanding of evolution even decentered us as a species. In the early twentieth century evolution was interpreted as showing humans to be the culmination of a process that had inexorably moved life from single-celled organisms to the creature whose brain is the most complex thing in the universe. But that interpretation faded and evolution came to be interpreted not as a movement toward complexity, but a random walk. And more recently we have found that we share ninety-eight percent of our DNA with chimpanzees, fifty percent with bananas, and twenty-six percent even with yeast.

Some Developments in 20th Century Science

We have reiterated throughout this book that culture is the stage on which we act out our lives and exercise our creativity. There are of course many ways we can describe cultures, from religious views of the cosmos to the ways meals are eaten and everything in between. In this book we are focusing on a culture's scientific worldview, the notions of space and time within which people live their lives, both literally and figuratively, and we have looked in some detail at the Newtonian world. What about our world today; what is the cultural stage of our emerging twenty-first century, the stage on which we will be living our lives, and on which our Visionary Creatives will be doing their work? The achievements of twentieth century science are vast, but here we will just briefly mention geology, cosmology, relativity, quantum theory, and mathematics to get a sense of this loss of fixed frames of reference and a notion of the world in which Visionary Creatives are working today.

Geology

Let's begin with the Earth on which we live. At the end of the nineteenth century, the Earth was stable and the continents fixed. The Earth was believed to have formed over a period of about a hundred million years and it had reached equilibrium. By the end of the twentieth century the Earth was four and a half billion years old and was violent, dynamic and constantly changing. Its interior roiled with convection currents of lava trying to dissipate the six thousand degree heat of its iron core, and magnum pushed up into the ocean floor moving the continents apart in what is called plate tectonics. Even the ground on which we stand is in motion.

And then with the Apollo Moon shots we were able to look back on the Earth as a "big blue marble," much smaller than we had previously imagined it, a "Spaceship Earth" in need of an "operating manual."

Cosmology

As we discussed earlier, in the fifteenth and sixteenth centuries Copernicus and Galileo put forward the notion that the Sun, not the Earth, was at the center of our solar system, an idea disturbing not only to astronomy, but to our notion of our place in the cosmos. We had begun our process of decentering. By the beginning of the twentieth century we were no longer in a solar system surrounded by a thin shell of fixed stars, but located in the Milky Way galaxy that perhaps had always existed, and that was the entire universe. Vast, but still somewhat cozy. Then in the 1920s the astronomer Edwin Hubble discovered that some nebulae, fuzzy objects that had been thought to be clouds of gas in our galaxy, are actually other galaxies. Eventually billions and billions of other galaxies. And then Hubble discovered that far from being static, the universe is expanding, and by the 1960s it was established that the expansion had begun with a "Big Bang," now thought

168

to be about fourteen billion years ago. And the vastness of our universe had just begun. We can "see" out only as far as those stars whose light has had time to reach us since the Big Bang, about forty-six billion light years away, but the universe is presumed to be perhaps billions of times larger than that. And now it is suggested that we live in a "multiverse" of countless universes of which ours is just one. The part of the universe we occupied became smaller, but at the same time our grasp of its extent and even its details grew.

Physics: Relativity

Late nineteenth century physics was content in the belief that it had comprehended all of physical reality. Newton's laws of motion and gravity were at the foundation, thermodynamics explained heat, and Maxwell's equations enabled us to understand electromagnetism. There were just some minor loose threads to attend to, but those loose threads, when pulled, unraveled the entire fabric of physics, leading to relativity theory and quantum theory.

There are many ways to look at Einstein's relativity theory—let's try one that addresses our interests in this book. Recall Newton's absolute space that we might think of as being marked with a grid like a three dimensional chess board. Now recall Maxwell's fields with their lines of force that were made apparent by the iron filings on a piece of paper laid over a magnet. Then came the question, where are those fields located, or more precisely, against what are they oriented? And how do light waves propagate through these fields? Waves propagate through something—sound waves through air, ocean waves through water; how could they be transmitted through the vacuum of space? A substance called the ether, a massless "ethereal" medium, was hypothesized for the transmission of light. The ether was thought to be fixed within space—within Newton's grid—so movement of light or even

169

our Earth through the ether would be movement with reference to this grid of absolute space. (The Jello was nailed to the wall.) That model provided the security of a fixed frame of reference within which we could position ourselves, but it led to problems. It implied that different observers moving in different ways would measure the speed of light differently: faster for those moving toward a light source, and slower for those moving away. But experiments showed that the speed of light was always the same for all observers no matter their motion.

In 1905 Einstein published a paper presenting what is now called *special relativity*, in which he showed that there is no ether (no Jello) and no absolute space (no wall). One of Newton's fundamental axioms was gone, and Maxwell's fields existed in... well, nothing. They were self-referential, just like the modern condition in which there are no fixed frames of reference against which we can orient ourselves. Einstein also showed that time is dependent on our observations. So neither space nor time exist except as arrangements of objects or events as we perceive them, and different observers can perceive them differently. Then in 1915 Einstein's *general relativity* showed that gravity is not a force, but the dynamic contortions of a no longer uniform space-time.

We might be tempted to say that these notions are abstractions of advanced physics, not applicable to our lives, but is that the case? Visionary Creatives swim in their cultures, experiencing them, while the rest of us experience what we have been taught, which is often out of date. In much of modern art the approach to space-time is similar to what we have been discussing. The Surrealist painter, Salvador Dalí, writes of sitting at a table and feeling it move upwards against the flow of the space-time that was rushing through his body, pouring into the Earth. Recall the Copernican-Galilean-Newtonian revolution. It did not just exchange the Earth with the Sun at the center of the solar system, it eliminated any fixed center for existence. But how can there be existence without a fixed center around which to orient it? Today we have seen enough outer space in science fiction movies not to be bothered by this, but for many post-Copernicans it was all very distressing. Likewise, those rooted in Newton's world, on encountering Einstein's space-time continuum, experienced the loss of a fixed frame of reference as highly disconcerting. How can we exist on a stage if there is no reference to tell us where we are? We would be slipping and sliding all over the place. And we are! It's called modernism.

What does relativity tell us? *That there is no fixed space or time; there is nothing to which we can anchor ourselves.*

Physics: Quantum Theory

Over the course of the twentieth century, physicists developed quantum theory and made some very strange discoveries, including that a subatomic "particle" exists as a cloud of probability until we observe it, when it chooses a location. And even then, due to Heisenberg's uncertainty principle, the particle can have a precise location or a precise velocity, but not both. For some time popularizers of science, unable to accept this "quantum weirdness," attempted to keep these disturbing features of quantum theory contained by saying that the particle always has a precise position and velocity; we were just not able to measure them. But that contention is wrong. Quantum theory shows that this "weirdness" is a feature of reality, not a feature of our limited measuring ability. Worse, when a particle is faced with the choice of following one of two paths, it can follow either or both depending on how we observe it, and it can change its choice even after is has taken one of the paths. The American theoretical physicist, John Archibald Wheeler states, "No phenomenon is a real phenomenon until it is an observed phenomenon."

And these quantum effects apply at cosmic scales, even extreme cosmic scales. We ask, exactly what happened approximately fourteen billion years ago at the moment of the Big Bang? Since the Big Bang was a quantum phenomenon, some physicists, including Stephen Hawking, contend that what happened depends on how we look at it, and some say that how we look at it is changing the future of the universe. Wheeler contends that, "We are participators in bringing into being not only the near and here but the far away and long ago."

What exactly is going on with these quantum phenomena? There are several contending attempts at explanations, including what is called the *Von Neumann-Wigner* position that it is experience by a conscious being that leads to what we see in quantum phenomena. Wow! Hard core science saying that our consciousness plays a role in forming reality.

Does any of this have application in our creative disciplines? Of course most of us will not be doing anything that involves relativity or quantum theory. Likewise, the artists of Newton's time did not do anything that involved planetary orbits. Or did they? As we discussed earlier, Newton's space and time are potentials that are occupied by objects and events. But this is also the space and time of perspective painting, marked out by the grid of perspective lines, occupied by figures frozen in a moment of time. And it is the space of the Renaissance villa occupied by the human at the center. So there was a relationship between Newton's space and time and the space and time of the arts of his era. And there was a similar relationship between Einstein's space-time and the space-time of the arts of his day as we will see when we discuss Picasso's Cubism, Frank Lloyd Wright's architecture, and James Joyce's novels. And there is also such a relationship today, as we will see later.

What does quantum theory tell us? *That an observer, perhaps even consciousness, is necessary for the world to exist, and how we observe the world can change it, even in the past.*

172

In these few examples we see science presenting us with a world losing its fixed frames of reference, a world sliding into flux. But is not science built on mathematics, and is not mathematics rock solid in its rigor? The square of the hypotenuse of a right triangle does and must equal the sum of the squares of the other two sides. Or must it? In the mid-nineteenth century, several non-Euclidian geometries were developed that would hold for different kinds of surfaces, for example if a surface were curved like a sphere. One of the reasons we study Euclidian geometry in school is because it tells us that if ideas can be organized deductively, they have to be true. In other words Euclidian geometry is foundational to Western logical thought. But beginning in the late nineteenth century there were various possibilities from which we had to choose, such as what kind of curvature characterized the space of our universe, and we could only choose based on observation. Kind of shaky, since mathematics is not supposed to be contingent on observation, so mathematicians set out to secure their discipline. They explored three approaches, logicism, formalism, and intuitionism.

Logicism is the notion that mathematics is at its roots actually logic, and when all of mathematics is reduced to logic, it will be secure. In 1931 the Hungarian mathematician Kurt Gödel published what is called Gödel's incompleteness theorem, showing that all of mathematics has to be incomplete or self-contradictory, totally undermining the logicism enterprise. Formalism holds that mathematics is a formal game based on rules established by mathematicians. We are free to invent any rules as long as they are consistent. In 1936 the English mathematician and computer scientist, Alan Turing, established that there could be no such foundation for mathematics. Intuitionism holds that mathematics comes from our minds. Most mathematicians just don't like intuitionism, so they ignore it. But even while rejecting logicism and formalism, and ignoring intuitionism, mathematicians have continued their work and have made remarkable strides in generating new kinds of mathematics.

What does the continued progress of mathematics despite its loss of foundations tell us? *That we can build elegant sand castles in the sky, and that we can soar without a net.*

The Loss of Frames of Reference in Modern Art

Cubism

How did the artists of the twentieth century respond to a world losing its fixed frames of reference? Earlier we described Picasso's *Les Demoiselles d'Avignon* of 1907. Shortly after finishing it, Picasso began working with George Braque to develop Cubism, putting the final nail in the coffin of perspective, and therefore the point of view of a fixed observer. Recall our discussion of da Vinci's *Adoration of the Magi*, with its perspective lines converging in the distance to create a stage of uniform space and time for us as observers. Was not perspective a great discovery enabling us to reproduce in two dimensions the three-dimensional world that we see? No, perspective was not a discovery, and we do not see in perspective. Perspective is a convention used in Western European painting from 1400 to 1900. It was not used in other cultures, and few serious painters have used it since 1900.

But doesn't the camera see in perspective? Yes, because we have designed camera lenses to work that way, but today very different kinds of cameras and lenses are also being used.

Stand about ten feet from a friend and look at them, taking in all of them. You will need to move your eyes at least a half dozen times, and with each "snap shot" you get three vanishing points (depending on the approach to perspective we are using), giving you eighteen vanishing points just to see your stationary friend from one unmoving position. A far cry from the single vanishing point in da Vinci's *Adoration*. So how then did we arrive at the convention of perspective, and why did artists during the Renaissance think they saw in perspective, as some people still do today? Think about how you see. Your eyes flit around, catching tiny fragments, some of which are moving. All of this jumble is reported to the optical center of your brain, which then looks for stored precedents that it combines with these fragments to assemble *afterimages*, and these afterimages are what you "see." Ray Kurzweil, in *How to Create a Mind*, writes:

> *Although we experience the illusion of receiving high-resolution images from our eyes, what the optic nerve actually sends to the brain is just a series of outlines and clues about points of interest in our visual field. We then essentially hallucinate the world from cortical memories that interpret a series of movies with very low data rates that arrive in parallel channels.*

How these afterimages (or as Kurzweil calls them, high-resolution images) are assembled, which is a cognitive process, is *different in different cultures*. We tend to think that before the discovery of perspective, artists were struggling, not quite getting it. The period when perspective dominated was the time of real art. And modern artists who abandoned perspective still saw in perspective, but chose to "abstract" what they saw. That is a naive description. In a way, artists present what they see in a deep sense. The fact that the arts of different times and cultures are different is evidence that people in these different times and cultures saw differently.

The encounter between European Baroque painters who went to China in the 1700s and their Chinese counterparts presents an example of this. The Chinese painters appreciated the skills of the Europeans, but wondered why their figures had deformed limbs and skin diseases. The conventions of Chinese painting did not include foreshortening (a limb looking shorter if it is pointed at us) or chiaroscuro (the molding of the face with shadowing), and they therefore did not "see" these things in the "real world."

Now recall our complaint earlier about the lack of cultural awareness among sociologists and neurophysiologists who study creativity. The same is true of those who study perception. For example, there is currently much interest among psychologists and neurophysiologists in various neurological disorders, including visual agnosias, usually caused by some kind of brain damage. In some forms of the condition, a person can see only one thing at a time, for example only the spoon in a place setting. In another form, a person has trouble recognizing and naming objects, as described by the neurologist Oliver Sacks in his book, *The Man Who Mistook His Wife for a Hat*. This is part of a growing interest in how we form what we "see" out of the light that strikes our eyes, but that interest suffers from several limitations.

First, psychologists often assume that what they perceive is the "correct" perception. They see a hat, so there really is a hat; if someone else does not see a hat, they have a defect. Psychologists have not fully accepted that human cognition does not just make some interesting mistakes, it makes everything we experience. And they make no attempt to look for changes over time or differences in different cultures. Psychologists ask, "How do we perceive?" when they should ask, "How do people *in a particular culture at a particular time* perceive?" Much of our perceptual apparatus is malleable, formed as we grow up, and it is formed differently in different cultures. And even in our culture today, it has been formed differently in those who grew up reading books, those who grew up watching television, and now those who are growing up online with mobile devices.

The Impressionist painters presented what they in late nineteenth century Europe *saw* as opposed to what others *thought they knew was there*, and what they saw was light. In Monet's famous series of paintings of Rouen Cathedral he painted the light coming from the Cathedral at different times of day, in different weather, and in different seasons. What Monet saw changed, and looking at his paintings we can almost question whether there is a cathedral behind the light. Indeed Oscar Wilde, in his essay, "The Decay of Lying," contends that nature imitates art, not the other way around. He writes, "Where, if not from the Impressionists, do we get those wonderful brown fogs that come creeping down our streets, blurring the gas-lamps and changing the houses into monstrous shadows? ... The extraordinary change that has taken place in the climate of London during the last ten years is entirely due to this particular school of Art."

In Cubism, the flickerings our eyes pick up are assembled in a completely new afterimage, destroying the coherence of perspective and therefore the humanism that began with the Renaissance, and creating the fragmentation we call modernism. In his 1910 Cubist *Portrait of Ambroise Vollard*, Picasso shows Vollard's eyes cast downward and his head tilted slightly forward, calmly reading, providing a contrast to the violent fragmenting of the figure as though reflected in a shattered mirror and viewed from multiple angles.

Today we are yet again in a new world. We see differently, we paint differently, and we make our cameras differently. Look at some of the scenes in the *Lord of the Rings* and *Hobbit* movies. The camera moves over the landscape and among streaming warriors without the fixed point of view of conventional perspective. The climax scene at the volcano in *The Return of the King* pulls us into a totally new visual field. We have become accustomed to new ways of seeing through such

177

movies and through video games, and, as Oscar Wilde indicates, we want our "reality" to imitate it, so we have developed systems like the Skycam that maneuvers a camera in three dimensions over a sports stadium, allowing it to follow a ball in flight. In the early twentieth century, Cubism announced a revolution in how we saw, but we are today yet again in a totally new world. Our artists and other creatives keep us informed.

What does Cubism tell us? Let's go back to perspective painting. Perspective was not just a technique in the arts, it was a philosophical position stating that the world exists in a fixed space and time and that we are simultaneously a part of that world and also observers of it, each one of us with a unique point of view that establishes our individuality. With Cubism, we are in motion around an object that is not fixed. This is also a philosophical position, easier to state in the negative: *Cubism tells us that we are in a world that has no fixed frames of reference, and we have no fixed location in which to position ourselves or from which to have a point of view. We no longer exist as the kinds of individuals we previously were.* And once again, this was a hundred years ago; we are today in a very different world.

Frank Lloyd Wright

Frank Lloyd Wright had already expressed the ideas we discuss here in the houses he did in the early 1900s, but Fallingwater, which he did in 1937, is better known, so we will look at it. But before we do, let's go back to a Renaissance building, the Villa Rotonda by Andrea Palladio.

The Villa Rotonda, begun in 1550 in Vicenza, Italy, was designed for a retired clergyman as a weekend retreat. It is bilaterally symmetrical, with identical temple porticos on each of its four sides and a dome in the middle. While a dome is often meant to represent heaven, here it marks the referent point where the human being stands, fixed at the 0 point of Cartesian x, y, z coordinates, from which to survey nature.

Thus the building embodies the phrase, "Man is the measure of all things," a declaration by the Greek philosopher Protagoras that became a motto of the Renaissance. The Villa stands atop a hill, surveying the landscape around it, fully knowable, since from whichever side you approach it, you know the other sides—they are all the same.

Now contrast this with Fallingwater. Rather than sitting atop its hill, it is nestled into the side of its hill, cantilevered over a stream that runs under it. The building is anchored to the landscape not by a domed central space that we can occupy, but by a massive fireplace hearth, forcing the human being out of the center and into the spaces of the periphery. And these spaces are barely enclosed, divided from the outside only by floor-to-ceiling glass so that inside and outside flow together. And each time you approach from a different angle, you encounter a different building, as you also do when you move through the inside in different ways. In effect there is not one building; rather a different building unfolds each time we move around it or through it in a different way.

What does Wright tell us? *That we no longer have a fixed home, nor a fixed identity, that we are pushed put of the center to meander in the periphery as a part of the flux of nature. We make and remake our Selves and our world depending on how we observe it, reminiscent of Einstein's relativity and of quantum theory.*

Other 20th Century Art Forms

Having looked at Cubism and Wright's Fallingwater, we can see other twentieth century art forms through the lens of the loss of a fixed frame of reference. In painting, Dali's melting watches in his *Persistence of Memory*, that we discussed earlier, are illustrative of the dissolution of uniform time. In music, Igor Stravinsky's 1913 *The Rite of Spring*, with its wildly asynchronous beat, left its audience with nothing to hang on to. Paul Rosenfeld, in 1920, wrote of it "pound[ing] with the rhythm

179

of engines, whirls and spirals like screws and fly-wheels, grinds and shrieks like laboring metal." That, combined with its sexuality and depiction of human sacrifice, led to the riot in its opening night. Arnold Schoenberg's later atonal music would leave audiences with even less to hang on to.

In literature we see this loss of fixed frames of reference in Marcel Proust's *Remembrance of Things Past*, which is organized not by an objective chronology, but by memories that come flooding forth from the aroma of a madeleine dipped in tea. Proust writes:

> *No sooner had the warm liquid mixed with the crumbs touched my palate than a shudder ran through me and I stopped, intent upon the extraordinary thing that was happening to me. An exquisite pleasure had invaded my senses, something isolated, detached, with no suggestion of its origin.... Whence did it come? What did it mean? How could I seize and apprehend it?... And suddenly the memory revealed itself. The taste was that of the little piece of madeleine which on Sunday mornings at Combray (because on those mornings I did not go out before mass), when I went to say good morning to her in her bedroom, my aunt Léonie used to give me, dipping it first in her own cup of tea or tisane. The sight of the little madeleine had recalled nothing to my mind before I tasted it. And all from my cup of tea.*

What do these works of modernism tell us? *That despite slipping and sliding on a stage with nothing to hold on to, we have found new ways to orient our new Selves.*

Internalizing Archetypes

There is a strong materialist, even nihilist quality to much of the modernism of the twentieth century, but this materialism is only one thread of modernism. Certainly many modernists rejected the myths and religions of the past, but others asked, what if those myths and religions have not gone away, but have become internalized in our psyches? Then we could see our own religion and other religions as mythologies that contain insights into the human condition that are as powerful and useful as those offered by psychology, sociology, etc. Let's look at some twentieth century approaches that do just that.

While Sigmund Freud saw the unconscious as containing an individual's past, his younger colleague, the Swiss physician Carl Jung, proposed in his analytical psychology that the unconscious contains the entire past of the culture, with the individual linked to that past by dreams, myths, art, and literature. Based on this insight Jung developed a psychology that used access to this material as a means of achieving a fully integrated Self.

We also see this internalization of the richness of the world into the Self in James Joyce's novel, *Ulysses*, written between 1914 and 1922 and regarded as one of the most important novels of the twentieth century. The book, employing Joyce's method of "stream of consciousness," is built on Homer's *Odyssey*, and uses colors, parts of the body, and different arts and sciences, all woven into his characters. *Ulysses* follows Leopold Bloom, representing Odysseus; his friend and Joyce's alter ego, Stephen Dedalus, representing Odysseus's son, Telemachus; and Leopold's wife, Molly, representing Odysseus's wife, Penelope, through one day, June 16, 1904, the day of Joyce's first date with his future wife, Nora. And Joyce claimed that his descriptions of Dublin are so accurate that the city of that date could be rebuilt from them. All of this richness reveals to each of us our own potential richness.

After finishing *Ulysses*, Joyce began *Finnegans Wake*, publishing it seventeen years later in 1939. In it he continued his stream of consciousness writing and added layer upon layer of literary allusions, dream associations, and the play of words from a dozen languages. But not much plot. The book is structured around Giambattista Vico's *New Science*, which sees history as a cycle of animism, aristocracy, democracy, and anarchy, to begin again with animism, just as Joyce begins his book with the completion of the last sentence. The book exists on familial, historical, legendary, Biblical, symbolic, and psychological levels. The central character, Humphrey Chimpden Earwicker, or HCE for Here Comes Everybody, announces an exuberant embrace of the common person.

Joseph Campbell, who had coauthored *A Skeleton Key to Finnegans Wake*, refers to this internalization of our myths when he writes in *The Hero with a Thousand Faces*:

> *The latest incarnation of Oedipus, the continued romance of Beauty and the Beast, stand this afternoon on the corner of Forty-second Street and Fifth Avenue, waiting for the traffic light to change.*

Campbell approaches mythology in terms of archetypes, which he sees as universal patterns that manifest with local inflections in particular cultures. In religion, a dying and resurrecting god, born of a virgin, and associated with a cross is one example of a universal pattern. In local inflection, we see this archetype as Christ for Christians, but also Osiris for Egyptians, Dumuzi for Sumerians, Orpheus and Dionysus for Greeks, Krishna for Indians, and Quetzalcoatl for Meso-Americans. Thus the archetype is a pattern that stands outside of time, while its manifestations occur within specific historical and cultural contexts.

Another prominent archetype is the hero journey. As described by Campbell in *Hero*, a figure hears the call to adventure, leaves ordinary reality, journeys to a realm of fabulous forces, wins a decisive victory, and returns to enrich the world. This is the structure of *Star Wars* and hundreds of other movies, but it is also the structure of each of our lives. We are born into a wondrous world, encounter adventures and overcome adversities, and hopefully leave the world enriched by our contributions.

Earlier we mentioned J. K. Rowling's Harry Potter books. What is the reason for their phenomenal success? Of course there are many reasons, but one is that they embody the archetypes of the hero journey and of death and rebirth, and re-present them for the northern European spirit. Recall that we said Rowling had absorbed the stories of Merlin, who could not be killed, and T. H. White's *The Once and Future King*, titled after the inscription on King Arthur's tomb, "Here lies Arthur, king once, and king to be." These mythic archetypes are embedded in the northern European psyche as we see for example in J. R. R. Tolkien's *Lord of the Rings* series of books. European culture generally and British culture specifically are today dismissive of this archetypal material, going so far as to rewrite children's fairytales to eliminate it. But these archetypes remain alive in children, are internalized in them, and their hunger for its manifestation is one of the drivers of the popularity of these books.

Note again that there are two parts to archetypal structures: the universal pattern and the local inflection. A Visionary Creative must be able to navigate between them. The legendary Chinese mystic, Lao Tzu, writes in the *Tao Te Ching*:

Without desire, one can see the mystery.
With desire, one can see the manifestations.

But Lao Tzu then says that they are ultimately the same:

These two are twins, differing only in name...

183

A Visionary Creative should avoid making imitations of the past, and should not mistake the local inflection for the universal pattern, as happened, for example, with the French academic painters at the time of the Impressionists. Later, when Kandinsky, Mondrian, Brancusi, and many other modern artists produced "abstract" art, they stated that one of their intentions was to embody the archetypal spirituality of the great religious arts of the past in a form free of outdated cloaks. In Mondrian's paintings, we can see the horizontal black lines as representing death, and the vertical lines, resurrection. The paintings explore the balance between them. James Joyce, T. S. Eliot, Thomas Mann, and other modernist writers also presented archetypal themes in modern settings. In Eliot's play, *The Cocktail Party*, a contemporary social ritual is, at the same time, an incarnation of a sacred ritual.

Thus in the twentieth century we could engage with our myths, even live them if we were bold enough to do so, rather than just having them dictated to us.

What does this process of internalization tell us? *It tells us that works of Visionary Creativity in art, literature, and sometimes even science can become supra-psychologies, representative of the cosmos and of our unfolding individual lives. Embedded in these works are the accumulated wisdoms of the past, available to us like words in a book if we know how to read them. Or, more importantly, how to live them.*

How Did the World Come Apart?

There are of course many circumstances underlying the emergence of our contemporary world without fixed frames of reference. Let's look briefly at one of them. The media theorist, Marshall McLuhan, shows that behind the Newtonian clockwork world that was to come undone in the twentieth century were the workings of minds bred on the printed phonetic alphabet. Think of the text of a book that is made up of paragraphs, that are made up of sentences, that are made up of words, that are made up of letters. Then think of the habits of mind acquired by moving one's eyes across uniform lines of type to recreate an author's intensions. McLuhan points out that doing so rewires the brain, preparing it for linear-logical thought and ushering in the mechanistic production we saw in the industrial world.

By the late nineteenth century, print as the dominant technology of communication was being challenged by electricity and the information it carried. As we mentioned earlier, telegraph, telephone, and radio communications were developed throughout the nineteenth century, and communications that had been interiorized by reading were now being externalized. Modes of communication are extensions of our nervous systems, and in the late nineteenth and early twentieth centuries electric communications contributed to our decentering as our nervous systems spread over the globe. Hold a telephone to your ear and your neurons, by way of electric extensions, reach around the planet and now even out to satellites in orbit and beyond, flowing out from the Earth and following the *War of the Worlds* and *I Love Lucy* broadcasts that are now reaching the seventy and sixty light year marks respectively, engulfing thousands of stars. The dissolution of our linear-logical Selves was a reflection of the dissolution of our linear-logical world. And of course we can begin to think about what will be the effects on us of our current online mobile digital media.

What Was the 20th Century All About?

Over the course of the twentieth century we moved from a world that was solid, static, and knowable, to one that was fluid, dynamic, and indeterminate; a world without fixed frames of reference. We lost our privileged position as humans, as Westerners, as objective knowers of the world through science; as the favored children of the creator, and as the culmination of evolution. The patterns of our culture become internalized in each of us and our nervous systems become spread out around the globe and beyond in an electronic web.

How should we describe the stage on which we exercised our creativity and lived out our lives by the end of the twentieth century? *As one on which we slipped about with nothing to hang on to. What was it like to exist on this stage? That is what modern art tells us.*

Marcel Duchamp

Let's end our discussion of the twentieth century with Marcel Duchamp (1887–1968). Beethoven began his career in the context of the Viennese classicism of Haydn and Mozart, and his later work opened the way to Romanticism, but at the same time he was uniquely Beethoven. We might say the same for Duchamp, whose early work was in the modernist tradition, derivative of Cubism, Futurism, and Surrealism, and who was later part of the Dadaist movement, opening the way to the art of our time. But at the same time Duchamp was uniquely Duchamp. And, despite his having died in 1968, a transition from the twentieth to the twenty-first centuries.

Duchamp began his art career in the early 1900s experimenting with various Post-Impressionist styles and hanging out in French artistic circles. In 1912 he completed an ambitious painting, *Nude Descending a Staircase No. 2*. It features repeated abstracted fragmented images of a figure to capture its motion, and partakes of Cubism and Italian Futurism. He submitted it to the *Salon des Indépendants* in Paris where a juror asked that he change its name. Refusing, he took it home in a taxi and stated that he was finished with being a part of a group, although he did eventually become associated with the Dadaists. Later he submitted the painting to the 1913 Armory Show in New York where it was accepted. An art critic for the *New York Times* wrote that it resembled "an explosion in a shingle factory." Duchamp lost interest in painting, got a job as a librarian, and started working on other things, including *The Large Glass*, a piece that looks like a double glazed storm window with images sandwiched between the panes of the glass.

In 1917 Duchamp was on the board of the Society of Independent Artists in New York, which announced an exhibition that, they said, would show all work submitted. Duchamp went to a plumbing supply, bought a men's room urinal, signed it "R. Mutt 1917," and anonymously submitted it to the exhibit. The exhibition committee debated whether the *Fountain*, as it is now known, was art and whether they should show it. They decided they had to have it at the exhibit because of their announcement, but put it behind a curtain in the hope that no one would notice it. Bad move for a gallery claiming to be progressive, as the *Fountain* was to become one of the most important works of modern art. Duchamp then announced that it was his and resigned from the gallery, as did several other prominent figures. Today we can see the *Fountain* only in replica, as the gallery threw it out after the exhibition closed.

An article about the matter titled "The Richard Mutt Case" stated that, "Whether Mr. Mutt made the fountain with his own hands or not has no importance. He CHOSE it. He took an article of life, placed it so that its useful significance disappeared under the new title and point of view—created a new thought for that object." Duchamp called the things he chose "readymades." At New York's Museum of Modern Art you can sometimes see a snow shovel that he bought at a hardware store, hanging by a wire and looking just like an old snow shovel you might have in your garage. Some critics tried to talk about the erotic curves of the urinal, or the fact that the art form of pragmatic America was plumbing, but you can't say that about a snow shovel.

Duchamp spent the last decades of his life focusing on chess, assembling references to his earlier work, meeting with young artists, and not making art. Except secretly. For twenty years he worked in his New York studio on *Étant donnés*, which was unveiled at the Philadelphia Museum of Art a year after his death.

You enter the section of the museum that has the most comprehensive Duchamp collection in the world and make your way to a very small room that has a worn wooden door with two holes in it. You press your eyes up to the holes and you see a mannequin of a naked woman lying in the brush, her head obscured from your view, her legs spread open, and a lantern in one hand.

When you look at the *Fountain* or the readymade snow shovel, a voice in your head might say, "But that's not art!" Exactly what the exhibition committee of the Society of Independent Artists decided. And you might also wonder about *Étant donnés*.

An artist has an intention; he or she wants to convey an insight about the time or the human condition. He or she creates something, usually requiring craft and an aesthetic sense, but as we now know, not always, and places it where an audience can encounter it—in a gallery, between the covers of a book, in a concert hall. An audience experiences the piece, sometimes with consternation. The work, the initial response of the audience, subsequent responses of that audience, responses of subsequent audiences, and ongoing evaluations by critics and historians reverberate through the years, decades, and centuries. Duchamp's point was that art is not just the object—the "something, usually requiring craft and an aesthetic sense"—but this *entire process*. We can no longer separate the artist, the audience, and the work of art. They have become one interpenetrating organism.

Duchamp was one of the first to bring this new vision to our attention, and in so doing engaged in one of the most powerful Visionary Creative processes of modern times. Many artists today, especially artists about whom politicians object when their work receives federal funding, are working in the world created by Duchamp.

With his *Les Demoiselles d'Avignon* of 1907, Picasso launched the twentieth century. With his *Fountain*, just ten years later, Duchamp presciently launched the twenty-first.

CREATING THE 21ST CENTURY

In which we ask, what is the nature of the world in which we are creating today? We see that the developments of the late twentieth century continue and are accelerating, putting us in the midst of rapid technological change. And we see that new networked digital media, acting as extensions of our Selves, are bringing about a new environment, and perhaps even a new kind of person.

A wondrous net hangs in Indra's heavenly abode, stretching in all directions infinitely. At each intersection of the net is a multifaceted jewel, each facet of each jewel reflecting all of the other jewels. And the image in each facet of each jewel contains not only all of the other jewels, but in those images all of the jewels, again and again, as deeply as we look.

A Continuation of the Twentieth Century

We should begin our discussion of the twenty-first century by noting that in many ways it continues the twentieth. Physics still has no framework of space or time, mathematics no foundation, and art no fixed observer. We are still creatures in flux, slipping about on a stage with no frames of reference, a stage now intermingled with our consciousness.

The twenty-first century is accelerating scientific and technological developments and we are seeing incredible advances in computers, artificial intelligence, robotics, materials, nanotechnology, biotech, and fabrication. But here we will look briefly at just a few developments that have the potential to change not only the world around us, but also who we are. Most of the fields we look at below began in the twentieth century, but are now seeing rapid ongoing development.

Science and Technology

Information Theory

As we stated earlier, at the end of the eighteenth century, matter was real and energy was derivative; energy was what you got when matter moved. By the end of the nineteenth century, energy was quite real, and in 1905 Einstein's paper presenting his special theory of relativity included the equation, $E=mc^2$ (energy equals mass times the speed of light squared). Matter and energy were equivalent, two forms of the same thing, like water and ice. By the mid twentieth century, energy had gained supremacy, and we were tempted to say that subatomic particles were vortices in an energy field, a notion we already saw in the late nineteenth century in the paintings of Van Gogh.

Then in 1948 the electrical engineer Claude Shannon published "A Mathematical Theory of Communication," laying the foundations of information theory. Shannon, whom we looked at earlier, wanted to quantify information, and coined the term "bit" for an irreducible unit of information, which in a binary system, is represented by a 0 or a 1. John Archibald Wheeler suggests that information is fundamental to the physics of the universe. He titled his notion "it from bit:"

> *It from bit. Otherwise put, every "it"—every particle, every field of force, even the space-time continuum itself—derives its function, its meaning, its very existence entirely—even if in some contexts indirectly—from the apparatus-elicited an-*

192

*swers to yes-or-no questions, binary choices, bits. ... in short,
that all things physical are information-theoretic in origin and
that this is a participatory universe.*

So physics moved from seeing matter as fundamental, to seeing energy as fundamental, and now to seeing information as fundamental. And biology? The discovery of the mechanism of DNA put information at the heart of life. The evolutionist Richard Dawkins writes:

What lies at the heart of every living thing is not a fire, not warm breath, not a "spark of life." It is information, words, instructions. If you want a metaphor, don't think of fires and sparks and breath. Think, instead, of a billion discrete, digital characters carved in tablets of crystal. If you want to understand life, don't think about vibrant, throbbing gels and oozes, think about information technology.

And psychology? David Chalmers, a philosopher who studies the mind, writes:

We are led to a conception of the world on which information is truly fundamental, and on which it has two basic aspects, corresponding to the physical and the phenomenal features of the world.

So physics, biology, and psychology are being rethought in terms of information. And some think at an even larger scale. Edward Fredkin, who refers to himself as a digital philosopher and is at the center of important developments in computer science, is a proponent of the idea that the universe itself is a computer doing some immense calculation.

What does information theory tell us? *That the fundamental component of reality is information—translatable, storable, and trans-*

193

mittable at the speed of light. And as we will see, that includes us.

Chaos Theory

In 1961, Edward Lorenz, an American mathematician and meteorologist, wanted to skip having his computer run an entire weather simulation from the beginning, so he typed in the results from the midpoint of a previous simulation. The output was completely different from what it had previously been. After eliminating other possibilities, Lorenz realized that the printout he was working from had rounded off the numbers in the information slightly differently from the way the computer did it internally, and these tiny differences led to the completely different results.

A situation that produces this kind of result is said to be nonlinear, highly sensitive to initial conditions, and led to the title, "Does the flap of a butterfly's wings in Brazil set off a tornado in Texas?" for one of Lorenz's talks. The implication was that while in theory science was deterministic, in many situations in practice, theory was of little use, since the slightest error or variation in entering initial conditions into a scientific procedure could lead to wildly different results.

As others began to explore the implications of this, an entirely new field emerged which is now called chaos theory and which shows orderly disorder created by simple processes leading to patterns. Scientists in different fields began to find similar patterns in very different phenomena leading to profound new insights, but at the expense of the dream of controlling or even predicting the future.

In the 1940s the science fiction writer Isaac Asimov was beginning his monumental *Foundation* series of novels based on "psychohistory," the idea that science could predict history thousands of years into the future. Around the same time scientists were beginning to believe they were on the verge of having sufficiently powerful computers to predict all kinds of things, including the weather, which they were also confident they would soon be able to control. Chaos theory shattered such dreams.

What does chaos theory tell us? Quantum theory told us that the world is indeterminate on the level of sub atomic particles, but scientists could hold on to the belief that in the realm of classical physics, that is the realm of large things, their deterministic theories still held. Now even that was denied them. But in return, whole new realms were opened up. *Chaos theory tells us that "forces" we do not yet understand, called such things as "strange attractors," are driving the behavior of chaotic systems—which means our world and our Selves—bringing us wondrous patterns.*

DNA and Genomics

In 1953 James Watson and Francis Crick cracked the DNA code, showing that it is an alphabet of four letters, chemical bases referred to as A, C, G, and T. These bases are strung along a twisted backbone made from phosphate and sugar molecules, and follow two simple rules: A and T can link, and G and C can link. Two strands of DNA, linking their bases, form the famous double helix. Add a few more rules, including those that allow DNA to make RNA and RNA to organize the assembly of proteins, and all of life, from the simplest microorganisms to human beings, can be built. We are learning to master DNA to the point where we can read, write, engineer, and recode it almost as easily as we do computer code. The results so far include new high-yield, high-nutrition, disease resistant crops, new treatments for diseases, custom organisms, designer children, new species, DNA computers, and the prospect of extreme life extension as we come closer to identifying the genetic causes of aging and turning them off. Today a virologist can design a new virus, have its DNA synthesized for a few dollars, and create the organism. Should we find this exciting, chilling, or both?

At the same time that Watson and Crick were decoding DNA, the Hungarian-American physicist and polymath John von Neumann and the Polish-American mathematician Stanislaw Ulam, both at the Institute for Advanced Study in Princeton, were using cellular automata to explore machines that could reproduce themselves. More recently, the technology entrepreneur, mathematician, and computer scientist, Stephen Wolfram, has been exploring a particular form of cellular automata. Draw a checkerboard-like grid of all white squares and establish rules for making some of the squares black. The patterns generated by very simple rules can be highly complex, containing little worlds. Wolfram contends that such rule-based systems provide a better approach to understanding and modeling nature than does Newton's mathematics. Working out from the rule-based approach of cellular automata, Wolfram explores our universe as one in a vast space of possible universes, and our logic as one in a vast space of possible logics. He likes to say that Newton made a mistake when he sought to describe the workings of nature using differential equations. Such equations work well for the orbits of the planets, but not so well for describing or understanding clouds or trees, or indeed much of anything we see around us. He contends that nature uses simple sets of rules, like software code, to generate the world, and he says, "I think when I find the code that generates our world, it will be about six lines."

If you wanted to make an oak tree, you would not nail sticks to a pole and glue leaves to the sticks. You would put some rules (the DNA in an acorn) in the ground and let the oak tree make itself in a process called generative genomics. Soon we may make our smart phones that way.

In life and throughout all of nature we see patterns, many interesting, many beautiful. Neo-Darwinism holds that when these patterns appear in life, they have emerged randomly by natural selection. And our reductive physical sciences insist that such patterns in inanimate things come from bottom-up processes such as the way molecules assemble. But so many of the patterns we see in nature seem so intense, and similar patterns occur so often, both in living and non-living things systems. Suppose there are forces at work that we do not yet understand, such as those being studied in chaos theory. Gravity and atomic forces can arrange matter in such patterns as spiral galaxies and crystals. Might other forces be behind the patterns on a butterfly's wing, a lobster's symmetries and asymmetries, or a human hand? Biologists cringe at the thought, fearing that even discussing the topic will leave them open to the insistence by advocates of intelligent design that these patterns must come from the mind of a creator. But we see these patterns everywhere, we now understand that many of them can be genomicly generated, and we hope that their study will someday be permitted in biology.

What do DNA and genomics tell us? *That simple rules can create richly complex patterns. The rules encoded in DNA constitute tiny computers at the heart of life, storing the blueprint for building and reproducing the organism. And similar simple rules may even build the universe in which we live.*

Bell's Theorem and Entanglement

Although he was one of its founders, Einstein never accepted the "weirdness" of quantum theory, insisting that the theory was incomplete, and once it was completed, the weirdness would go away. Einstein kept challenging Niels Bohr, quantum theory's designated defender, with problems to prove this incompleteness, all of which Bohr parried, until in 1935 Einstein with two colleagues came up with what is called the EPR paradox. This paradox shows that once two particles become "entangled" by both being part of the same event, a later action on one should affect the other instantly even if it is on the other side of the universe. Since this is absurd—it negates distance and causality—Einstein felt the EPR paradox would show that quantum theory was incomplete. Niels Bohr dismissed it and most scientists were happy to ignore it.

In the 1960s, John Bell, a Northern Irish physicist, decided it was time to resolve the EPR paradox. He took a leave from his job at the European Organization for Nuclear Research and spent a year at Stanford and other American universities to think through the problem. In 1964 he published what is now called Bell's Theorem, finally bringing the problem into focus so that it could be resolved by experiment. In 1982 Alain Aspect, a young French physicist, performed experiments confirming that separated entangled particles *do* instantly influence each other, because in a way, they are the same phenomena. (Just put this in the category of more quantum weirdness.) When Aspect approached Bell for advice on what would be the definitive experiment supportive of Bell's Theorem, Bell, in surprise, asked him, "Do you have tenure?" Aspect replied that he was only a graduate student, which is perhaps the reason he could do the experiment.

Bell had shown that Einstein was totally wrong about quantum theory. Just as Einstein had a natural intuitive feel for a different geometry of space-time sixty years earlier, Bell had a natural intuitive feel for a quantum world totally different from any that had existed before, and he had the courage to follow his instincts. Now in the twenty-first century we routinely use entanglement in encryption and quantum computing.

What do Bell's Theorem and entanglement tell us? *That particles reflect each other across the universe. Or, stated another way, that existence is made up of* relationships *rather than of space, time, and causality. It is all Indra's net.*

Symbiogenesis

How does evolution come about? Neo-Darwinism, which is Darwin's theory of natural selection combined with Mendel's

198

genetics and updated with today's understanding of DNA and random mutations, says that mutations continually occur, and in subsequent generations those mutations that are beneficial are selected to be passed on to the next generation, while those that are detrimental die off. It is the slow accumulation of these mutations, usually in populations that become geographically separated, that leads to the emergence of new species. However, the sudden appearance of many species and the lack of evidence of substantial gradual change within many species, from their first appearance until their extinction, was always a problem.

In 1972 the evolutionary biologists Niles Eldredge and Stephen Jay Gould put forward the theory of *punctuated equilibrium*, stating that most species remain stable for long periods of time and then undergo rapid short bursts of evolutionary change. But while punctuated equilibrium *names* rapid change, it does not provide an *explanation* for it. Evolutionary biologists don't like to talk about this, because it leaves them open to attack by creationists.

There is a possible explanation. Mitochondria, the units in all cells that generate energy, and chloroplasts, the units in plant cells that engage in photosynthesis, both contain their own DNA, different from and independent of the DNA in the cell's nucleus. How did they come about, and why do they have their own DNA? In 1967 the biologist Lynn Margulis published a paper suggesting that both mitochondria and chloroplasts evolved from bacteria that merged with other cells. At first controversial, this idea is now widely accepted.

But Margulis, whose specialty was bacteria, eventually went much further, putting forward the theory of symbiogenesis. She observed that bacteria are very facile at exchanging DNA and that viruses reproduce by injecting their DNA into host cells. She contends that the wholesale movement of DNA from one species to another, often carried by bacteria or viruses, is the driving force in evolution. Symbiogenesis provides an explanation for the leaps in evolutionary change that are observed in the fossil record but are not adequately explained even by punctuated equilibrium. The theory received support from the discovery of a substantial amount of bacteria and virus DNA in humans when the human genome was sequenced. As more and more species get sequenced, we find more and more of everybody's DNA in just about everybody else. What we are finding is a huge web of interpenetrating elements, each reflecting all of the others. Margulis states:

All visible organisms are products of symbiogenesis, without exception. The bacteria are the unit. The way I think about the whole world is that it's like a pointillist painting. You get far away and it looks like Seurat's famous painting of people in the park. Look closely: The points are living bodies—different distributions of bacteria…. Symbiogenesis recognizes that every visible life-form is a combination or community of bacteria.

As many as a hundred species and as much as two pounds of microbes live in and on our bodies. And we now recognize that much of our health depends on our relationship with these microbes. If we take all of the sequences of DNA of ourselves and our microbes together, ninety percent of it belongs to the microbes, and we now realize that this microbial DNA interacts in important ways with our own. And all we have to do is sneeze to spread our microbes to everyone else in a room.

While neo-Darwinism emphasizes a nineteenth century mechanistic model of competition between discrete organisms as the primary driving force of evolution, symbiogenesis sees all of life as a complex web of interpenetrating genomes and *it proposes cooperative, symbiotic, and parasitic relationships as equally important as competition in evolution.* According

200

to Margulis and her son Dorion Sagan, "Life did not take over the globe by combat, but by networking." This networking is fundamental to our emerging creativity.

What does symbiogenesis tell us? *That species that once seemed to be discrete entities are interconnected, each element containing and reflecting the rest. It is all a huge cluster of interactive networks. It is all Indra's net.*

Paradigms and Metaphors

Once more we might ask, why so much attention to science in a book on creativity? As we said before, in part because scientists are often Visionary Creatives. Einstein found himself in a new world and was driven to create works that would allow others to experience what he experienced. But beyond that, science helps us understand the cultural context for our creativity, the stage on which it takes place. Let's look at the term "stage" that we have been using. Kuhn uses the term "paradigm" for something related to what we mean by stage. Kuhn is a philosopher of sciences, but some theoretical physicists are also thinking this way. In their 2010 book, *The Grand Design*, Steven Hawking, one of the leading physicists of the latter half of the twentieth century, and his coauthor, Leonard Mlodinow, use the term "model-dependent reality" for what we have been calling paradigms. They write:

Strict realists often argue that the proof that scientific theories represent reality lies in their success. But different theories can successfully describe the same phenomenon through disparate conceptual frameworks. In fact, many scientific theories that had proven successful were later replaced by other, equally successful theories based on wholly new concepts of reality.... According to model-dependent realism it is pointless to ask whether a model is real, only whether it agrees with observa-

201

tions... One can use whichever model is more convenient in the situation under consideration.

Kuhn uses the term "paradigm." Hawking and Mlodinow use the term "model." Let's see if the term "metaphor" will also work. When you cannot describe something directly, which we surely cannot do with "absolute reality," what do you do? Often you use a metaphor. A successful metaphor captures the essence of something and communicates it to a part of the mind that works outside of rational thought.

It is easy to see how we might refer to Michelangelo's *David* as metaphorical. It represents—or rather gives us an experience of—the humanist notion of a person. Can we say the same about a scientific theory? At first it would seem that the answer should be no. As we said earlier, art is described as presenting the subjective insights of artists, while science is described as presenting an objective understanding of nature. This approach holds that, yes, our scientific understandings are continually evolving, but they are guided by principles of objectivity and rationality, and they constantly come closer to correct pictures of reality. But this is not what happens. Recall Newton's notions of absolute space and uniform time, and Einstein's theories of space-time in flux. In the terms we are using in this book, we might call both of these *metaphors*—descriptions that capture and communicate to us an experience of something that we can never fully comprehend. In that sense, science is metaphorical just as art is, and it is in that sense that they are linked.

We may or may not someday find firm roots for mathematics. We may or may not find evidence of parallel universes. Symbiogenesis may or may not become widely accepted among evolutionists. Our world may or may not be generated by simple rules. All of this awaits future developments in various scientific fields. But here we are interested in what these scientific metaphors tell us about the stage on which our Visionary Creatives will imagine the twenty-first century.

A NEW SELF

In which we ask, what kind of new Self is now emerging? We have shown that new technologies change not only the world around us, but also our Selves. We are being uploaded into webs of interconnected fractal networks computationally generating themselves.

Today, after more than a century of electronic technology, we have extended our central nervous system itself in a global embrace, abolishing both space and time as far as our planet is concerned.
~ Marshall McLuhan, Understanding Media

Social Media

Now that we have described the stage on which twenty-first century creativity will be taking place we will want to look at some examples of this creativity. But rather than looking at the arts, let's look at an example in technology and see how it fits into the patterns we have established.

Recall that we began this book with the question, what do Michelangelo Buonarroti and Mark Zuckerberg have in common? After observing that both were Visionary Creatives and looking at the world of the private self that Michelangelo had helped to create, we went on to look at the world Mark Zuckerberg is now helping to create, and we observed that *we are more than our bodies, minds, and souls. We are also our memories, roles, relationships, friends, papers, photos, etc. Our identities began mi-*

205

grating outside of our skins as soon as we started making art, and the pace of that migration increased with writing and then again with printing. But the pace greatly accelerated in the late nineteenth century as we began to weave an electric net around our planet, and exploded with the Internet as we deposited vast parts of ourselves—our memories, records, images—in networked server farms around the world, known as the cloud. Zuckerberg's Facebook greatly extends our putting more and more of ourselves into the cloud and facilitates the sharing of this material, thus dissolving the private humanist vision created by the printed book and crystallized by Michelangelo and creating a new vision.

What do people do with Facebook and other social media? They post details of their lives: biographical profiles, minute-by-minute text and pictorial updates on what they are doing, information about relationships, what they are eating, and references to things they like—for their friends to see, respond to, and add their own links to. Before we go further, if you are not familiar with all that Facebook has to offer, you might want to ask a younger person to show you its features. While they are at it, ask them to show you Twitter, which allows networks of contacts between people, and BitTorrent, a service that lets you download all kinds of files, including pirated movies. (If you are reading this book some years after this writing, you might ask an older person to explain to you what Facebook, Twitter, and BitTorrent were.)

Before we go on with social media, let's stop for a moment and ask, how does BitTorrent work? (We'll see in a moment why we are asking this.) You might imagine that someone buys a DVD of a movie, obtains one distributed to the industry if it has not yet been released, or surreptitiously videos it in a theater, and then puts a digital file of it on a website from which others can download it. You would be right about the first part, but not the second. One of the ways the Internet works is by breaking information up into small "packets," labeling the packets with instructions on how to reassemble them to recreate the original file, and transmitting these packets through different channels depending on Internet traffic, letting the destination computer put them back together. BitTorrent goes one further. When you ask to download a movie, it finds copies of it on thousands of computers whose owners have joined BitTorrent, and sends you pieces from many of them for your computer to reassemble. Doing it that way makes the download much faster—the packets come to you in a torrent of bits. And at the same time you are downloading one movie, you might be contributing pieces of another movie already on your computer to someone else. (Of course the copyright holders of movies, music, etc. are not happy about this piracy of their material.) Thus when thinking about Facebook, Twitter, BitTorrent, and other online media, we might think of the Internet as a huge cluster of interactive computational networks. Think of Lynn Margulis's symbiogenesis in which all creatures are exchanging DNA.

BitTorrent doesn't just change how we download things, it completely changes the very nature of a "thing," which in this case happens to be a digital file. Likewise, social media don't just change the way people interact, social media change the very nature of social interaction, and since in some ways we are social creatures, they change what we are.

And central to that change is relationships. Let's look at Google for a moment. In 1996, Larry Page and Sergey Brin began Google as a research project on searching for information on the Internet at Stanford University in California. At the time many search engines ranked results by how many times the word you were searching for appeared on the page. If you were searching for shoes, for example, you would get pages that contained the word shoes several times. But then those selling shoes and wanting visitors would put the word shoes a hundred times at the bottoms of their pages. (Until some began putting it there thousands of times.) Page and

Brin developed an approach, sometimes referred to as their secret sauce or secret algorithm, that ranks results based on *relationships between websites*, including but not limited to how many other websites link to the website under evaluation, and how many links are made to those websites, etc. Notice something. The previous methods of Internet search looked at *characteristics* of websites to find those you might be looking for. Google's approach looks for *patterns of relationships*. It's a huge fractal, cluster of interactive computational networks.

How might all of this affect us? Notice the phrase we used above, *we are also our roles, relationships, friends, papers, photos, memories, etc*. The importance of these things is reflected in the Fourth Amendment in our Bill of Rights which states that, "The right of the people to be secure in their persons, houses, papers, and effects, against unreasonable searches and seizures, shall not be violated…." The Fourth Amendment is interesting in that it indicates the importance assigned to our papers, and that we would likely store them in our houses. Now we might store information that had once been in our papers in the cloud. The cloud can also do our computing, so that anyone can rent the computing power of Google or Amazon or Microsoft by the minute. And cloud computing means that what we have called "privacy," the right to be secure we demanded for our "persons, houses, papers, and effects" during the print era, will be changing. Privacy is dissolving. Parents and teachers are constantly warning youngsters that the things they put on the Internet may haunt them later, as in "this will go on your permanent record," and youngsters are continually ignoring these warnings.

As we noted earlier, the objections to Facebook, Google, and other Internet services regarding privacy are, to a large extent, reactions against the ongoing destruction of the private Self that had been a function of the previous culture built on the book. We are experiencing a change from a private individual to a decentered networked person, electronically extended around and off of the globe, who slips the bonds of old institutions as new ones are built for a new environment. Marshall McLuhan writes:

> *After three thousand years of explosion, by means of fragmentary and mechanical technologies, the Western world is imploding. During the mechanical ages we had extended our bodies in space. Today, after more than a century of electronic technology, we have extended our central nervous system itself in a global embrace, abolishing both space and time as far as our planet is concerned... Rapidly we approach the final phase of the extensions of man—the technological simulation of consciousness, when the creative process of knowing will be collectively and corporately extended to the whole of human society, much as we have already extended our senses and our nerves by the various media.*

You might think of Facebook as a tool for kids to coordinate their partying and keep tabs on who is dating whom. You would be right, but that is just the beginning. You can put your entire life history on Facebook; relationships, pictures, news, etc., as well as everything you are doing at the moment—what you are eating for breakfast, what book you are reading and what page you are on, what song you are listening to. All of this can constitute recommendations for your friends, but suppose a handful of your friends are listening to the same song at the same time. This can be broadcast in real time as news to all of your friends. News becomes hyper immediate and hyper local, and you, your friends, the material you link to, and your activities become the nodes of totally new kinds of interrelated networks. You might object that the agglomeration of this information is not news, and for now you would be right; news is what a reporter and an editor filter, interpret, and say is news. But could not news be simply what is happening? In the near future, news may be understood very differently.

Many older people are concerned about who has access to their "data," fearing, for example, that an online bookseller might know they purchased a book about A and a book about B, and might send them an email offering them a book about A and B. In the meantime, many younger people are spending inordinate hours every day uploading every detail of their lives. As the online gadget review website, Gizmodo, says, "… your entire existence, Facebook-ified. It's terrifyingly amazing."

Imagine each of Facebook's billion plus users as a point. Now imagine lines connecting each of the points that are "friends." Further, imagine lines connecting all of the photos, events, and other items on Facebook to which there are interdependent links. If you are imagining this on a two-dimensional surface, you are going to have a lot of crossing lines. But that is not how computer scientists think. They can place their points in as many dimensions as they need, with no space, no extensions, *just relationships*. It is a world of parametric space in which the coordinates of a given point are not on a pre-existing Cartesian grid (the outdated Newtonian stage), but rather are defined *by each other*; as one value changes, the coordinates of another change at the same time. The static space and time of the literate world no longer exist, and now all is interrelationship, free of any matrix, free of any fixed frames of reference. All is Indra's net, as we become a part of a huge fractal, a cluster of interactive computational networks. What kind of stage, what kind of world are we dealing with here?

Books

How do we feel about social networking, about people in movie theaters tapping away at small glowing screens, oblivious to the big screen, about couples in restaurants looking at

210

their mobile devices and not each other (are they texting each other?), and about young people who do not read books? Our first reaction must be discomfort if not worse. What will the world be like when it is occupied by people who "live online?" They will be without depth knowledge, without real world social skills, without critical thinking skills.

At the beginning of this book we contrasted Mark Zuckerberg with Michelangelo. Now let's contrast Mark Zuckerberg with Edward Gibbon, the English author of *The History of the Decline and Fall of the Roman Empire.* Beginning in 1776, Gibbon took twelve years to complete his six-volume work covering the period from 180 CE to 1453 CE, and focusing on the behavior and decisions of the Romans that led to the decay and eventual fall of their empire. Gibbon's study, using primary sources wherever possible, is the first history of the Roman Empire, still used today as a model of scholarship, and brings us the quip from the Duke of Gloucester, "Another of those damned fat, square, thick books! Always scribble, scribble, scribble, eh, Mr. Gibbon." And all done without Wikipedia. Or a word processor. Or even a typewriter.

The columnist and novelist, Anna Quindlen, writes in her memoir *How Reading Changed My Life*:

In books I have traveled, not only to other worlds, but into my own. I learned who I was and who I wanted to be, what I might aspire to, and what I might dare to dream about my world and myself.... There was waking, and there was sleeping. And then there were books, a kind of parallel universe in which anything might happen and frequently did, a universe in which I might be a newcomer but was never really a stranger. My real, true world. My perfect island.

How many young people today feel this way about books? A book—a real book, not a contrived book for people to buy as a holiday gift—can take years to write. Books represent a way of knowing and existing; a person with a point of view is interested in something and wishes to understand it more deeply. From their point of view, they research it, think about it, and come to conclusions. Then they present their findings in a book, a medium that communicates with other persons who invest their time in reading it, following the arguments, perhaps disputing them. But all of this is dependent on the existence of literate individual persons capable of knowledge, insights, and emotions, *with points of view*. McLuhan describes the printed book as a source of individualism, of a private and fixed point of view.

As literacy is replaced by *electronacy*, "individual," "person" and "point of view" as we have known them are replaced by something new. Those attached to literacy cannot see the new and therefore see only dissolution. Reviewing Russell Banks's *Lost Memory of Skin*, a novel she describes as canonical for our time, the *New York Times* book critic Janet Maslin, writes that it describes characters unable to tell the difference between "reality" and "imagery," and that it presents the dehumanizing consequences of our "creepy times" and our new-found means of "ruination."

In an article in the *New York Times* titled "Growing Up Digital, Wired for Distraction," Matt Richtel writes about 17-year-old Vishal who was assigned by his school to read Kurt Vonnegut's *Cat's Cradle* over the summer. Distracted by making videos to post on YouTube and "hanging out" on Facebook, he only makes it part way into the book. Fourteen-year-old Allison Miller, Richtel continues, provides Vishal with serious competition, sending 27,000 text messages per month.

We could lament the activities of Vishal and Allison, just as Socrates lamented what he saw as the destructive effects of reading on the Athenian youth of his day, who, he said, would lose the ability to memorize. Or we could celebrate the entry of Vishal and Allison into new words of interactive discourse and visual thinking based on their immersion in video making, a kind of thinking those from a literate past may never fully experience.

For Maslin these are creepy times. For Richtel, 27,000 texts in a month are too many. But those who live in a world of electronacy cannot for the life of them see the problem. Today, some young children, when given a magazine, run their fingers over the pictures and wonder why they don't move the way they do on a tablet computer. Many young people today may not share Anna Quindlen's experience of books, but they have visual experiences far richer than the visual experiences of their literate forebears. Let's look again at the *Lord of the Rings* movies. The point here is not the hobbits and wizards, the elves and dwarves, the orcs and battle mastodons. A reader of the *Lord of the Rings* books can imagine these. But the movies give us new points of view from ever moving cameras that swoop through the scenes. Perspective gave us an observer who was outside of the scene and who had a fixed position. In these movies, as in video games, we are integral with the scene and we are in motion with the action. The verbal richness that literate generations swam through in print is now replaced by a visual richness we do not yet know how to fully describe.

We are now in a world of networked creatures, our persons, papers, and effects perhaps not secure, but always instantly accessible along with all of the world's information, interconnected with our friends and colleagues, swimming in seas of information, having migrated from inside our skins out to the electronic cloud, destroying the literate, humanist world and opening a new one with new kinds of interrelationships.

Now let's look at an example of all this in the experience of one Visionary Creative, David Karp, founder of the social

213

networking site, Tumblr. Karp didn't drop out of college, he didn't go to college—he didn't even finish high school. His site allows users to create all kinds of content—blogs, pictures, videos—and to link them to those of others.

Tumblr was bought by Yahoo for over a billion dollars. Obviously luck and timing played a role in the success of Tumblr, along with Karp's skill as a programmer. But perhaps more important is that Karp is immersed in, lives in, a networked mobile digital world—he is a "networked mobile digital native." He does not "understand" our new world, *he lives it*. When an early employer asked him to create a video platform for computers, he refused, remarking that doing it was "so 2000." Video, he explained to his employer, would, in the future, be experienced on mobile devices.

At the beginning of this book we said that Visionary Creatives feel that our world is no longer what we had thought it to be and that a new world is struggling to be born. They wonder what is wrong with everyone else that they do not also feel this, and they are driven to produce works that will help others feel what they feel. Karp lives in a new world and he created a vehicle to allow others to experience it as he does.

Are we happy with the world that Facebook, Tumblr, and other social media bring us? If we are literate, private, discrete individuals, living on a stage of uniform space, time, and causality, we are very likely unhappy with this world. If we exist as interconnected networks on a stage that is made up of other networks, an Indra's net, each jewel reflecting all of the others, we are very likely happy with it.

Recall that we earlier described the advent of electric communications—the telegraph, telephone, radio, etc.—as in part responsible for the coming apart of the late nineteenth and early twentieth centuries. Now our communications technologies are digital, allowing everything—text, voice, images, and even the instructions for fabricating material products on

3D printers—to be stored and disseminated, to travel instantly, to be infinitely reproduced, and to rapidly approach zero cost. We have for some time been plugged into this new world through our computers, but now we walk about with mobile devices far more powerful than the supercomputers of just a few years ago interconnecting all of us. So, what does this mean for the new human being, for the new Self?

A New Self Beyond Humanism

Is Humanism Anachronistic?

Let's delve some more into this new creature we are becoming. Recall that at the beginning of this book we referred to the "humanist vision that some anachronistically still hold today." In what way is that vision anachronistic?

Stand in the Accademia Gallery in Florence where Michelangelo's *David* is now situated and look for a while at the sculpture. Its recently cleaned marble gleams pale white. We feel an empathy for—a relationship with—the figure, it is our image of a young man, and we perhaps recall how young men looked when we were that age, or might have wished to look, as it is quite idealized. We look at his furrowed brow and intense eyes and imagine his thoughts, and then look at our own thoughts. But while *David* is thinking, there is no emotional depth, no backstory. We do not yet fully see ourselves. So let's move forward through the history of Western art and add some layers to our notion of a human being, of a Self. The inner sorrows we see in Rembrandt self-portraits reflecting the sadnesses in his life add emotional depth. And then add the rationality brought to us by the great successes of science, and the application of that rationality to ourselves that the Enlightenment brought us. We see all of this in the 1765 painting, *A Philosopher Lecturing on the Orrery* by Joseph Wright of Derby, with its demonstration of the orbits of the planets viewed by children who are fascinated and who we feel will grow up to become scientists. And finally let's add a dose of respect for the powers of nature and the human passions that Romanticism gave us and that we see in the paintings of Caspar David Friedrich and J. M. W. Turner that we referred to earlier, as well as in Henry Fuseli's 1781 *The Nightmare*, depicting a sleeping woman beset by strange creatures, and we have rounded out a portrait of the humanist Self.

But is that humanist Self still us today? Look at Edvard Munch's paintings *The Scream*, done in several versions between 1893 and 1910. Referring to his paintings, Munch writes:

> *I was walking along a path with two friends—the sun was setting—suddenly the sky turned blood red—I paused, feeling exhausted, and leaned on the fence—there was blood and tongues of fire above the blue-black fjord and the city—my friends walked on, and I stood there trembling with anxiety—and I sensed an infinite scream passing through nature.*

Do we today sometimes feel more like Munch's poor terrified figure than Michelangelo's confident youth? But even Munch's image is from a distant past, *over a hundred years ago*.

A Mixed Metaphor

Let's try to visualize our Selves today with an awkward agglomeration of mixed metaphors. We will begin our agglomeration with Georges Seurat's Pointillist painting, *A Sunday Afternoon on the Island of La Grande Jatte*, the painting that inspired the musical, *Sunday in the Park with George*. Recall that for Lynn Margulis, the painting represents biological life. From a distance, we see solid, almost classical figures. But as we move up close, we see the figures, indeed all of the paint-

216

ing, to be made up of dots. Lots of dots. Margolis says that we as biological creatures seem distinct from a distance, but on moving in close we see seas of bacteria all carrying DNA—computers generating the organism and its progeny. Let's extend this metaphor in attempting to understand our Selves today. Living our lives, walking about each with our tasks for the day, we seem to be the same distinct humanist Selves that Michelangelo and later Rembrandt had portrayed. But we are in fact far different creatures living on a far different stage.

Let's extend our agglomerated metaphor. Go online and find an animation of a Mandelbrot set that continually zooms in on it. A Mandelbrot set is a richly complex fractal that exhibits patterns that remain similar at any scale. Laced through it are rich webs of Arabesque filigree binding all together. And all generated from a simple formula, just as our simple DNA of just four letters generates us.

We have dots, they exhibit fractal-like self-similarity as we zoom in on them, and they are all linked together. But there is one more step. Recall our description of Stephen Wolfram's cellular automata, self-computing patterns, and his notion that the full richness of our world comes from simple rules. ("I think that when I find the code that generates our world it will be about six lines.") Now our dots are not only linked together, they are also computing, generating themselves and their progeny!

So, in our twenty-first century world we are digital, mobile, and networked, but that is just the beginning. We are storable, translatable, and transmittable at the speed of light. And while from a distance we look like the classical figures in the Sunday in the Park painting, we are in fact made up of the dots that you see when you look close up, and the dots are interconnected fractal networks computationally generating themselves. Some don't like this new world. Some love it. And

217

what will be the consequence of all of this? We await our Visionary Creatives.

HUBRIS

In which we look at the role of Visionary Creatives in global problems, and question whether it is our place to remake the universe.

Standing on the world's summit we launch once again our insolent challenge to the stars!
~ F. T. Marinetti, Italian Futurist poet,
The Futurist Manifesto

I think when I find the code that generates our world, it will be about six lines.
~ Stephen Wolfram, British-American computer scientist,
mathematician, and entrepreneur

Global Problems

In the previous section we described the emergence of a new Self, a new kind of person. How will this new person live in the world and respond to its challenges? We are acutely aware of the problems facing our world today: environmental degradation, epidemics, poverty, repression, ethnic conflicts. At the same time, if we follow cutting edge advances in computers, information, biotech, and new materials, we are aware that we are on the verge—even in the midst of—startling developments. What are we to make of these conflicting trends? The first thing that comes to mind has to be Charles Dickens's, "It was the best of times, it was

219

the worst of times..." which after a long list of contrasts, ends, "in short, the period was so far like the present period, that some of / its noisiest authorities insisted on its being received, for good or for / evil, in the superlative degree of comparison only."

Sounds like today. But we might also think in terms of a parable from the futurist designer, William Katavolos, who describes a fetus developing in the womb. This fetus is special in that it comes to consciousness around its third month. It is happy in its environment, and by the fifth month has begun to check things out. In the sixth month it concludes that something alarming is happening, it appears to be growing exponentially. By the seventh month it has confirmed that its growth is exponential and it becomes frantic. It sends out sound waves to determine the structure of its external environment and finds that it is not going to stretch indefinitely. It measures nutritional intake and waste output and finds that its situation is not sustainable, it will soon run out of resources and be knee-deep in waste. In the eighth month, finding that it is still growing, it panics and goes on a full-blown sustainability program, limiting nutritional intake, researching ways to recycle waste, and doing everything it can to stop its growth. Of course, what our fetus does not know is that in the ninth month its situation will change completely. It will be born.

The role of Visionary Creatives in all of this? The late literary critic Lionel Trilling proposed that literature—we could say Visionary Creativity in general—should be a corrective to political and economic thinking. Trilling sympathized with those who sought to right the injustices of the world, writing:

Life presses us so hard, time is so short, the suffering of the world is so huge, simple, unendurable—anything that complicates our moral fervor in dealing with reality as we imme-

220

diately see it and wish to drive headlong upon it must be regarded with some impatience.

But what if current received wisdoms regarding our problems are wrong? Trilling advocates that the creative imagination should be free to explore problems in unconventional ways. Stated another way, rather than established thinking telling those with creative imaginations what to imagine, suppose we make openings for those with creative imaginations to influence established thinking; suppose we allow our Visionary Creatives to envision our world beyond the "ninth month."

Recall our mention earlier of a caterpillar morphing into a butterfly. Evolution assures that the transition will be successful, but the caterpillar does not know that, and surrendering to the process takes an act of faith. As we look at our world and its problems today, we are tempted to latch on to current solutions and say, "this is the safe way forward." That approach will only assure a stagnant future that may not even be safe, as we have seen time and again with attempts at planned societies. The alternative, allowing Visionary Creatives to envision things the rest of us cannot imagine, seems risky, and of course it is, it might not work, or it might work and we might not like the results. And it might also yield things that most today cannot imagine. In 1993 few in the communications industry were aware of the Internet. In 1994, the industry was abuzz with its possibilities. Very few, even in the communications industry, could see the most world-changing technology of the late twentieth and early twenty-first centuries coming just a year before it struck.

Of course those invested in current understandings and solutions may be no more happy with the challenges openness might bring than the nineteenth century French art establishment was with the Impressionists, the 1960s physics estab-

221

lishment was with Bell's theorem, or today's evolutionists are with Lynn Margulis's symbiogenesis. In the case of the Internet, it started so small, looked so much like a hobby, and seemed so unlikely to become a threat, that established industries ignored it. By the time it became apparent that the Internet was changing everything, it was too late to stop it, and industries that had been successful in using their monopoly powers and their allies in government to stop previous advances are now being swept away.

Recall our earlier discussion of Virginia Postrel's notion of "stasists" and "dynamists." Stasists are amenable to the future only if they can control and regulate it. They abhor an open society and an unknowable future. Dynamists embrace exploration, change, individual choice, and creativity and the open future and messy progress it brings us. Predictability presents a promise of safety that is an illusion. All it can assure is stagnation. Openness and the freeing of Visionary Creatives lead to risk, but also the possibility of flourishing. These are the choices.

Expanse

Watch the opening sequence for the television series, *Star Trek: Voyager*. A long plume of luminous gas arches diagonally across the screen, and as the camera pans we see the Voyager spacecraft plunge through a jet from a sun as it fills the screen and passes over us. It then plows through a blue mist, stirring it in its wake, and exits, arching over an ice moon of a large, Jupiter-like planet, a tiny rock moon hanging nearby and the Pillars of Creation in the background. Then Voyager approaches a Saturn-like planet, passes through the plane of its ice rings, and races its reflection as it rides over the rings. Finally it pulls away from the solar system as the sun emerges from an eclipse, passes an Earth-like planet, and jumps into warp drive, heading toward a brilliant nebula.

Today we are able to look out over the vast expanses of our known universe, now bordered only by the distance from which light has had time to reach us since its beginning. Our large Earth telescopes, orbital telescopes, solar system flybys, and computer enhancements give us magnificent views of planets, stars, and billions of galaxies. But short of the hyper-drives and wormholes of science fiction, we are trapped in our little solar system and will never travel to see most of these places up close. It will take months or years to reach planets in our solar system, and it would take hundreds of years to reach nearby stars and tens of millions of years to reach nearby galaxies. Depressing? Perhaps, but suppose we reject the idea that these places are inaccessible and assert that anywhere our imagination can go, we can eventually go.

The Singularity

Earlier we referred to cutting edge advances in computers, information, biotech, nanotechnology, materials, and methods of fabrication. Is our embrace of these technologies hubris? Of course it is, and this is only the beginning.

Ray Kurzweil, a technology entrepreneur, futurist, and a director of engineering at Google, is an advocate for what is called the Singularity, a future time when human and machine intelligence merge. Moore's Law observes that the number of transistors that can be placed on computer chips doubles about every two years. If this rate continues, in twenty years a single chip can have more circuitry than the human brain, and in forty years more circuitry than all of the brains of all of the people who have ever lived. Kurzweil, like many scientists, equates circuitry with intelligence, and intelligence with consciousness. We might question Kurzweil's understanding of consciousness, but we should not question the potential of this exponential growth, which he points out is taking place not only in electronics, but in all information technologies—and more and more technologies are becoming information technologies. For Kurzweil, the ultimate outcome of all this will first be a merging of human and machine intelligence and then a migration of intelligence outward from the planet. He writes:

> *The explosive nature of exponential growth means it may only take a quarter of a millennium to go from sending messages on horseback to saturating the matter and energy in our solar system with sublimely intelligent processes. The ongoing expansion of our future superintelligence will then require moving out into the rest of the universe, where we may engineer new universes.*

Kurzweil is not speaking metaphorically. He has carefully mapped technological growth over the past hundred years, and he closely monitors today's technological developments. He is predicting the continued acceleration of technological growth to the point where intelligence, human and machine combined, encompasses the Earth, then our solar system, then our galaxy, and eventually the entire universe. Indeed he is seeing far beyond the opening of *Star Trek: Voyager.*

Kurzweil is not the only one thinking this way. MIT professor Seth Lloyd, who calls himself a "quantum mechanic," titled his 2006 book *Programming the Universe: A Quantum Computer Scientist Takes on the Cosmos.* A task too complex to even imagine? Perhaps not. Recall Stephen Wolfram's remark, "I think when I find the code that generates our world, it will be about six lines." The Windows computer operating system contains around fifty million lines of code, but those fifty million lines are a part of the world, so they themselves could ultimately be generated by Wolfram's six lines. We are in the

224

realm of a totally new way of thinking.

At the turn of the twentieth century the architect and planner of cities, Daniel Burnham, wrote: "Make no little plans. They have no magic to stir men's blood and probably will not themselves be realized." Kurzweil, Lloyd, and Wolfram might have read that somewhere.

Values and Technology

But should we be thinking these hubristic ways? Lao Tzu in the *Tao Te Ching* writes:

> *Do you believe you can conquer the universe?*
> *Do you believe you can improve it?*
> *I do not believe it.*
> *The universe is sacred.*
> *It cannot be improved.*
> *If you try to change it, you will ruin it.*
> *If you try to hold it, you will lose it.*

Who is right, Kurzweil or Lao Tzu? What is a good technology; what is a bad technology? What should be our response to all of this? These questions are today hotly debated; how might we address them? Here we might imagine how those from different cultural traditions might view this. In the Biblical tradition it was the pursuit of knowledge and the fear that we would seek eternal life that led to the expulsion from the Garden of Eden, and it was human aspiration that led to the destruction of the tower of Babel. In this tradition, such aspirations distract us from our true task, which is submission. In ancient Hindu traditions, universes are continually born and continually end in fire, and if we want to set ours ablaze, it will matter little in the long run, which is long indeed. In this tradition it is better to renounce the fruits of action. In

225

ancient Chinese tradition where the superhero, Monkey, must serve the larger whole, this might be done, but only with permission. In the tradition of ancient Greece, Prometheus stole from the gods and brought to us not only fire but also the arts and sciences. Our minds, our imaginations, our ambitions exist for tasks such as these. However, the Greek tradition cautions that we should not delude ourselves into believing that any of this will change our fates.

And what of those living in the West today? We are descendants of those who built the Gothic cathedrals, circled the globe, and ventured into space. We need not accept modesty. We can indeed aspire to improve the universe, but the motivation to do so and the judgment of such actions must come from within the heart of each individually. Sounds scary. Do we trust people, or do we need to control them? Are we shamans, or the subjects of priests? The story of Percival implies that we are each here to use our own judgment, to realize our own potentials, to set not just the universe but ourselves ablaze. If we harness our potentials and set ourselves ablaze, we are liberated. If we decline, we are in a wasteland.

We may someday travel to the stars or we may find, through quantum entanglement, that we are already there. We may extend our physical lives to centuries through the manipulation of DNA, or we may find that we value a life like a work of art, not by its length but by its luminosity. We may reprogram the universe, or we may find new inner worlds. We await our Visionary Creatives to let us know on what new stage we will act out our lives.

PART FOUR:
■ POSTSCRIPT

CREATING YOURSELF

In which we ask, is it time to make of your life an outrageous work of art, to set yourself ablaze?

Life isn't about finding yourself. Life is about creating yourself.
~ George Bernard Shaw, Irish playwright and
*   social philosopher*

Oh wow! Oh wow! Oh wow!
~ Steve Jobs, last words

Is it Time for Visions to be Born in You?

I ask you, the reader; is it time for visions to be born in you; is it time for you to begin building our world anew? Is it time to make of your life an outrageous work of art, to set yourself ablaze?

Recall Nietzsche's "The Three Metamorphoses of the Spirit" that we quoted earlier in this book. It began:

I will tell you of the three metamorphoses of the spirit: how the spirit becomes a camel; the camel, a lion; and the lion then a child.

The camel takes on the load of its culture. It then runs out into the desert where it becomes a lion whose task it is to kill the dragon whose name is "Thou shalt;" to destroy the culture it has mastered. Then it is time to create anew, and this is the task of the child. But, Nietzsche says, before you create the world anew, you must create your Self. How might you do that? Of course in a sense that is what this entire book is about, but let's look at one example.

Over and Over

The movie, *Groundhog Day*, a romantic comedy directed by Harold Ramis and staring Bill Murray and Andie MacDowell, was well received at the time of its release, but as is often the case with significant movies, it took a while to really sink in. Recall our earlier discussions of how our experience of a work of art can change over time. The movie critic, Roger Ebert, raised his estimation of *Groundhog Day*; the literary critic, Stanley Fish, includes it as one of only two movies since 1958 on his top ten list; and spiritual leaders in several traditions use the movie in their teaching. Ramis states, "At first I would get mail saying, 'Oh, you must be a Christian because the movie so beautifully expresses Christian belief.' Then rabbis started calling from all over, saying they were preaching the film as their next sermon. And the Buddhists! Well, I knew they loved it because my mother-in-law has lived in a Buddhist meditation centre for 30 years and my wife lived there for five years."

In the movie, Bill Murray plays Phil Connors, an obnoxious, self-centered, and unhappy television weatherman at a local Pittsburgh station who is assigned to go to the small town of Punxsutawney, Pennsylvania to cover Groundhog Day, the day when a groundhog emerges from hibernation and does or does not see its shadow, thus predicting when winter will end and spring will come. Andie MacDowell plays Rita, his patient producer and eventual love interest.

They leave Pittsburgh in a van driven by their cameraman—the journey to adventure—and arrive in the charming little town. After their Groundhog Day broadcast, they attempt to leave for home, but are blocked by a snowstorm that has also cut off all communications with the outside world. They have left ordinary reality and are now in a magical realm where something transformative might happen.

For no reason given in the movie, Phil finds himself repeating February 2nd, Groundhog Day, over and over. He wakes up each morning to find that it is not tomorrow, but once again February 2nd. He remembers "yesterday's" February 2nd, but no one else does. At first he is terrified. Perhaps he has a brain tumor. He sees a doctor. No brain tumor, but the day keeps repeating. It starts to get wearing. Sitting in a bar, he remarks, "I was in the Virgin Islands once. I met a girl. We ate lobster, drank pina coladas. At sunset, we made love like sea otters. That was a pretty good day. Why couldn't I get that day, over and over and over?"

Then he realizes that if tomorrow will be unchanged by anything he does today, there will be no consequences for his actions, and he declares, "I'm not going to live by their rules anymore." His repeated broadcasts of the groundhog coming out of its burrow become more and more cynical, to the disgust of Rita and his cameraman. He engages in hijinks, steals money, exploits people, has casual sex, cons Rita, and stuffs himself with pastries. But after a while that stops working for him, and in despair, he commits suicide, again and again. But despite being in the morgue at the end of the day, he wakes up again and again on the same morning.

The film does not specify how many times Phil repeats the day, but from what he eventually masters—playing the piano, reciting French Romantic poetry, ice sculpting, flipping cards into a hat—it must be the equivalent of years.

Finally, in desperation, Phil decides to use his situation to become a decent person. He becomes genuinely interested in Rita, not just in exploiting her. He uses his situation to help people. Having heard that a boy falls out of a tree that day, he rushes off from his now poetically profound Groundhog Day television broadcasts to catch the boy as he falls, wrenching his back and good naturedly shouting after the boy as he runs off, "You little brat. You have never thanked me!" And then, "I'll see you tomorrow... maybe!"

He seeks to use his situation to help an old homeless man whom he had initially ignored each morning. Finding out that the man dies at the end of the day, he intervenes, feeding him at a diner, giving him CPR, and looking at his chart in the hospital for clues to what intervention might help. But despite being able to help others, for example the Mayor and master of ceremonies at the Groundhog Day celebration, on whom he performs a Heimlich maneuver, he is unable to help the old man. The nurse at the hospital attempts to comfort him, saying, "Sometimes it's just their time." Earlier Phil had stated, "I'm a god. Not 'the' God, but a god." But now as he realizes his limitations, Phil comes more deeply in touch with his humanity.

Our protagonist is Phil Connors and the groundhog is Punxsutawney Phil. Like the groundhog, Phil Connors has been in his own burrow, one of despair, "hibernating" in a personal wasteland of self-centered negativity. At the end of the movie, he has emerged. Spring is coming. He wins Rita, escapes the repeatedly cycling day, and, after she accepts his marriage proposal, having found joy, says, referring to the cute little town that he had disparaged at the beginning of the movie, "Let's live here."

The meaning of Phil's repeating day? Here is one thought. In his book, *The Gay Science*, Nietzsche asks:

What if one day or night a demon were to steal after you into your loneliest loneliness and say: "This life as you now live it and have lived it, you will live again and again innumerable times"... Would you throw yourself to the ground and gnash your teeth and curse the demon? Or have you once experienced a moment of such joy that you would have answered him: "You are a god. This is the most divine thing to hear."

Some have said that Nietzsche is proposing a theory of how time works, that it consists of eternally recurring cycles. But that is not right. He is not saying, "In this theory, this is how time and your life work," but rather, "How would you live your life if it *were* to work this way?" If you were going to relive your life or this day over and over forever, you would want it to be a very good life or very good day. A day of pleasure, as in "I was in the Virgin Islands once?" Perhaps. But how about even better than that, the climactic day of *Groundhog Day*, a day of not only pleasure, but of the joy of having done a good job of creating yourself as a decent person. Nietzsche suggests that we should regard our lives as so precious that we should live as though we were going to be living our lives over and over. If we would not want to repeat this life again and again, why are we putting up with it now? Steve Jobs put it slightly differently in his 2005 Stanford commencement address a year after being diagnosed with cancer and six years before his death when he said, "I have looked in the mirror every morning and asked myself: 'If today were the last day of my life, would I want to do what I am about to do today?' And whenever the answer has been 'No' for too many days in a row, I know I need to change something."

When a movie has a strange premise, such as a day repeating over and over, what are we to make of it? We might say, "Well, that's an entertaining story, but it doesn't mean anything to me, as that would never actually happen in real life." But in the best of such movies, the strange premise is a metaphor for something that actually does happen in real life. Like Phil Connors in *Groundhog Day*, we are stuck experiencing the next day, again and again, if not over and over. And we have a choice of what we are going to do with our situation. We can be cynical, as Phil is at the beginning of the movie, or we can be joyful and create the most amazing creation, a luminous Self, as Phil does at the end of the movie. Roger Ebert, in his essay revisiting *Groundhog Day*, concludes: "We see that life is like that. Tomorrow will come, and whether or not it is always Feb. 2, all we can do about it is be the best person we know how to be. The good news is that we can learn to be better people."

Stand in the Sun

Stand in the Sun and feel its energies flow through you. Recall the description earlier of the Furyan, the Purifier, in the movie, *The Chronicles of Riddick*, burning in the light of twin suns until white bone began to show. This is the white bone of the shaman who is stripped of all flesh, who dies to be reborn and thereafter has no fear of death. You feel a nascent world, struggling to be born. What is wrong with others that they do not also feel this? It becomes clear what you must do, what you must create, so that others will feel what you feel. They will object. But after they encounter what you have created, they will be changed, and they will be in a new world in a new way. The late British fashion designer, Alexander McQueen writes:

> *This is the birth of a new dawn. There is no way back for me now. I am going to take you on journeys you've never dreamed were possible.*

And if you take the path of the Visionary Creative, is success assured? Of course not ... or perhaps it is. Dr. Seuss's tells us in his last book, *Oh, the Places You'll Go!* that success is "98¾% guaranteed."

DETAILED CONTENTS

Following is a more detailed table of contents. The numbers before the items correspond to those in the appendices and footnotes that follow.

APPENDICES

Some of the ideas in this book expanded.

Appendix a. Are We All Geniuses?

Related to the material in: 1.1.2.a. *Mastery*

In his book, *The Genius in All of Us: New Insights into Genetics, Talent, and IQ*, David Shenk tells stories of figures like Ted Williams, who, he says, achieved his success through dedicated practice, and implies that all of us can achieve such success. He does not tell the story of Srinivasa Ramanujan, born in India in 1887. By the age of ten he was immersed in mathematics, and later supported himself as a clerk while studying on his own and producing groundbreaking proofs. Ramanujan was invited to England to work with the English mathematician, G. H. Hardy at Cambridge. Unable to handle English food and the English climate, he died in 1920 at the age of thirty-two, but before his death he did work in mathematics that some say puts him in a league with Newton and Archimedes. Think of Will in the movie, *Good Will Hunting*, on steroids, but real. Hardy writes: "Here was a man who could work out modular equations and theorems... to orders unheard of, whose mastery of continued fractions was... beyond that of any mathematician in the world..."

If we accept Shenk's contention and that of others who take similar positions that we can all be geniuses, Ramanujan's accomplishments were not that special and we can all be Ramanujans if we work hard enough. Ramanujan made contributions to number theory, infinite series, mathematical analysis, and continued fractions, some of which are just now being understood, as well as laying the foundations for the mathematics of string theory. I have calculated thin shell structures in school using indeterminate equations, but I don't even know what the areas of mathematics on which Ramanujan worked are. I don't know how strong Shenk is in mathematics, but if I were to put in ten thousand hours, I might learn what some of these areas of mathematics are, but I could never make contributions to any of them. So maybe there are exceptionally creative people, and maybe we can't all be geniuses.

David Shenk's book, *The Genius in All of Us: New Insights into Genetics, Talent, and IQ*, was published in 2010.

The Hardy quote, "Here was a man..." is from Wikipedia: Wikipedia contributors, "Srinivasa Ramanujan," *Wikipedia, The Free Encyclopedia*, http://en.wikipedia.org/w/index.php?title=Srinivasa_Ramanujan&oldid=643366401 (accessed February 1, 2015)

Appendix b. *The Structure of Scientific Revolutions*

Related to the material in: 1.1.2.d. *Visionary Creativity*

I refer several times in this book to Thomas S. Kuhn's 1962 book, *The Structure of Scientific Revolutions*, and it is important to my approach, so I am quoting the introduction to the Wikipedia entry on the book: *"The Structure of Scientific Revolutions* is a 1962 book about the history of science by Thomas S. Kuhn. Its publication was a landmark event in the history, philosophy, and sociology of scientific knowledge and triggered an ongoing worldwide assessment and reaction in—and beyond—those scholarly communities. Kuhn challenged the then prevailing view of progress in 'normal science.' Normal scientific progress was viewed as 'development-by-accumulation' of accepted facts and theories. Kuhn argued for an episodic model in which periods of such conceptual continuity in normal science were interrupted by periods of revolutionary science. The discovery of 'anomalies' during revolutions in science leads to new paradigms. New paradigms then ask new questions of old data, move beyond the mere 'puzzle-solving' of the previous paradigm, change the rules of the game and the 'map' directing new research. For example, Kuhn's analysis of the Copernican Revolution emphasized that, in its beginning, it did not offer more accurate predictions of celestial events, such as planetary positions, than the Ptolemaic system, but instead appealed to some practitioners based on a promise of better, simpler, solutions that might be developed at some point in the future. Kuhn called the core concepts of an ascendant revolution its 'paradigms' and thereby launched this word into widespread analogical use in the second half of the 20th century. Kuhn's insistence that a paradigm shift was a mélange of sociology, enthusiasm and scientific promise, but not a logically determinate procedure, caused an uproar in reaction to his work. Kuhn addressed concerns in the 1969 postscript to the second edition. For some commentators it introduced a realistic humanism into the core of science while for others the nobility of science was tarnished by Kuhn's introduction of an irrational element into the heart of its greatest achievements."

Wikipedia contributors, *"The Structure of Scientific Revolutions," Wikipedia, The Free Encyclopedia,* http://en.wikipedia.org/w/index.php?title=The_Structure_of_Scientific_Revol utions&oldid=612431257 (accessed October 20, 2014).

Appendix c. The West and other Cultures

Related to the material in: 1.3.1. Creativity and the West

This book is about creativity in our Western culture today, but it is useful to contrast our culture to other historical cultures to see that our attitude toward creativity is unique.

We might start with the assumption that we as human beings are creative by nature. But are we? Yes, we see all around us evidence of dynamism, change, imaginative arts, individual expression, creativity. But it would be a mistake to characterize human nature as creative based on the past six hundred years of European and American culture. We should also recall the thousands of years of human history with little change. So what is different about our culture over the past six hundred years?

To answer that question, we must start with cultural differences. Social scientists and historians have, for the most part, adopted a materialistic view that humans are everywhere and in every time essentially the same, and that the differences we see from one group to another and from one time to another are due to the availability of material resources and the state of the technologies used to manipulate those resources. But perhaps something else is at work. Perhaps we as human beings are as much symbolic creatures as we are material creatures, and we live in cultures, and cultures are not characterized solely by material means of production, but primarily by symbolic meaning systems. What do we mean by symbolic meaning systems?

Let's begin by looking at some familiar stories and then examine what they tell us about their cultures.

The Ancient Greeks: The Greek tragedian Aeschylus writes: *Worship him, pray to him; flatter whatever today's king; tell Zeus I spit in his face.*

In *Prometheus Bound,* the Titan Prometheus is empowered to choose the successors to the gods and chooses humankind, stealing from the gods and giving to humans not only fire, but the arts and sciences so that humans can eventually supplant the gods. For this, Zeus punishes him by having him chained to a rock on a mountain where an eagle comes each day to eat out his liver, which regrows each night. When an opportunity to ask for Zeus's pardon is presented to him, Prometheus is defiant, yet rails at his fate. Prometheus is defined by his resignation to his fate and his defiance of the gods as he helps bring humankind to the fore.

The Ancient Middle East: God said to Job: *Canst thou draw out leviathan with an hook?... Hear, I beseech thee, and I will speak: I will demand of thee, and declare thou unto me....* Job responded: *I have heard of thee by the hearing of the ear: but now mine eye seeth thee. Wherefore I abhor myself, and repent in dust and ashes.*

In the Old Testament story of Job, God, in a wager with Satan, claims that his subject Job will remain faithful even if subjected to torment. God allows Satan to take Job's children, wife, crops, livestock, lands, health, and finally the respect of others. Yet Job still bows down before God. Job is defined by submission.

Ancient India: Vishnu exclaimed: *I am time, destroyer of the worlds. These men are already dead! Arjuna replied, O Vishnu, I see You devouring all people from all sides into Your flaming mouths. You covering all of the universe with terrible, scorching rays.*

The throne of the Indian prince, Arjuna, has been usurped, but when he is about to enter battle to regain it, he sees teachers, friends, and family among the usurpers and he declares that he will not fight. His charioteer then reveals himself as Krishna, an avatar of Vishnu, the supreme being, telling him that he cannot change fate, that these men are already dead, and that it is his duty to fight. In the *Bhagavad-Gita,* a section of the Indian epic poem, *the Mahabharata,* Krishna then instructs Arjuna on proper action in the world and that an aspect of ourselves reincarnates. Arjuna comes to identify with the duty of his station in this life and with immortal transcendence. His attitude is expressed by the German philosopher, Arthur Schopenhauer who writes, "if you deny the will, then this world, seemingly so real with its suns and galaxies—is nothing."

Ancient China: The *hunter and Tripitaka* [a Chinese monk traveling to India for sacred texts] *were still wondering who had spoken, when again they heard the voice saying, "The Master has come." The hunter's servants said, "That is the voice of the old monkey who is shut up in the stone casket of the mountain side."* ... [Monkey cried out,] *"Welcome,*

245

Master! Welcome! Get me out of here, and I will protect you on your journey to the West....
Five hundred years ago I made trouble in the Halls of Heaven, and Buddha clamped me
down in this place. Not long ago the Bodhisattva Kuan-yin, whom Buddha had ordered to
look around for someone to fetch Scriptures from India, came here and promised me that if I
would amend my ways and faithfully protect the pilgrim on his way, I was to be released, and
afterwards would find salvation...."

In Wu Chery'en's Chinese tale, *Journey to the West*, Monkey is a powerful but
mischievous figure who makes trouble as often as helping. While in the West,
heroes act out of their own volition according to their inner moral sense of
what is right, in China this is not tolerated, and Monkey must be caged, to be
released only when China needs his powers.

Five Eurasian Cultures: We are usually presented with history as progressing
from the caves, through the ancient cultures, to Greece and Rome, then to the
Middle Ages and the Renaissance, and finally to our modern era. And then some
non-Western cultures, but we typically look at them only when they get
colonized by the West. But history does not unfold continuously. Each culture is
distinct with its own historical arc and its own inner symbolic structure; its own
set of stories. The stories we refer to here represent four of Eurasia's great
culture fields. More on a fifth, our own, later.

In what we now call the Middle East, the culture was one of submission.
The creator had given instructions on how to live recorded in the patterns of
the sky and in the written word. One's worth came in conforming to these
instructions and to the dictates of the community. Those who disobeyed these
instructions and dictates put not only themselves, but the entire community,
perhaps even the entire world, in jeopardy.

In India this world was seen as transitory, even illusory, with a transcendent
oneness beyond appearances standing behind it. Our individual existence is
perhaps a mistake, like a drop of dew that condenses out of the fog off the
great water, and that desires to flow back into the great water and reunite with it.
Existence has no beginning and no end. The world was not created, but has
always been and will always be, as have and will we in our infinite previous and
future incarnations. We are to seek harmony by acting in accordance with our
role, identify with the perfection of the universe, and work toward eventually
achieving unity with transcendent oneness.

In China, Confucianism required one to conform to the social order, and
Taoism held that the social order should be in harmony with nature, so one's
individual expression was constrained not only by the society, but also by nature.
For the greater harmony, unpredictable individual creativity was to be
suppressed.

Two thousand years before classical Greece, the Egyptians built a great
civilization but it was not based on a concept of the individual human being.
The Greeks did have that concept, and in Greece there emerged a totally new
notion of what human life was for and what the human mind could do. The
Greek temples stood apart from nature, representing the emergence of human
society, their freestanding columns representing the emergence of human
individuals. The Greek poet Pindar writes: "One is the race of gods and of
men; from one mother we both draw our breath." The Greek gods were not all-
knowing and all-powerful; they were subject to the same foibles as humans and

were destined to eventually be overthrown by humans. This Greek humanism is sometimes called the tragic tradition, as the individual stands in defiance knowing that death is inevitable, and accepts that fate. Contrast this to the Western hubris that death might be just another disease that we will some day conquer. In northern Europe, emerging just a thousand years ago, is a fifth great Eurasian culture, the European West that five hundred years later was extended to the Americas, that we still live in today, and that places the moral and creative center in the heart of each individual. We will look at this culture, our culture, in some depth below and see that creativity is at its core.

Before we go farther, we should pause and admit that these are highly simplified portraits of ancient cultures, and ask, even if we accept these characterizations, do they hold today? China has in some ways become like the West, but has China westernized or has it modernized? And what is the difference? The West is once again in a "clash of civilizations" with the Middle East. What role do the underlying natures of the Middle East, India, China, and the West—their stories—play in their actions today? There are no simple answers to these questions, but they are worth thinking about.

Cultures as Symbolic: All creativity, in art, design, science, technology, business, takes place in layers of culture, and cultures are symbolic meaning systems. The notion that cultures are symbolic differs from the materialist position common today, a position that we see for example in Jared Diamond's popular book, *Guns, Germs, and Steel: The Fates of Human Societies.* Diamond sees material causes for the courses of history, but does not recognize symbolic ones. In so doing, he brings us the surface, but misses the depth that is stored in stories and in the arts.

One way to approach the symbolic nature of cultures is to look at "The Needham Question." Joseph Needham, a Cambridge scholar who fell in love with China and who died at age ninety-four in 1995, complied a vast encyclopedia of the scientific and technological achievements of ancient China showing that China was far in advance of Europe until the 1400s and was in many ways still on its own technological path even at the time of the communist takeover. China had developed advanced agricultural techniques, printing with movable type, paper, silk, porcelain, cast iron, optics, gunpowder, the compass, decimal mathematics, and even airborne gliders. Then beginning in the late 1400s, Europe leaped ahead with outgoing explorations of the globe and scientific and eventually industrial revolutions, while China stagnated. Needham's question was, why did the West advance and China stagnate?

China and the West. Needham himself proposed that the answer lay in Confucianism, the Chinese ethical system, and Taoism, a Chinese mystical veneration of nature, that he said led to Chinese science being defused into the culture rather than existing as independent disciplines the way it eventually did in the West. Others blame the difficulty of managing knowledge in a language that required 250,000 different bronze movable type characters to create an encyclopedia.

But the answer lies elsewhere. Let's look at one example. Between 1405 and 1433 China launched a series of voyages of ocean exploration under the leadership of Admiral Zheng He. The first consisted of a fleet of sixty-two nine-masted treasure ships, each far larger than a football field and fifteen times the tonnage of Columbus's ships, along with hundreds of other substantial ships and a crew of 28,000. Seven voyages explored oceans and lands, but the voyages were halted by an Emperor who destroyed the ships and many of the records of the entire affair. It was less than a hundred years later that Hernán Cortés left Europe with five hundred men, eleven ships, thirteen horses, and several cannons, and conquered the Aztec Empire whose capital, Tenochtitlan, had a population greater than that of any European city of the time. No one can say that Europe began its global conquests and colonizations just as China began its stagnation because of Europe's material or technological superiority.

The answer to Needham's question lies in the differences in the characters—the symbolic meaning systems—of the two cultures. China was insular, with a concentric notion of space that put the imperial court in the center, surrounded by the royal domains, then the tributary feudal princes, then the zone of pacification, then the zone of allied barbarians, and finally the zone of cultureless barbarians. (That's us.) Indeed this center for the imperial court was not just locational, it was directional. There were five directions in ancient China: north, south, east, west, and center. Center was fundamental to the Chinese symbolic orientation and China was not comfortable with anything beyond its boundaries. In the West, there was a very different feeling. Standing in the nave of a Gothic cathedral and looking up at the soaring vaults, one could already see the European spirit that would circle the globe and eventually go to the Moon. So we have two very different worlds in China and the West with regard to their notions of space, which established the stages on which their courses of action would unfold.

Second, something occurred in Europe beginning in the 1400s that had never occurred anywhere before. In a way, Needham's question is misstated. The question should not be why the difference between the West and China, but rather why the difference between the West and all other cultures. If you had traveled the world in the early 1400s you would have see the Forbidden City under construction in the midst of the splendors of Ming Beijing; the Ottomans in conquest of Constantinople in the Near East; the Aztec capital, Tenochtitlan in Mesoamerica, teaming with people. And Europe? At this time England was a miserable backwater of bad sanitation and constant war, ravaged by plagues. The kingdoms of Aragon, Castile, France, Portugal, and Scotland were also miserable places. And before 1400 not only was the West technologically, economically, and artistically behind China, it was also behind where India had been until the Islamic invasions and destructions beginning around 1000 CE, behind where Rome had been before it fell, and even in many ways behind Ancient Egypt.

What happened in Europe beginning in the 1200s and coming to flower in the 1400s that changed this? As we will see below in the literature of the Arthurian Romances (the tales of King Arthur and the Knights of the Round Table), there was a separation of the individual from the group, and a requirement that the individual discover and follow their own path. Thus individuals began, with less and less restrictions, to be freed to pursue their own interests, and their own visions. And to be rewarded for their efforts.

Who We Are in the West: Freeing the Individual. There are three ideas in this concept of individuals free to pursue their own interests and be rewarded for doing so: the notion of an individual with interests, the notion of freedom, and the notion of the possibility of reward, sometimes great reward, for one's efforts. Each needs some exploration.

There are many reasons why this individualism flowered in Europe. One was the rediscovery of the humanism of classical Greece and Rome, a key part of the Renaissance, but that was only an influence. The classical world of Greece and Rome was a separate culture from the world of Western Europe, and while it had superficial influences on the West, as we see in the adaptation of classical styles in architecture, the inner symbolic systems of the two cultures are very different. Far more important is the symbolic meaning system of Europe itself, which we can see in the stories Europeans told themselves.

Next is freedom. We have to realize that individual freedom is simply not a concept in most cultures, where one is required to identify with the role one is born into, and to perfect one's Self as a farmer, warrior, or ruler; as a daughter, son, mother, or father; as a practitioner of the craft of one's family. By contrast, in the West we are expected each individually to find and then manifest our own potential.

And then the idea of great reward. In most cultures throughout history what you could achieve was usually limited by the position into which you were born. But with the Renaissance in Europe, this began to change as we see, for example, in finance, where banking families like the Medici could achieve wealth and power; in art where a figure like Leonardo da Vinci could achieve towering recognition that stands to this day, and in science where Newton could become one of the most prominent people in all of Europe.

Of course this eventual freedom to pursue one's own choices often came with conflict. Michelangelo wrote, "When I told my father that I wished to be an artist, he flew into a rage, saying that 'artists are laborers, no better than shoemakers.'" His father wanted him to become a man of letters, a scholar. With the Renaissance, European artists began to sign their names to their art, and we recall the story that Michelangelo, upon hearing that his sculpture of Mary holding the dead Christ, *La Pietà*, was being to attributed another artist, went out at night and carved on the sash across Mary's breast, "Michelangelus Bonarotis Florent Facibat" (Michelangelo Buonarroti, Florentine, made this). And yes, many, such as Galileo, who spent the last years of his life under house arrest for asserting that the Earth moved around the Sun, were persecuted, but little by little, restrictions fell away, and artists, writers, merchants, bankers, architects, and scientists could pursue things that interested them, even if their interests were different from those of their parents and outside of the accepted orthodoxy. And, if they were fortunate, they could also gain great wealth or recognition for their accomplishments.

Artists during the Renaissance were seldom able to support themselves through independent commissions and often needed patrons, but Leonardo, in his travels from patron to patron, always kept his notebooks with him, preserving them. Did he anticipate that today we would admire his studies of anatomy, his observations of nature, and his visions of flying machines, that we would pore over his notebooks in museums and value them monetarily at tens of millions of dollars?

Agricultural innovations that would not have been permitted in China were

249

put into effect in the 1500s in the Veneto near Venice, which was turning to agriculture in response to its decline as a sea power, producing great wealth and the farm villas designed by the architect Andrea Palladio, villas that led him to become the most influential architect in history. The Flemish physician, Andreas Vesalius, pursued an obsession to understand anatomy and produced *On the Fabric of the Human Body* in 1543, his great book of drawings that we still use today and that now inspires online anatomical representations. Copernicus, Brahe, Kepler, Galileo, and Newton studied the motions of the planets in increasing detail until they understood the principles behind these motions, and Newton produced the mathematics we still use today to calculate the orbits of our spacecrafts. When ground control asked during an Apollo mission, "Who is navigating," those on the craft could respond, "Newton."

Voltaire's freedom was restricted in France, but he was able to accumulate a small fortune from his plays and financial speculation, and then, by staying away from France and later occupying a chateau near the border in the mid 1700s, he could continue his writing, ridicule rulers, entertain luminaries, and build a magnificent library. He aided his mistress, Émilie du Châtelet, in experiments in physics supportive of Newton's theories, and she produced the definitive French translation of Newton's *Principia Mathematica*. We do not see a figure who parallels Voltaire or Émilie du Châtelet in India or China, even in times of greater wealth and cultural sophistication than that of Voltaire's Europe.

Just before his untimely death in 1791, Mozart began earning a living by staging his own productions, culminating in *The Magic Flute*, thus freeing himself of the need for patronage. In the late eighteenth century in science, Joseph Priestly was able to conduct experiments that led to the discovery of oxygen, even while his attempt to combine his science with his theology led to his leaving England for America. In the early nineteenth century in England, Michael Faraday, despite having little formal education, was able to lay the foundations for the study of electromagnetism and invent the electric generator and electric motor, gaining recognition as one of the most influential scientists in history. In industry James Watt, working in Scotland in the late eighteenth century, was able to improve the steam engine and profit from it. Samuel Morse was able to paint the *Gallery of the Louvre* that was to eventually sell for a then-record amount for a painting by an American. Later in the mid nineteenth century, when he was unable to be with his wife when she died because a letter did not reach him in time, he was able to develop the telegraph and invent Morse Code.

In the late nineteenth century, industrialists were able to create fortunes by building new industries and then were able to use their fortunes to build great museums, universities, libraries, and foundations. In our own time, the pioneers of Silicon Valley have been able to build yet again new industries and reinvent how we live. And today, celebrities are able to gain fame and fortune for, well, being celebrities.

The freedom to create, whether in art, literature, science, technology, or industry, may seem natural, and we may be tempted to think that cultures that did not host such creativity failed to do so because of their position in time. The necessary affluence or technology was not there. But that is simply not the case. Most cultures throughout history expended great efforts to repress the individual imagination. Look at an Egyptian mural from the time of the pyramids, then one from the time of Ramesses II, and finally one from the time of Cleopatra. To anyone other than an Egyptologist, they look quite similar. But Ramesses II lived over a thousand years after the time of the pyramids, and Cleopatra over a thousand years after Ramesses II. We do not expect our art to remain unchanged for twenty years, much less two thousand. Ancient Egypt provides an excellent example of a highly conservative culture in more than its art. In the 1300s BCE, the Pharaoh Akhenaten introduced monotheism, replacing Egypt's vast pantheon of gods with a single Sun god, Aten. The Egyptian priesthood resisted his efforts, and he had to create a new capital, Akhetaten, to escape their objections. As soon as Akhenaten died, his new capital was buried and the traditional pantheon restored. And of course ancient Egypt is not the only example of a culture suppressing the individual imagination. Shogun Japan, Ming China, Nehru's India, and the Soviet Union quickly come to mind.

So it was a belief that individuals should be free to create and to be rewarded for their creations, a belief not present in other cultures, that led to the rise of the West, and to the freedom, affluence, mobility, knowledge, and the understanding and control of nature, down to single subatomic particles, that we enjoy today. Even what we now call science originated at the beginnings of Western culture with Adelard of Bath. Adelard, in his twelfth century *Natural Questions*, laid down the elementary principles of modern science: natural phenomena are to be explained by natural causes, nature is a closed system (matter can neither be created nor destroyed), and we should rely on experiment rather than authority in seeking to know the world. To this day these principles remain fundamental to the scientific method.

Note that this does not necessarily mean that Western culture is better than others. "Better" is a matter of trans-cultural valuation and takes us back to the stories we referred to above. Each of these stories has elements of beauty, and several of them may contribute to our future, but for now let's look at the individual.

How did this individual come about? What is different about the symbolic systems of the West? On what understandings do we build our lives? What are the stories we tell ourselves? We could skip these questions, taking Lucy's position in the Peanuts cartoon in which she says that she thought we were just supposed to keep busy. But for those who want to delve into themselves and understand our culture and therefore Visionary Creativity, the question is pertinent.

The quote, "*Worship him...*," is from Aeschylus' *Prometheus Bound*. Impressionistic translation with inspiration from Joseph Campbell.

The quotes from the Old Testament, "*Canst thou draw out leviathan...*," are from the King James Version of the Bible.

The quote, "*I am time, destroyer...*," is from the *Bhagavad-Gîta*. Impressionistic translation.The quote from Arthur Schopenhauer, "if you deny the will...," is from his 1818 and 1844 *The World as Will and Representation*. Impressionistic translation.

The quote from Wu Chery'en, "*The hunter and Tripitaka...*" is from the Chinese tale, *Journey to the West*, and is from a translation by Arthur Waley titled *Monkey*.

The quote from Pindar, "One is the race of gods...," is translated by H. D. F. Kitto and appears in his 1951 book, *The Greeks*.

The book, *Guns, Germs, and Steel: The Fates of Human Societies*, by Jared M. Diamond, was published in 1999.

"The Needham question" is discussed in the 2008 book, *The Man Who Loved China: The Fantastic Story of the Eccentric Scientist Who Unlocked the Mysteries of the Middle Kingdom*, by Simon Winchester.

The story of Zheng He's ocean explorations is told in Louise Levathes' 1997 book, *When China Ruled the Seas: The Treasure Fleet of the Dragon Throne, 1405-1433*. It is also well documented in Wikipedia:

http://en.wikipedia.org/wiki/Zheng_He

Wikipedia contributors, "Zheng He," Wikipedia, The Free Encyclopedia, http://en.wikipedia.org/w/index.php?title=Zheng_He&oldid=613019487 (accessed June 15, 2014).

The quote from Michelangelo, "When I told my father...," can be found in William E. Wallace's 2011 book, *Michelangelo: The Artist, the Man and His Times*.

Appendix d. Has Science Discovered All it is Going to Discover?

Related to the material in: 1.5.1.c. *Science*

Despite continued evidence that science changes through paradigm shifts, we are continually told that our science today is "settled." In 1900, Lord Kelvin is reported to have said, "There is nothing new to be discovered in physics now. All that remains is more and more precise measurement." Just in time to herald relativity and quantum physics that overturned everything. When I asked Carl Sagan in the 1970s about the relevance of quantum theory to cosmology, he was immediately dismissive, remarking that quantum theory applies only at the subatomic level, and has no relevance at cosmic scales. Today quantum theory is fundamental to cosmology. It has a central role in our attempts to understand black holes, which are at the center of every galaxy, and a central role in our attempts to understand the Big Bang, which we now realize was a quantum phenomenon. Similar statements continue. In 1996, John Horgan in his book, *The End of Science* contended that the foundations of science, including the Big Bang theory, the structure of DNA, and evolution by natural selection, are settled, and are not going to change. In just two decades all were undermined, with the notion that our Big Bang universe might be one of an infinite number of bubble universes and that our universe is composed of ninety-five percent dark energy; with theories of DNA being challenged by the notion that much DNA is shared and what makes species different is not which DNA they have, but which is turned on or off; and with evolution by natural selection being challenged by Lynn Margulis's symbiogenesis theory that we discuss in this book. The science journal *Nature*, in 2009, hosted a discussion on the future of science in which the biologist Lewis Wolpert stated that fundamental biology is essentially complete and that the "fundamental architecture" of life is not going to change. Yet we still have no idea how we go from a single cell to the form of creature we become.

The quote from Lord Kelvin, "There is nothing new...," is often repeated, but has not been definitively sourced.

Wikiquote contributors, "William Thomson," Wikiquote, http://en.wik quote.org/w/index.php?title=William_Thomson&oldid=1740568 (accessed June 7, 2014).

Appendix e. The Shaman and the Priest

Related to the material in: 1.6.3. The Creative and the Bureaucrat

What are the origins of this fear of people acting for themselves; what are the origins of the long tradition of conflict between "the individual" and "society?" Let's go way back.

We might think of people in hunting-gathering societies as "freelancers." They have to work, but can do so on their own terms. In these societies, the figures who negotiate transcendent realms are shamans, spiritual practitioners who gain their abilities through personal visions, often hallucinations from fever during an illness or fasting. That vision will inform the shaman of his or her role—hunter, warrior, healer—and of his or her special powers. Thus the shaman was also a freelancer.

As cultures built on hunting and gathering were replaced by those built on agriculture, the independence of hunters and gatherers was replaced by the well organized hierarchical social order necessary for agriculture, and humans were "domesticated"; tied down to tending crops according to the dictates of the seasons, and the rituals of the calendar were created as one of the means of enforcing this domestication. Freelancing was replaced by the necessity of planting and harvesting according to strict schedules and procedures. In this agricultural order, shamans were replaced by priests who are agents of institutions, trained and ordained by those institutions, deriving their authority from their titles. Their effectiveness comes from performing the proscribed rituals properly, not from any abilities of their own. Agriculture brought the need for masses of people to act in organized ways according to the dictates of authorities, and priests helped serve that need. Industrialization continued that pattern, but as our economy today moves from industry to creativity, and work again becomes more and more freelance, the patterns of the herd no longer suit us, and the potential for the independence of the shaman reemerges. The priesthood is not happy. The shaman and the priest represent two totally different ways of being in the world that exist in opposition to this day: shamans experience the energies of the cosmos flowing through them, while priests work in institutions that claim to be the source of those energies. But are not.

This notion of the opposition between the shaman and the priest comes from Joseph Campbell who addressed it in his essay, "The Symbol without Meaning," which he presented in 1957 at Eranos. Eranos is a European discussion group addressing psychology, religion, philosophy, and spirituality, that is attended by major figures in these fields. The essay was published in Campbell's 1968 book, *The Flight of the Wild Gander: Explorations in the Mythological Dimension*.

Joseph Campbell, *The Flight of the Wild Gander*. Novato CA; New World Library, 2002, p. 154, 155.

Appendix f. Great Managers

Related to the material in: 1.6.3. The Creative and the Bureaucrat

Two examples of great managers: The late David Evans. In 1964 he started a program in computer science at the University of Utah focused on computer graphics. Evans recruited, nurtured, and supported researchers who created much of the digital world we know today, including computer games, digital recording, computer animated movies, Internet browsers, computer aided design, and the graphical user interfaces we use today on our Macs, PCs, tablets and smart phones. All from one small university department that supported individuals who pursued their visions. This was around the same time that managers at General Motors were placing layer upon layer of clones of themselves over their engineers and designers until the company was making such mediocre cars that it had to pay people to buy them. These managers eventually bankrupted the company.

We see another case of an academic manager exercising great leadership in the case of G. Holmes Perkins, dean of the architecture school at the University of Pennsylvania from the early 1950s through the mid 1970s. Perkins was brought to Penn to bring the school into the modern era, and was given the opportunity to bring in an entirely new faculty. To avoid the danger of building a school on expired ideas, which often happens when big names are brought in, Perkins relied on his extraordinary intuition about people and appointed mostly young unknowns. He then created an environment, both in the school and in the city, in which these young figures were able to develop in interaction with each other. The result was one of the finest schools of architecture of the twentieth century, and "The Philadelphia School" is now recognize as a brilliant moment in the discipline of architecture. Its faculty included the architects Louis Kahn and Robert Venturi, the city planners Edmund Bacon and Denise Scott Brown, the landscape architect Ian McHarg, and the cultural critic Lewis Mumford.

Appendix g. *Ressentiment*

Related to the material in: 1.6.4. Who Owns Your Creativity?

A bit more on why there would be those who are enemies of creation: In The Rational Optimist: How Prosperity Evolves, Matt Ridley documents the growth in material wealth over thousands of years, focusing with increasing detail on the past few hundred years and then more intently on recent decades. He shows that, despite continued pessimistic predications of immanent collapse, every material aspect of life has been improving, including life span, health, the availability of food, and general prosperity. And he shows that the rate of improvement is accelerating and is spreading across the globe. A discussion of the growth of affluence is outside the scope of this book, but very briefly, a lower middle income person in a developed country today lives in better material conditions than did monarchs two hundred years ago, an African youth today with a smart phone can access more information than could the president of the United States twenty years ago, and in the past thirty years over a billion people have moved from abject poverty to the lower rungs of a middle income lifestyle. Ridley proposes that specialization, trade, and what he calls "sex between ideas" are behind this improvement, but that is theory. The increase in prosperity is fact. So why, in the face of this fact, is there such a wide-spread denunciation of our lives today among intellectuals and academics?

In *The Future and its Enemies: The Growing Conflict Over Creativity, Enterprise, and Progress,* the cultural writer, Virginia Postrel, describes a conflict between two approaches to progress, "stasism" and "dynamism." Stasists fall into two categories, reactionaries who fear an unknown future and value stability, and technocrats who value the future but only if it conforms to their plans, who fear chaos, and who wish to control and regulate the future. Both abhor an open future and an open society.

Dynamists embrace the messy progress that takes place in the context of exploration, change, and creativity that brings us individual choice, an open future, and an open society. In other words, they embrace Visionary Creativity.

A desire to protect the commons from the dangers of the unknown, fear of potentially disruptive change, and the desire to retain power among those who are on top of the culture at a given moment certainly underlie much of the resistance to the prosperity that Ridley describes, the dynamism that Postrel describes, and the Visionary Creativity that we describe in this book. But there has to be more. Hundreds of years of growth in affluence, liberty, opportunity, and the miracle of our ever deepening knowledge of nature would seem to present a strong argument for dynamism and creativity. So what else could be at work among those who reject all of this, and to sometimes even deny that it has occurred?

Ressentiment is a term used by the late nineteenth century German philosopher, Friedrich Nietzsche (whom we revisit several times in this book), that is meant to in part evoke "resentment," but that also has other reverberations. We all have limitations and suffer frustrations and various degrees of injustice in our lives. Nietzsche says that we can accept our limitations, get over our frustrations, deal as best we can with injustices, and move forward with our lives, or we can wallow in our misfortunes, allow them to create our identities, and construct edifices of blame toward others. Those who choose to wallow find justification for their existence in the hostility and *ressentiment* they direct at those who are successful and whom they blame for their frustrations. And of course the cause of their frustrations is never themselves. Some even go on to construct entire moral systems that label their limitations as good and the qualities of their real or imagined tormentors as evil. Active, strong-willed people, Nietzsche says, will have impulses of *ressentiment*, but they are too busy living their lives to dwell on them. As Emily Dickinson writes: "To live is so startling it leaves little time for anything else."

The early nineteenth century Danish existential philosopher, Søren Kierkegaard, had a notion of *ressentiment* similar to that of Nietzsche. According to Kierkegaard, *ressentiment* occurs in a "reflective, passionless age," that seeks to stifle creativity. Kierkegaard writes:

> *The* ressentiment *which is establishing itself is the process of leveling, and while a passionate age storms ahead setting up new things and tearing down old, razing*

and demolishing as it goes, a reflective and passionless age does exactly the contrary: it hinders and stifles all action; it levels. Leveling is a silent, mathematical, and abstract occupation which shuns upheavals.... If the jewel which every one desired to possess lay far out on a frozen lake where the ice was very thin, watched over by the danger of death, while, closer in, the ice was perfectly safe, then in a passionate age the crowds would applaud the courage of the man who ventured out, they would tremble for him and with him in the danger of his decisive action, they would grieve over him if he were drowned, they would make a god of him if he secured the prize. But in an age without passion, in a reflective age, it would be otherwise. People would think each other clever in agreeing that it was unreasonable and not even worthwhile to venture so far out....

Although this was written over a hundred and fifty years ago, it sounds remarkably contemporary. We are called to our lives and we can enter the fray, engage, struggle, compete, produce, create, help others, succeed or fail, find joy or suffering. Or we can refuse the call and remain where it is safe. If we refuse, if we do not engage, we can still champion those who do. Or we can practice resentment (or *ressentiment*) of these who do engage; we can make up moral systems that justify our inactions and demonize those who do act. But if we do that, if we resent those who engage and repress our Visionary Creatives, then we are all impoverished.

Matt Ridley's book, *The Rational Optimist: How Prosperity Evolves*, was published in 2011.

Virginia Postrel's book, *The Future and its Enemies: The Growing Conflict Over Creativity, Enterprise, and Progress*, was published in 1999.

Friedrich Nietzsche discusses *ressentiment* in his books *Beyond Good And Evil* of 1886, and *On the Genealogy of Morality* of 1887.

The Emily Dickenson quote, "Life is so startling...," can be found on the Internet, but is not sourced.

The quote from Kierkegaard, "The *ressentiment* which is...," is from Wilipedia, which credits *The Present Age,* Dru 1962 p. 49-52
Wikipedia contributors, "Ressentiment," *Wikipedia, The Free Encyclopedia,* http://en.wikipedia.org/w/index.php?title=Ressentiment&oldid=593442019 (accessed April 12, 2014).

Appendix h. Relativity

Related to the material in: 3.1.3.c. Physics: Relativity

Looking at relativity in some more depth: Recall Newton's absolute space that we might think of as being marked with a grid like the one we see in a perspective painting. Now recall Maxwell's fields with their lines of force that were made apparent by the iron filings on a piece of paper laid over a magnet. This was a revolutionary idea—that seemingly empty space was filled with invisible but real lines of force. Then the question comes, where are those fields located, or more precisely, against what are they oriented? And how do light waves propagate through these fields? Waves propagate through something—

sound waves through air, ocean waves through water; how could they be transmitted through the vacuum of space? A substance called the ether, a massless "ethereal" medium, was hypothesized for the transmission of light. The ether was thought to be fixed within space (the Jello was nailed to the wall), so movement through the ether would be movement with reference to absolute space. That model provided the security of a fixed frame of reference within which we could position ourselves, but it lead to problems. It implied that different observers moving in different ways in the space would measure the speed of light differently. Faster for those moving toward a light source, and slower for those moving away. But experiments by two American physicists in 1887, Albert Michelson and Edward Morley, as well as many experiments to follow, showed that the speed of light is always the same for all observers, no matter their motion relative to the light source.

Albert Einstein had since childhood been interested in the question of the relative motion of an observer, wondering what a clock would look like to someone looking back at it while riding on a wave of light streaming away from it. In 1905 Einstein published a paper presenting what is now called special relativity, in which he showed that the fact that the speed of light is always constant, 186,000 miles per second, for all observers no matter their motion toward or away from a source of light, meant that there is no ether, and no absolute space—there was no Jello and there was no wall. One of Newton's fundamental axioms was gone, and Maxwell's fields existed in… well, not in anything. They existed in themselves; they were self-referential. Just like the modern condition in which there are no fixed frames of reference against which we can orient ourselves.

Einstein then asked, how would an observer on a moving train and another standing in a station see two closely timed flashes of light? This gets involved, but in short, the order of the flashes depends on the motion of the observer. Time is dependent on our observations. So neither space nor time exist except as an arrangement of objects or events as we perceive them, and different observers can perceive them differently.

Einstein's general relativity of 1915 went a step farther. For physicists it showed that gravity and acceleration are the same thing; that there is no experiment a physicist in a windowless room could perform, for example dropping a stone, to determine if the room where sitting on the Earth and subject to "gravity," or in space being accelerated at thirty-two feet per second (one g) by a cable attached to the room. The consequences of gravity and acceleration are the same—the stone accelerates toward the floor at thirty-two feet per second squared in either case. As part of general relativity, Einstein produced the equations that described the dynamic contortions of our no longer uniform or constant space-time. But for the rest of us general relativity does something more. In special relativity, matter tells space-time how to curve while space-time tells matter how to move. In other words, the answer to which came first, the chicken or the egg, is both. General relativity tells us that the stage on which we live, on which we move about both figuratively and literally, is mutually interactive and ungrounded.

We might be temped to say that these notions are abstractions of advanced physics, but in everyday life, a stone is still pulled towards the floor by gravity when we let go of it, but is it? Visionary Creatives swim in their cultures, experiencing them, while the rest of us experience what we have been taught, which is often out of date. In much of modern art, including Surrealism, the approach to space-time is similar to what we have been discussing. The Surrealist painter, Salvador Dalí, writes of sitting at a table and feeling it move upwards against the flow of the space-time that was rushing through his body, pouring into the Earth. Recall the Copernican-Galilean-Newtonian revolution. It did not just exchange the Earth with the Sun at the center of the solar system, it eliminated any fixed center for existence. How can there be existence without a fixed center around which to orient it? Today we have seen enough outer space in science fiction movies not to be bothered by this, but for many post-Copernicans it was all very distressing. Likewise, those rooted in Newton's world, on encountering Einstein's space-time, experienced the loss of a fixed frame of reference as highly disconcerting. In fact the great physicist, Hendrik Lorentz, who was a supporter of Einstein, always insisted on one correction to relativity, that absolute space does exist.

Oh, and Einstein's childhood question about what would a clock look like to someone looking back at it while riding on a wave of light streaming away from it? It's complicated, but if you think it all the way through, you come up with the theory of special relativity.

Appendix i. Quantum Theory

Related to the material in: 3.1.3.d. Physics: Quantum Theory

Some more thoughts on quantum theory: In 1900 the German physicist Max Planck proposed that energy would always be measured as radiated and absorbed not as continuous but as distinct units now called quanta. In 1905 Einstein proposed that it was not just an issue of measurement, but in fact a fundamental characteristic of energy. And it was eventually proposed that all phenomena—energy, matter, and even space and time—are not infinitely sub-dividable, but exist as discrete quanta.

Over the course of the twentieth century, physicists developed quantum theory and made some very strange discoveries. At first, popularizers of science were able to keep the most disturbing features of quantum theory contained by saying that they applied only to the subatomic world; in our larger world, classical physics still held. And these popularizers contended that Heisenberg's uncertainty principle, which states, for example, that if we know the velocity of a particle, it has no exact position, was only a problem of observation. The particle, they contended, actually has a definite position, but we cannot know it because in observing the particle, we disturb it. But that contention is wrong. Quantum theory applies to our macro world as well as to the subatomic world, and a particle truly has no definite position or velocity before we observe it. The American theoretical physicist John Archibald Wheeler states, "No phenomenon is a real phenomenon until it is an observed phenomenon."

There are several ways we can approach quantum theory, but let's use a simplified description of what is called the double-slit experiment. The American physicist Richard Feynman liked to say that everything you need to know about quantum theory can be found in the double-slit experiment. Feynman also liked to say that nobody really understands quantum theory, so if

258

what follows is not completely clear, don't be too bothered.

Shine light at a sheet of opaque material that has two parallel slits in it about a quarter-inch apart. Bands of light and dark will appear on a photo detector screen placed behind the slits, indicating what is called wave pattern interference. Waves of light go through both slits. Where the peaks of these waves overlap, they reinforce each other and cause greater brightness, and where a peak and a trough overlap, they cancel each other out and cause darkness. We see something similar when we drop two stones in a pond and the waves they generate intersect. Experiments like this were done as early as 1800 by the English polymath Thomas Young, indicating that light propagates as waves. But by the early twentieth century, physicists came to understand that light is also made up of individual particles we call photons, and light is now understood to have a dual nature. It is waves when we set up an experiment to detect waves, and photons when we set up an experiment to detect photons. This was disturbing enough—light decides to be waves or particles depending on how we look at it—but something even more disturbing was to develop.

It is possible to fire a single photon at a time at the two slits. Obviously, the photon has to go through one slit or the other, and there should be no interference, as only one photon is involved and there is nothing for it to interfere with. But something weird happens. If you keep firing photons one at a time at the two slits, the pattern that builds up as they continue to hit the photo detector screen is the same wave interference pattern we saw when we shined a lot of light all at once. Each photon is being interfered with by something, although it is not clear what. But it gets even weirder. If we put detectors at the slits so that we know which slit each photon went through, the photons get petulant and choose to act like particles instead of waves. We now know which slit each photon goes through, but there is no wave pattern interference; the impacts on the detector screen just build up behind each slit.

So let's try to fool the photons. We place detectors after the slits, so we do not detect what each photon has done until after it has made its choice of which slit to go through. But the photons again outsmart us. They notice the detectors and call for a do-over, changing how they went through the slits after they already had gone though them, and there is again no wave pattern interference. The term "quantum weirdness" is used to describe this.

But we are dealing with small distances and particles moving at the speed of light. Perhaps we made mistakes in the way we set up the experiment, or perhaps there is some way the photon at the beginning of its trip was tipped off about the detectors. So let's try an experiment with bigger distances. Identify a quasar (a very bright light source) twenty million light years away in space that has a galaxy lying halfway between it and us. The gravity of the galaxy bends the light from the quasar, so light going to the left of the galaxy and to the right of the galaxy can be bent so that both beams come together at a light detector we set up on Earth. If we set up our detector one way, a photon from the quasar will come to us having gone around just one side of the intervening galaxy. If we set up our detector another way, a single photon can come to us having gone around both sides of the galaxy. (Quantum weirdness allows this.) The way we set up our detectors on Earth now, determines the path a photon took twenty million light years away, twenty million years ago. We can affect the past by what we do today. We ask, exactly what happened approximately fourteen billion years ago at the movement of the Big Bang? Since the Big Bang is a quantum phenomena, some quantum physicists contend that what happened depends on how we today look at it. Interesting stuff.

The first double-slit experiments were done with photons and then electrons, but now they have been done with Buckyballs made up of sixty carbon atoms, and plans are in the works to try it with living tardigrades, microscopic creatures. If it works, the tardigrades will be in two places at the same time, reminiscent of Schrödinger's hypothetical cat, famous for being both dead and alive until we look at it.

There are currently about a half dozen proposals for what this quantum weirdness might mean. One of them is the many worlds theory first put forward by Hugh Everett, whom we discuss in this book, which is championed by the British quantum computer pioneer David Deutsch among others. This theory holds that when the photon reaches the two slits, the universe divides and in one universe it goes through one slit, and in a parallel universe it goes through the other. Another proposal is the Von Neumann-Wigner position that it is experience by a conscious being that leads to the results we see in quantum phenomena. In his book, *Symmetries and Reflections*, Eugene Wigner observes that reference to consciousness is necessary to the formulation of quantum theory. Wow. Hard core science saying that our consciousness plays a role in forming reality.

We are indeed in a very different world than we were at the opening of the twentieth century. Space, time, and even reality are not what we have thought them to be. So what are they? That is what modern artists have been telling us for the past hundred years, and that is one of the ways science and art are joined.

Since the experiments described above require sophisticated laboratories, here is a quantum experiment you can easily do at home. Set up two polarized lenses like the ones in polarized sunglasses, one in front of the other, with their polarization at right angles. One lets through only light with vertical waves and the other lets through only light with horizontal waves. Together, they block out all light and you see black. Now insert a third lens between them with its polarization at a 45-degree angle to the other two. Light reappears. In discussing this polarization experiment, the physicist Nick Herbert presents the following analogy: cows and horses approach a gate that allows horses through but not cows. Then the horses pass through a gate that rejects all white animals and allows only black animals to go through. So only black animals and horses can pass through both gates. But when we survey the animals that passed through both, we find that half of them are cows.

We might object that this weird logic is fine for quantum physics, but everyday life works by the logic we learned in school. But does it, or do we just try to convince ourselves that it does? In fact there are all kinds things in our lives that do not conform to conventional logic, but we have been taught to dismiss them. Now other logics are emerging, and the mathematician and computer scientist, Stephen Wolfram, developer of the software tool Mathematica, says that the logic we commonly use is about the fifty-thousandth in a list of all possible logics.

Does any of this have any application in our creative disciplines? Of course most of us will not be doing anything that involves relativity or quantum theory. Likewise, the artists of Newton's time did not do anything that involved planetary orbits. Or did they?

As we discussed earlier, Newton's notion is that space is absolute and uniform in all directions, a featureless infinite container, independent of anything in it, and with no special center. And time is a universal clock that ticks away at the same rate through all of space and all of eternity. Space and time are potentials to be occupied by objects and events. But is this not the space and time of perspective painting, marked out by the grid of perspective lines, occupied by figures frozen in a moment of time? And is it not the space of the Renaissance villa occupied by the human at the center? So there was a relationship between Newton's space and time and the space and time of the artists of the era. And there was a similar relationship between Einstein's space-time and the space-time of the artists of his day as we see in Picasso's Cubism, Frank Lloyd Wright's architecture, and Joyce's novels. And there is also such a relationship today, as we will see later.

Appendix j. Mathematics

Related to the material in: 3.1.3.e. Mathematics

A few more thoughts on mathematics: In the nineteenth century there were tremendous strides in all of the sciences, for the most part built on the foundation of mathematics, itself rock solid in its rigor. But where did that rigor come from? In 1960, the Hungarian-American theoretical physicist and mathematician Eugene Wigner published a paper titled "The Unreasonable Effectiveness of Mathematics in the Natural Sciences" in which he asks how it is that mathematics is so useful to the natural sciences, and finds no explanation.

Two plus two not only does equal four, it always must. And the square of the hypotenuse of a right triangle must equal the sum of the squares of the other two sides. Or must they? In the mid-nineteenth century, several non-Euclidian geometries were developed that would hold for different kinds of surfaces, for example, if a surface were curved like a sphere. The reason we study Euclidian geometry in school is not so that we can rebuild a wagon wheel for which we have only a segment of the rim, but because it tells us that if ideas can be organized deductively, they have to be true. In other words, Euclidian geometry is foundational to Western logical thought. But beginning in the late nineteenth century there were various possibilities from which we had to choose, such as what kind of curvature characterized the space of our world, and we could only choose based on observation. Kind of shaky, since mathematics is not supposed to be contingent on observation, so mathematicians set out to secure their discipline. They explored three approaches: logicism, formalism, and intuitionism.

Logicism is the notion that mathematics is at its roots actually logic, and when all of mathematics is reduced to logic, it will be secure. The great document of logicism is the three-volume work, *Principia Mathematica*, by Alfred

North Whitehead and Bertrand Russell, published between 1910 and 1913. In 1931 the Hungarian mathematician Kurt Gödel published what is called Gödel's incompleteness theorem, showing that all of mathematics has to be incomplete or self-contradictory, totally undermining the logicism enterprise. Russell ignored it. Whitehead went on to other things.

David Hilbert, one of the most important mathematicians of the late ninetieth and early twentieth centuries, championed formalism, which holds that mathematics is a formal game based on rules established by mathematicians. We are free to invent the rules, such as what numbers mean, as long as these rules are consistent. Mathematics might or might not correspond to the world; it just has to be self-consistent. In 1900 Hilbert issued a set of twenty-three propositions for mathematicians to prove, some of them intended to establish mathematics on a solid and consistent foundation of axioms, from which, in principle, all mathematical truths could be deduced by rigorous procedure. In 1936 the English mathematician and computer scientist Alan Turing established that there could be no such foundation for mathematics.

Intuitionism, the notion that mathematics comes from our minds, remained. Some philosophers contend that perhaps the world we experience also originates in our minds. If both mathematics and the world originate in the mind, that might explain the remarkable correspondence between them. Most mathematicians just don't like intuitionism, so they ignore it. But even while rejecting logicism and formalism, and ignoring intuitionism, mathematicians have continued their work and have made remarkable strides in generating new kinds of mathematics, even with no secure foundation.

Appendix k. A New Self Beyond Humanism

Related to the material in: 3.3.3. A New Self Beyond Humanism

The private, literate, separated Self, the person that we criticize young people for no longer being, was a product of the print universe. That universe had made possible, had encouraged, had valued the private act of taking up to several years in solitude to write a book, and reading books in solitude. That Self is fast fading, and is being replaced by a Self that lives in the cloud, is interconnected with its environment and with its friends anywhere in the world, getting entertainment and instant updates on news, stocks, traffic, and restaurant and product reviews. What might life under these circumstances be like? We are just beginning to live it, but we might think of something like *Cloud Atlas*, a film directed by Lana and Andy Wachowski and Tom Tykwer. It presents a world of interconnectedness, features multiple plotlines with parallel characters that are perhaps reincarnations of each other set across six different eras. The producers describe the film as: "An exploration of how the actions of individual lives impact one another in the past, present and future, as one soul is shaped from a killer into a hero, and an act of kindness ripples across centuries to inspire a revolution."

Of course the interconnectedness we see in *Cloud Atlas* is not new. We see it in Buddhism and in the writing of the German philosopher, Arthur Schopenhauer, who asks in his essay, "On the Basis of Morality," "How is it

262

possible that when once compassion is stirred within me then another's well-being or distress go straight to my heart, exactly in the same way, if not always to the same degree, as otherwise I feel only my own. Consequently the difference between myself and him is no longer an absolute one." But perhaps today we feel that interconnectedness more directly.

Appendix 1. A Bibliography

Related to the material in the entire book.

Below are some books that contributed to the ideas in my book:
The Decline of the West, by Oswald Spengler
Spengler presented several ideas: History cannot be understood as a linear development from primitive, to today. Rather, each culture—Egyptian, Greek and Roman, Indian, Chinese, Western, etc.—is independent of the others, and has its own historical arc.

Each culture has a life cycle, which Spengler describes using a seasonal analogy and an organic analogy. Each culture goes through a spring, summer, fall, and winter. After winter a culture has lost its creativity and enters what Spengler calls a civilization phase; it has no more creative juices and is focused on engineering and money rather than on religion and art. Spengler also describes this development in terms of birth, youth, maturity, and old age. Each of these periods is characterized by a different kind of art, architecture, philosophy, political system, etc. Each culture has its own inner symbolic structure which Spengler refers to as its Prime Symbol, a sort of cultural personality.

The Masks of God, four volumes: *Primitive Mythology, Oriental Mythology, Occidental Mythology*, and *Creative Mythology*, by Joseph Campbell
As with Nietzsche's, Campbell's influence can be seen throughout my book. *The Hero With a Thousand Faces* is Campbell's most influential book, presenting the pattern of the hero journey that can be found in many of today's movies. I briefly refer to *Hero* in my book. The best brief overview of Campbell's ideas can be found in his *Myths to Live By*.

Phenomenology of Perception, by Maurice Merleau-Ponty
Merleau-Ponty comes from the tradition in phenomenology that sees our consciousness as taking an active role in generating the world we experience. He sees perception as active, not passive. The passive model sees stimuli coming in from the world, and we interpret it, for example, as a chair. Merleau-Ponty sees us, through "intentionality," projecting the meaning, "chair."

In addition, Merleau-Ponty sees this meaning projected not just by the mind, and not just by the senses, but by the body as a whole, for which he posits "the body-subject." Thus a chair is a chair not only because we see it and we have the category chair in our minds, but because we can sit on it. If we were some alien creature with a very different body, it would not be a chair.

Understanding Media: The Extensions of Man, by Marshall McLuhan
McLuhan shows how our technologies change not only our external
environments, but also our interior environments, that is the workings of our
minds—what I call our structures of consciousness. The invention of the
printing press brought about cheap books, gave the common person access to
the Bible, etc. But it also lead to many people reading, that is moving their eyes
across lines of print made up of words made up of letters. Doing so exercised a
different part of the brain than the one that had been exercised by listening to
speech. The brain was changed, leading to visually centered linear-logical
thinking, leading to perspective painting, humanism, and eventually the
industrial revolution.

Electric communications, including the telegraph, telephone, etc., lead to
other changes in the working of the brain. And now computers, the Internet,
and social media are yet again changing not only our external environment, but
also the workings of our brains.

For a brief illustrated presentation of these ideas, see *The Medium is the
Massage* by Marshall McLuhan and Quentin Fiore, produced by Jerome Agel.
(That's *Massage*, not *Message*.)

Man's Rage for Chaos: Biology, Behaviour and the Arts, by Morse Peckham
Peckham presents the notion of the discontinuity in the arts. He begins by
looking for defining characteristics of the arts, and shows that there aren't any.
We might try to say that art is beautiful, but many things are beautiful that are
not art, and much art is not beautiful. Similarly for order, etc. Peckham then
shows that the only way to define art is to say that art produces an art
experience. Now two things happen. We realize that something might be art for
one person and not for another. And we have to describe the art experience.

Peckham looks at the things we call art and shows that the one feature all
art has in common is that it changes. Flip through the pages of an art history
text, or go to the galleries season after season, and the one constant you will see
is change. And he shows that this change is often unrelated to changes in the
function of the item. Peckham therefore calls this *non-functional stylistic dynamism*.
So, what is the purpose of this non-functional stylistic dynamism? To produce
discontinuities—differences between what we anticipate and what we
experience. Usually our minds work hard to cover over discontinuities—we see
this in lots of optical illusions. But in the art experience we agree to be open to
them. However, in order to be open, we have to let down our guards that usually
protect us from them. But, in letting down our guards, we become vulnerable to
assaults from the environment. So we usually only let our guard down—we only
have art experiences—in protected environments such as art galleries, museums,
concerts halls, etc.

What is the purpose of art—of the discontinuity? Peckham says the only
purpose is to keep our minds agile so that we can adapt to changes in the world.
Here I disagree with Peckham. I feel that for the most part the discontinuities
produced by art are not random, they are not discontinuities for the sake of
discontinuities. Rather, they are directed. As I say in my book, Visionary
Creatives swim in the culture of their day and manifest in their work the spirit

of their age. The things they create—in art, design, science, technology, business—embody that spirit, and at the same time are a little off center for us, somehow not what we anticipated, presenting discontinuities that stretch us, re-form our neural paths, and pull us into the future. So I feel that discontinuities are intended to bring us into a new emerging culture. And that they occur not only in the arts, but also in other fields, including design, science, technology, and business.

The Psycho-Analysis of Artistic Vision And Hearing: An Introduction to a Theory of Unconscious Perception, by Anton Ehrenzweig
Our perception brings us fleeting broken images. We then put those fleeting broken images together in an "after image." Ehrenzweig shows that art demonstrates how those after images are different in different cultures and at different times.

The Structure of Scientific Revolution, by Thomas Kuhn
Kuhn is known for presenting several ideas regarding science. First, that science does not present us with an absolute objective truth about the world. Nor does it present us with an almost truth that continually gets closer to the absolute objective truth. Rather, science works within paradigms, or models. Paradigms are underlying assumptions that are widely accepted, but that cannot be proved, sort of like Euclid's axioms. The Newtonian paradigm held that space and time are absolute, uniform, and continuous. All of Newtonian science then unfolded within these assumptions. The Einsteinian paradigm held that space and time change based on the orientation of the observer and the presence of matter.

Second, Kuhn held that science does not move from one paradigm to another gradually as new evidence accumulates, but in jumps that he calls paradigm shifts. Newtonian absolute space and time did not slowly become refined into Einsteinian relativistic space-time due to the accumulation of more accurate measurements. There is no relation between these two concepts; one cannot evolve into the other. The change was a discontinuous jump, a paradigm shift.

And third, that there are two kinds of science, *revolutionary science* and *normal science*. Revolutionary science brings about paradigm shifts involving changes in philosophical visions about reality. Normal science works within a paradigm, not questioning the underlying assumptions.

Kuhn's paradigms are parallel to what I call worldviews in my book. Now comes an interesting question: what causes changes in Kuhn's scientific paradigms? Most interpretations of Kuhn claim that he says that paradigms change due to accumulated anomalies. Too many things that don't fit pile up, and a new model is needed to accommodate them. These interpretations are wrong. Kuhn says that paradigm shifts are not due to accumulated anomalies; anomalies are there from the beginning of a new paradigm. At first they are ignored. Then one day they no longer are. Kuhn does not say why. I do. I say that the world changes. Most of us try to deny those changes, but a few accept them, live in them, swim in the new world. They wonder why others do not experience what they experience, and are driven to create works that will enable others to experience what they experience. These people are Visionary Creatives. My book is about them.

I refer to Kuhn in my book because of his important insights, but primarily because when people think of science as a cultural expression rather than as a statement of objective truth, they think of Kuhn and his paradigms. But this idea was around long before Kuhn. It is central to what is called Continental Philosophy, which sees us as cultural creatures. In particular, we see this approach in the work of Ernst Cassirer. And we see it today in Steven Hawking's and Leonard Mlodinow's *The Grand Design*, in which they use the term "model-dependent reality."

Quantum Reality: Beyond the New Physics, by Nick Herbert
A highly accessible explanation of quantum physics. No heavy science or math required.

The Singularity Is Near: When Humans Transcend Biology, by Ray Kurzweil
What is our world like today? In part, it is one dominated by digital technologies. And the capabilities of these technologies are rapidly increasing. In generalized terms, Moore's law observes the power of computer chips doubles every two years, but Kurzweil observes that this kind of exponential growth applies to all information technologies, not just computer chips. Kurzweil then projects this exponential growth forward, and predicts that in just a few decades our intelligence will merge with machine intelligence, and eventually that combined intelligence will spread throughout the universe. Kurzweil's book provides the best summary of current futurist thinking.

A New Kind of Science, by Stephen Wolfram
I present the idea that the universe computes, and that it is perhaps fundamentally a computational process. This book is a major source for that idea.

Friedrich Nietzsche
Nietzsche's influence can be seen throughout my book, primarily his exhortations that we live life as it is. Yes, Nietzsche is a self-help writer. There is no one book presenting all of Nietzsche's thought—his aphorisms are scattered throughout his work.

Science Wars: What Scientists Know and How They Know It, by Steven L. Goldman
An audio course form The Great Courses. From their website: "Choose one: (A) Science gives us objective knowledge of an independently existing reality. (B) Scientific knowledge is always provisional and tells us nothing that is universal, necessary, or certain about the world. Welcome to the science wars—a long-running battle over the status of scientific knowledge that began in ancient Greece, raged furiously among scientists, social scientists, and humanists during the 1990s, and has re-emerged in today's conflict between science and religion over issues such as evolution."
    http://www.thegreatcourses.com/courses/science/history-philosophy-of-science/science-wars-what-scientists-know-and-how-they-know-it.html

Science in the 20th Century: A Social-Intellectual Survey, by Steven L. Goldman
An audio course from The Great Courses. From their website: "As the 19th
century drew to a close, the age-old quest to understand the physical world
appeared to be complete except for a few minor details. 'It seems probable that
most of the grand underlying principles have been firmly established,' said
Albert Michelson, the first American scientist to win a Nobel Prize.

But when Michelson made that prediction, he never dreamed that one of
the 'details'—his own curious discovery that the speed of light is constant no
matter how fast an observer is moving—would soon be explained by a
revolutionary theory that redefined the very concepts of space, time, matter, and
energy."

http://www.thegreatcourses.com/courses/science/history-philosophy-of-
science/science-in-the-20th-century-a-social-intellectual-survey.html

FOOTNOTES

Rather than have footnote numbers in the text, I have organized notes to correspond to the Detailed Table of Contents. My citation style is informal, although for Wikipedia and Wikiquote citations I am using the Chicago style format. When I give dates for books, I give the date of first publication so that the reference can be seen in historical context.

Below you will find the Detailed Table of Contents with notes under those sections in which the material they refer to appears in the book. I have included those sections in the Contents under which there are no notes so that it is easier to keep track.

Note that some of the translations I have used in the text are built on established translations. I indicate such cases with the remark, "Impressionistic translation."

The introductory quote by Percy Bysshe Shelley, "Poets are the unacknowledged...," is from his 1821 essay, "A Defence of Poetry." It can be found online at: http://www.bartleby.com/27/23.html

Salvador Dalí did his painting with the melting watches in 1931. It is titled *The Persistence of Memory.*

Marshall McLuhan's *Understanding Media: The Extensions of Man* was published in 1964.

The J. K. Rowling quote, "I had been writing almost continuously...," can be found on her website at:

http://www.jkrowling.com/en_GB/#/timeline/it-all-started/

The notion of the world as a great thought rather than as a great machine comes from the English physicist and astronomer James Jeans. Jeans states: "...the universe begins to look more like a great thought than like a great machine." You can find the quote on Wikiquote.
Wikiquote contributors, "James Jeans," *Wikiquote*, , http://en.wikiquote.org/w/index.php?title=James_Jeans&oldid=1691041 (accessed April 12, 2014). Wikiquote credits Jeans's 1930 book (1939 edition), *The Mysterious Universe.*

The Steve Jobs quote that Microsoft had "no taste...," is from *The Triumph of the Nerds*, a 1996 British/American television documentary, written and hosted by Robert X. Cringely (Mark Stephens), based on his 1992 book, *Accidental Empires.*

The introductory quote from an imagined thought of a sixteenth century Florentine, "Yes, that's it!...," was made up by the author.

1.1.1. Michelangelo and Mark Zuckerberg . . . 17

1.1.2. From Mastery to Visionary Creativity . . . 20

1.1.2.a. *Mastery* . . . 21
K. Anders Ericsson is the editor of the book, *The Road To Excellence: The Acquisition of Expert Performance in the Arts and Sciences, Sports,* which was published in 1996.

Malcolm Gladwell's book, *Outliers: The Story of Success,* was published in 2008

David Shenk's book, *The Genius in All of Us: New Insights into Genetics, Talent, and IQ,* was published in 2010.

1.1.2.b. *Innovation* . . . 22
Steven Johnson's book, *Where Good Ideas Come From,* was published in 2010.

Tony Wagner's book, *Creating Innovators: The Making of Young People Who Will Change the World,* was published in 2012.

1.1.2.c. *Ordinary Creativity* . . . 24
A survey of recent scientific literature on creativity can be found in *New Scientist* magazine, 29 October 2005, issue number 2523.

Nancy C. Andreasen's book, *The Creating Brain: The Neuroscience of Genius,* was published in 2005.

1.1.2.d. *Visionary Creativity* . . . 26
Thomas S. Kuhn's book, *The Structure of Scientific Revolutions,* was published in 1962.

For big-C and little-c creativity, see:

"What exactly is creativity? Psychologists continue their quest to better understand creativity," by Karen Kersting. November 2003, Vol 34, No. 10. Quoting psychologist Dean Keith Simonton, PhD, of the University of California, Davis. It can be found online at: http://www.apa.org/monitor/nov03/creativity.aspx

The quote from Friedrich Nietzsche, "Lack of a historical sense...," is from his 1879 book, *Human, All Too Human.* Impressionistic translation.

1.1.3. Abandoning Assumptions . . . 30
The quote from Eugene Wigner, "Hungary has produced...." is from Amir D. Aczel's 2001 book, *Entanglement: The Greatest Mystery in Physics.*

"Walk on the Wild Side" is a Lou Reed song from his 1972 album *Transformer,* produced by David Bowie.

1.2. CREATIVITY IN CULTURAL CONTEXT . . . 35
The introductory quote from Leonardo da Vinci, "Perspective is nothing more..." is from Wikiquote, which cites *The Notebooks of Leonardo Da Vinci,* translation by Jean Paul Richter in 1888. Wikiquote contributors, "Leonardo da Vinci," *Wikiquote,* , http://en.wikiquote.org/w/index.php?title=Leonardo_da_Vinci&oldid=1727610 (accessed June 4, 2014).

1.2.1. Culture as a Store of Ourselves . . . 35
The quote, "I've seen things you people..." is from the 1982 science fiction movie *Blade Runner* directed by Ridley Scott and staring Harrison Ford.

It was based on Philip K. Dick's 1968 novel, *Do Androids Dream of Electric Sheep?*

1.2.2. Spirit of the Age . . . 36
The Percy Bysshe Shelley quote, "It is impossible to read...," is from his 1821 essay, "A Defence of Poetry." It can be found online at:
http://www.bartleby.com/27/23.html

The Frank Lloyd Wright quote, "Every great architect...," is from his London lectures of 1939 and is published in his 1953 book, *The Future of Architecture*. It can be found online on Wikiquote at:
Wikiquote contributors, "Frank Lloyd Wright," *Wikiquote*, ,
http://en.wikiquote.org/w/index.php
?title=Frank_Lloyd_Wright&oldid=17
10157 (accessed April 18, 2014).

The Ludwig Mies van der Rohe quote, "Architecture is the will of an epoch...," is from Ludwig Mies van der Rohe's 1923 "Aphorisms on Architecture and Form," translated from the German by Philip Johnson in *Mies van der Rohe*, 1947. It can be found at:
http://modernistarchitecture.wordpre
ss.com/2010/10/25/ludwig-mies-
van-der-rohe's-"aphorisms-on-architec
ture-and-form"-1923/

Marshall McLuhan's reference to art as an early warning system can be found his 1964 book, *Understanding Media: The Extensions of Man*.

The Oswald Spengler quote, "The means whereby...," is from his book, *The Decline of the West*. The first volume was published in 1918 and revised in 1922. Impressionistic translation.

The Ananda Kentish Coomaraswamy

quote, "[Metaphor is] ... the representation...," is a paraphrase by Joseph Campbell in his 1983 *Historical Atlas of World Mythology, Volume I: The Way of the Animal Powers*. Campbell is referencing Coomaraswamy's 1946 book, *Figures of Speech or Figures of Thought? The Traditional View of Art*.

Joseph Campbell, *The Historical Atlas of World Mythology. Volume I: The Way of the Animal Powers*, New York, NY; Perennial Library, Harper Row 1988, p.9.
We make several references to Joseph Campbell (1904-1987) in this book. He was an American mythologist, writer and lecturer. More on Campbell and his books in a later note.

1.2.2.a. *Galileo's Heliocentric Solar System* . . . 39
Regarding Galileo Galilei's *Dialogue Concerning the Two Chief World Systems*: We refer in this book to the toleration of personal freedom and new ideas in the West in comparison to other cultures. While this is the case, this toleration and freedom has been won with struggle. We read in Wikipedia:
"*The Dialogue* was published in Florence under a formal license from the Inquisition. In 1633, Galileo was convicted of 'grave suspicion of heresy' based on the book, which was then placed on the Index of Forbidden Books, from which it was not removed until 1835 (after the theories it discussed had been permitted in print in 1822). In an action that was not announced at the time, the publication of anything else he had written or ever might write was also banned."
Wikipedia contributors, "Dialogue Concerning the Two Chief World Systems," *Wikipedia, The Free Encyclopedia*,
http://en.wikipedia.org/w/index.php
?title=Dialogue_Concerning_the_Tw

o_Chief_World_Systems&oldid=6277 96751 (accessed October 20, 2014).

Note that there are two versions of Leonardo da Vinci's *Adoration of the Magi*, both from 1481. In this book we are referring to: LEONARDO da Vinci Perspectival study of the Adoration of the Magi Pen and ink, traces of silverpoint and white on paper, 163 x 290 mm Galleria degli Uffizi, Florence.

The Leonardo da Vinci quote, "Perspective is nothing more..." is from Wikiquote, which cites *The Notebooks of Leonardo Da Vinci*, translation by Jean Paul Richter in 1888.
Wikiquote contributors, "Leonardo da Vinci," *Wikiquote*, , http://en.wikiquote.org/w/index.php ?title=Leonardo_da_Vinci&oldid=17 27610 (accessed June 4, 2014).

1.2.2.b. *Beethoven's Third Symphony* ... 41
The Heiligenstadt Testament is a letter written by Ludwig van Beethoven to his brothers Carl and Johann when he was living in Heiligenstadt (today part of Vienna) on 6 October 1802.
Wikipedia contributors, "Heiligenstadt Testament," *Wikipedia, The Free Encyclopedia*, http://en.wikipedia.org/w/index.php ?title=Heiligenstadt_Testament&oldid =570400689 (accessed October 20, 2014).

The William Kinderman quote, "What Beethoven explores...," is from his 1995 book, *Beethoven.*

The quote, "Just as the behemoth..." is from Beethoven's funeral oration, written by Franz Grillparzer and read by Heinrich Anschütz on March 29th

1827. The full text can be found at: http://www.lvbeethoven.com/Bio/Bi ographyFuneralOration.html

The William Blake poem, "Now I fourfold vision see..." is from a letter to Thomas Butt, 22 November 1802. Quoted in Geoffrey Keynes (ed.), *The Letters of William Blake* (1956).
Wikipedia contributors, "Newtons Sleep," *Wikipedia, The Free Encyclopedia*, http://en.wikipedia.org/w/index.php ?title=Newtons_Sleep&oldid=561868 974 (accessed July 13, 2014).

1.2.2.c. *Van Gogh's* The Starry Night ... 43

1.2.2.d. *Frank Gehry's Guggenheim Bilbao Museum* ... 44

1.3. CREATIVITY IN OUR CULTURE ... 47
The introductory quote, "All right, then..." is from Mark Twain's *The Adventures of Huckleberry Finn*, first published in the United Kingdom in 1884 and in the United States in 1885.

1.3.1. Creativity and the West ... 47

1.3.1.a. *The Arthurian Romances* ... 48
The approach to the Arthurian Romances we take here is adopted from Joseph Campbell, as is the approach to the Percival story. The quote, "thought it would be a disgrace..." from *The Quest for the Holy Grail* comes from a lecture by Joseph Campbell given in New York in 1972. Joseph Campbell, lecture notes, 1972, New York, NY.

The quote, "'All right, then..." is from Mark Twain's *The Adventures of Huckleberry Finn*, first published in the United Kingdom in 1884 and in the United States in 1885.

272

1.3.1.b. *Gothic Cathedrals* . . . 49
The Winston Churchill quote, "We shape our buildings…," is from a remark in the House of Commons (meeting in the House of Lords), 28 October 1943. The full quote is: "We shape our buildings, and afterwards our buildings shape us. Having dwelt and served for more than forty years in the late Chamber, and having derived very great pleasure and advantage therefrom, I, naturally, should like to see it restored in all essentials to its old form, convenience and dignity." It can be found online at: http://www.winstonchurchill.org/lear n/speeches/quotations/famous-quotations-and-stories

1.3.1.c. *The Freedom to Create* . . . 50
The quote from Michelangelo, "When I told my father…," can be found in William E. Wallace's 2011 book, *Michelangelo: The Artist, the Man and His Times*.

1.3.1.d. *The Individual Today* . . . 51
Raymond Chandler's essay, "The Simple Art of Murder" was first published in *The Atlantic Monthly* in December 1944 and is available today in the 1950 collection of Chandler's short stories, *The Simple Art of Murder*. Wikipedia contributors, "The Simple Art of Murder," *Wikipedia, The Free Encyclopedia*, http://en.wikipedia.org/w/index.php ?title=The_Simple_Art_of_Murder& oldid=600695386 (accessed April 15, 2014).

Following the Raymond Chandler quote we list a few of the movies with the theme presented in the quote. We could also list the detective novels in this genre and their detectives, including, among many others,

Chandler's Philip Marlowe, Dashiell Hammett's Sam Spade and the Continental Op, Mickey Spillane's Mike Hammer, Lee Child's Jack Reacher, and Frank Miller's Marv. Apologies to those whose favorites I have left out.

The quotes, "We all began…" and "If only I could…" are from the 2004 movie, *The Chronicles of Riddick*, directed by David Twohy and staring Vin Diesel.

With reference to the Borg, we see in Wikipedia: "Borg is a collective proper noun for a fictional alien race that appears as recurring antagonists in various incarnations of the American television and film *Star Trek* franchise. The Borg are a collection of species that have been turned into cybernetic organisms functioning as drones of the Collective, or the hive. A pseudo-race, dwelling in the Star Trek universe, the Borg force other species into their collective and connect them to 'the hive mind'; the act is called assimilation and entails violence, abductions, and injections of microscopic machines called nanoprobes. The Borg's ultimate goal is 'achieving perfection'." Wikipedia contributors, "Borg (Star Trek)," *Wikipedia, The Free Encyclopedia*, http://en.wikipedia.org/w/index.php ?title=Borg_(Star_Trek)&oldid=6277 22164 (accessed October 20, 2014). Do you sometimes get a Borg feeling about our world today?

Brett Martin's book, *Difficult Men: Behind the Scenes of a Creative Revolution: From The Sopranos and The Wire to Mad Men and Breaking Bad*, was published in 2013.

1.3.1.e. *Creating an Original Self* . . . 54
Letters to a Young Poet is described on Wikipedia:

"... (original title, in German: *Briefe an einen jungen Dichter*) is a collection of ten letters written by Bohemian-Austrian poet Rainer Maria Rilke (1875–1926) to Franz Xaver Kappus (1883–1966), a 19-year old officer cadet at the Theresian Military Academy in Wiener Neustadt. Rilke, the son of an Austrian army officer, had studied at the academy's lower school at Sankt Pölten in the 1890s. Kappus corresponded with the popular poet and author from 1902 to 1908 seeking his advice as to the quality of his poetry, and in deciding between a literary career or a career as an officer in the Austro-Hungarian Army. Kappus compiled and published the letters in 1929—three years after Rilke's death from leukemia."

Wikipedia contributors, "Letters to a Young Poet," *Wikipedia, The Free Encyclopedia*, http://en.wikipedia.org/w/index.php ?title=Letters_to_a_Young_Poet&oldi d=595098079 (accessed April 15, 2014).

The quote, "I will tell you...," is from James Joyce's 1916 book, *Portrait of the Artist as a Young Man*.

The quote from Martha Graham, "There is only one of you..." is from Wikiquote. Wikiquote contributors, "Martha Graham," *Wikiquote*, , http://en.wikiquote.org/w/index.php ?title=Martha_Graham&oldid=16697 77 (accessed April 10, 2014). Wikiquote credits *The Life and Work of Martha Graham* by Agnes de Mille.

The Steve Jobs quote, "You've got to find...," is from his Stanford University 2005 commencement address and can be found at:

http://news.stanford.edu/news/2005 /june15/jobs-061505.html

1.3.1.f *Creating Original Work* ... 56
The quote from William Blake, "I must Create a System..." is from *Jerusalem The Emanation of The Giant Albion*, copy E, object 10 (Bentley 10, Erdman 10, Keynes 10). http://www.blakearchive.org/exist/bl ake/archive/transcription.xq?objectid =jerusalem.e.illbk.10

1.3.1.g *A Creative Economy* ... 56
The reference from Richard C. Levin, former president of Yale University, is from an address titled "The Rise of Asia's Universities" that he gave in 2010 to The Royal Society, London, England. It can be found online at: http://communications.yale.edu/presi dent/speeches/2010/01/31/rise-asia- s-universities

The Rise of the Creative Class is the title of a 2002 book by American sociologist and economist Richard Florida.

The reference from Deborah Wince-Smith is cited in many places, including a column by George F. Will in the *Washington Post* on January 2, 2011, titled, "Rev the Scientific Engine." http://www.washingtonpost.com/wp- dyn/content/article/2010/12/31/AR 2010123102007.html

1.4. ART, DISCONTINUITY, AND NEUROPHYSIOLOGY ... 59
The introductory quote, "Art in its execution...," from Richard Huelsenbeck is from the First German Dada Manifesto. It can be found on the website of The Center for Artistic Activism: http://artisticactivism.org/2008/06/r

ichard-huelsenbeck-1920/
They cite:
Richard Huelsenbeck (1920)
En Avant Dada: A History of
Dadaism
From En Avant Dada: Eine
Geschichte des Dadaismus, 1920
(reprinted in Art and Social Change,
Will Bradley and Charles Esche, eds.,
London: Tate, 2007, pp. 61-68)
It is interesting to note how non-
absurdist this quote is.

1.4.1. What is Art? . . . 59
William Faulkner's 1950 Nobel Prize
acceptance speech, "I feel that this
award...," can be found on the official
website of the Nobel Prize:
http://www.nobelprize.org/nobel_pri
zes/literature/laureates/1949/faulkne
r-speech.html

In this book we focus on art in
particular and creativity in general in
cultural context. But art also addresses
timeless human concerns, as we see in
Faulkner's speech.

1.4.2. Discontinuity, Neuroscience and
Perception . . . 61
The notion that the discontinuity is
rooted in neurophysiology is put
forward by Jeff Hawkins (although he
does not use that term) in his 2005
book, On Intelligence, coauthored with
Sandra Blakeslee.

The notion that the discontinuity is
rooted in neurophysiology is further
developed by Ray Kurzweil in his
2012 book, How to Create a Mind: The
Secret of Human Thought Revealed.
(Although he does not use that term.)

The concept of the discontinuity in art
is presented by Morse Peckham in his
1967 book, Man's Rage for Chaos: Biology,
Behaviour and the Arts.

Harold Bloom presents his notion that
there are no texts but only relationships
between texts in his 1973 book, The
Anxiety of Influence: A Theory of Poetry.

Apocalypse Now was directed by Francis
Ford Coppola and released in 1979.
The quote from Francis Ford
Coppola, "It was supposed to be...,"
comes from "Francis Ford Coppola:
The RT Interview: The great director
reflects upon his masterpiece
Apocalypse Now," by Tim Ryan, Friday,
Oct. 15 2010.
http://www.rottentomatoes.com/m/a
pocalypse_now/news/1920998/1/fra
ncis_ford_coppola_the_rt_interview/

1.4.3. Art Changes Who We Are
. . . 68
The quote, "Google is not a
conventional company...." is from a
2004 Founders' IPO Letter. It is in the
S-1 Registration Statement and is
titled, "An Owner's Manual" for
Google's Shareholders.
http://investor.google.com/corporate
/2004/ipo-founders-letter.html

1.5. CREATIVITY AS
DESTRUCTION . . . 71
The introductory quote from A. N.
Whitehead, "The major advances...,"
comes from Wikiquote.
Wikiquote contributors, "Alfred
North Whitehead," Wikiquote, ,
http://en.wikiquote.org/w/index.php
?title=Alfred_North_Whitehead&oldi
d=1709535 (accessed April 10, 2014).
Wikiquotes credits Whitehead's
Symbolism: Its Meaning and Effect (1927),
chapter 3, p. 88; final paragraph of the
book.

The introductory quote from Steve
Jobs, "Death is very likely...," is from
the Commencement Address he gave
at Stanford University in 2005.

http://news.stanford.edu/news/2005/june15/jobs-061505.html

1.5.1. Destruction . . . 71

Oppenheimer described the quote, "Now I am become death..." coming into his mind at the first atomic bomb test in a 1966 television documentary. Wikipedia contributors, "J. Robert Oppenheimer," *Wikipedia, The Free Encyclopedia*, http://en.wikipedia.org/w/index.php?title=J._Robert_Oppenheimer&oldid=609623073 (accessed May 26, 2014).

1.5.1.a. *Business* . . . 73

Joseph Schumpeter presents his concept of creative destruction in his 1942 book, *Capitalism, Socialism and Democracy*.

Clayton Christensen presents his concept of disruptive innovation in his 1997 book, *The Innovator's Dilemma: When New Technologies Cause Great Firms to Fail*.

1.5.1.b. *Art* . . . 76

1.5.1.c. *Science* . . . 77

The quote from Max Plank, "A new scientific truth...," comes from Wikiquote.
Wikiquote contributors, "Max Planck," *Wikiquote*, , http://en.wikiquote.org/w/index.php?title=Max_Planck&oldid=1846585 (accessed February 5, 2015).
Wikiquotes credits: *Wissenschaftliche Selbstbiographie. Mit einem Bildnis und der von Max von Laue gehaltenen Traueransprache. Johann Ambrosius Barth Verlag* (Leipzig 1948), p. 22, as translated in *Scientific Autobiography and Other Papers*, trans. F. Gaynor (New York, 1949), pp. 33–34 (as cited in T. S. Kuhn, *The Structure of Scientific Revolutions*).

1.5.2. Revisiting Our Examples, Finding Destruction . . . 80

1.5.2.a. *Galileo's Heliocentric Solar System* . . . 80

Arthur Koestler's book, *The Sleepwalkers: A History of Man's Changing Vision of the Universe*, was published in 1959.
The quote by Galileo Galilei is from his book, *The Assayer (Il Saggiatore* in Italian), published in Rome in 1623. The translation I quote is often quoted. A more accurate translation is: "Philosophy [i.e. physics] is written in this grand book—I mean the universe—which stands continually open to our gaze, but it cannot be understood unless one first learns to comprehend the language and interpret the characters in which it is written. It is written in the language of mathematics, and its characters are triangles, circles, and other geometrical figures, without which it is humanly impossible to understand a single word of it; without these, one is wandering around in a dark labyrinth." This version is on Wikipedia:
Wikipedia contributors, "The Assayer," *Wikipedia, The Free Encyclopedia*, http://en.wikipedia.org/w/index.php?title=The_Assayer&oldid=587555422 (accessed April 11, 2014).

1.5.2.b. *Beethoven's Third Symphony* . . . 83

The lines by William Blake, "Mock on, mock on...," are from one of the ten poems of 1800–1803 from The Notebook of William Blake. Quoted from Wikipedia:
Wikipedia contributors, 'Notebook of William Blake', *Wikipedia, The Free Encyclopedia*, http://en.wikipedia.org/w/index.php?title=Notebook_of_William_Blake&oldid=579452356 (accessed April 11, 2014).

276

1.5.2.c. *Van Gogh's* The Starry Night
... 86

1.5.2.d. *Frank Gehry's Guggenheim Bilbao Museum* ... 87
The Mies van der Rohe quote, "Architecture is the will...," can be found in his August 19, 1969 *New York Times* obituary.
http://www.nytimes.com/learning/ge neral/onthisday/bday/0327.html

1.5.3. Picasso and Matisse: Creativity as Struggle ... 88
The Hilton Kramer essay, "Reflections on Matisse," was published in the November, 1992 issue of *The New Criterion*.
http://www.newcriterion.com/art icles.cfm/Reflections-on-Matisse-4628

The quote from Joseph Campbell, "Life lives on life...," comes from a lecture by Campbell.
Joseph Campbell, lecture notes, 1972, New York, NY.

1.6. ENEMIES OF CREATIVITY ... 91
The introductory quote, "To restrict the artist...," by Egon Schiele was inscribed on one of his sketches done in 1912 while in prison. It can be found online at:
http://www.artchive.com/artchive/S/ schiele.html

1.6.1. The Man in the White Suit ... 91
The movie, *The Man in the White Suit*, is a 1951 British satirical comedy directed by Alexander Mackendrick and starring Alec Guinness.

We might be tempted to see the remark about "tuition for fashion school" as gratuitous, but we should note that Britain is today a world leader in fashion and design as well as in fashion and design education.

1.6.2. A Creative Realm ... 93
Joseph Campbell's book, *The Hero With a Thousand Faces*, was published in 1949.

Joseph Campbell, one of the major cultural figures of the twentieth century, worked with the idea that myth, religion, literature, and art are repositories of the workings of our deep psychology and of the cosmos, as well as our means of participation in our world. His most influential book, *The Hero With a Thousand Faces*, was published in 1949. While *Hero* focuses on one mythic theme, his monumental four-volume work, *The Masks of God*, published between 1962 and 1968, looks at cultures and mythology from around the world, from ancient to modern, emphasizing the differences in different cultures. The volumes are *Primitive Mythology*, *Oriental Mythology*, *Occidental Mythology*, and *Creative Mythology*. His most accessible work is *Myths to Live By*, published in 1972. Campbell often used the phrase, "Follow your bliss," in his lectures. Many people associate Campbell with this phrase as a result of the 1988 PBS documentary, *Joseph Campbell and the Power of Myth*. The documentary was originally broadcast as six one-hour conversations between Joseph Campbell and Bill Moyers. A companion book for the series titled *The Power of Myth*, by Joseph Campbell, Bill Moyers, and editor Betty Sue Flowers, was published in 1988.

The pseudo intellectual, Mortimer J. Adler, was so incensed with Joseph Campbell's admonition to follow one's bliss and with Campbell's high regard for religions besides Christianity, particularly Buddhism, that he wrote an entire book attacking Campbell. The book, *Truth in Religion: The Plurality of Religions and the Unity of Truth*, published in 1990, contends that the only religions that can be valid are those that claim to be revealed. Wikipedia calls Adler a "philosopher."

1.6.3. The Creative and the Bureaucrat ... 95
Susan Cain's book, *Quiet: The Power of Introverts in a World That Can't Stop Talking*, was published in 2013.

The Steve Wozniak quote, "Most inventors and engineers...," is from his 2006 book, *iWoz: Computer Geek to Cult Icon: How I Invented the Personal Computer, Co-Founded Apple, and Had Fun Doing It*.

This brief description of Francis Ford Coppola's conflicts with Paramount while making *The Godfather* is in part sourced from Wikipedia: Wikipedia contributors, "The Godfather," *Wikipedia, The Free Encyclopedia*, http://en.wikipedia.org/w/index.php ?title=The_Godfather&oldid=612784 675 (accessed June 16, 2014).

The Francis Ford Coppola quote, "The Godfather was a very unappreciated...," is from a 1994 interview for the Academy of Achievement, and can be found at: http://www.achievement.org/autodoc /page/cop0int-3

Alex Epstein's book, *Crafty Screenwriting: Writing Movies That Get Made*, was published in 2002.

Scott Collins's *Los Angeles Times*

column describing showrunners appeared on November 23, 2007. http://articles.latimes.com/2007/nov /23/entertainment/et-channel23

The David Chase quote, "I want to tell a story...," appears in the Wikipedia article on *The Sopranos*. Wikipedia contributors, "The Sopranos," *Wikipedia, The Free Encyclopedia*, http://en.wikipedia.org/w/index.php ?title=The_Sopranos&oldid=6033100 44 (accessed April 12, 2014).

1.6.4. Who Owns Your Creativity? ... 103

Ayn Rand's novel, *Atlas Shrugged*, was published in 1957.

Michael J. Sandel's book, *Justice: What's the Right Thing to Do?* was published in 2010. Sandel's approach is rich with questions like, what if you could save ten people by sacrificing one person. But he does not seem interested in approaching his questions through issues of character.

The Max Plank quote, "New scientific ideas...," comes from Wikiquote: Wikiquote contributors, "Max Planck," *Wikiquote*, , http://en.wikiquote.org/w/index.php ?title=Max_Planck&oldid=1685966 (accessed April 12, 2014). Wikiquote credits: Address on the 25th anniversary of the Kaiser-Wilhelm Gesellschaft (January 1936), as quoted in *Surviving the Swastika: Scientific Research in Nazi Germany* (1993) ISBN 0-19-507010-0

The Philip Guston quote, "When you're in the studio...," can be found in the 1988 book by his daughter, Musa Mayer, *Night Studio: A Memoir of*

Philip Guston. You can hear Guston speak these lines in the 1982 documentary film, *Philip Guston: A Life Lived*, directed by Michael Blackwood.

Virginia Postrel's book, *The Future and its Enemies: The Growing Conflict Over Creativity, Enterprise, and Progress*, was published in 1999.

PART TWO: BECOMING A VISIONARY CREATIVE

2.1. YOU BECOMING A VISIONARY CREATIVE ... 109
The introductory quote by Friedrich Nietzsche, "I will tell you of the three metamorphoses...," is from his 1883 to 1885 *Thus Spoke Zarathustra: A Book for All and None*. Impressionistic translation.

2.1.1. The Three Metamorphoses of the Spirit ... 109
The Friedrich Nietzsche quote, "I will tell you of the three metamorphoses...," is from his 1883 to 1885 *Thus Spoke Zarathustra: A Book for All and None*. Impressionistic translation.

Robert Venturi's book, *Complexity and Contradiction in Architecture*, was published in 1966.

2.1.2. Education ... 112

2.1.2.a. *A Framework* ... 112

2.1.2.b. *Schools* ... 113
You can find a list of popular musicians who died at age 27 on Wikipedia under "27 Club." Wikipedia contributors, "27 Club," *Wikipedia, The Free Encyclopedia*, http://en.wikipedia.org/w/index.php ?title=27_Club&oldid=612334488

(accessed June 18, 2014).

The full Arthur Rimbaud quote is: "What a life! True life is elsewhere. We are not in the world." Rimbaud (1854-1891), French poet. repr. In *Collected Poems*, ed. Oliver Bernard (1962). Une Saison en Enfer, "Délires I," (originally published 1874). http://www.poemhunter.com/arthur-rimbaud/quotations/page-2/?search=

The George Gamow reference to the ages of physicists when they made their major contributions is from his 1966 book, *Thirty Years that Shook Physics: The Story of Quantum Theory*.

The reference to David Karp's mother encouraging him to drop out of school can be found in an article titled "Before Tumblr, Founder Made Mom Proud. He Quit School." By Jenna Wortham and Nick Bilton, published in the *New York Times*, May 20, 2013.

Tumblr shows us that the world has already changed since the launch of Facebook. Facebook was originally created to be used on home computers, but young people now interact with each other through their smart phones and tablets. And while Facebook allows for continual updating of one's "status," it does not give users the tools to create videos and interactive web pages the way Tumblr does. Karp is a native to our new world in a way that Zuckerberg is too old to be, and Facebook is evolving into a valued old-line company like General Electric or Procter and Gamble.

The Michael Ellsberg quote, "If a young person...," comes from his book, *The Education of Millionaires*, published in 2011.

With reference to Alexander leading armies at sixteen, British naval officer Horatio Nelson commanded a ship in battle at seventeen, and today U.S. Navy nuclear powered aircraft crews have an average age of twenty-four.

The Steve Jobs quote, "None of us has any idea...," is from his Stanford University 2005 commencement address and can be found at: http://news.stanford.edu/news/2005/june15/jobs-061505.html

2.1.2.c. *Teachers* . . . 115
The Louis Kahn quote, "'How am I doing...," is from John Lobell's 1979 book, *Between Silence and Light: Spirit in the Architecture of Louis I. Kahn.*

2.1.2.d. *Colleagues* . . . 116
Linda Nochlin's essay, "Why Have There Been No Great Women Artists?" was, according to Wikipedia, "[f]irst published in *Woman in Sexist Society: Studies in Power and Powerlessness* (eds. Vivian Gornick and Barbara Moran; New York: Basic, 1971), it was later reprinted in ARTnews, January 1971. The essay was bundled with other essays and photographs and published as *Art and Sexual Politics: Why Have There Been No Great Women Artists?* (eds. Thomas B. Hess and Elizabeth C. Baker; New York, Macmillan, 1971)"
Wikipedia contributors, "Why Have There Been No Great Women Artists?," *Wikipedia, The Free Encyclopedia,* http://en.wikipedia.org/w/index.php?title=Why_Have_There_Been_No_Great_Women_Artists%3F&oldid=610423355 (accessed May 28, 2014).

2.1.2.e. *Take Control of Your Education* . . . 117

The Joseph Campbell quote, "opening through which...," is from his 1949 book, *Hero with a Thousand Faces.* Joseph Campbell, *The Hero with a Thousand Faces.* Novato CA; New World Library, 2008, p. 9.

2.2. YOUR WORK . . . 119
The introductory quote, "riverrun, past Eve and Adam's..." is from the opening of *Finnegans Wake* by James Joyce, published in book form in 1939.

2.2.1. Be in the World . . . 119
The quote, "Leaving there...," is from Italo Calvino's 1972 book, *Invisible Cities.* It was translated by William Weaver.

Franz Kafka's letter that contains "My last request..." was to his friend and literary executor Max Brod, and is quoted in Wikipedia:
Wikipedia contributors, "Franz Kafka," *Wikipedia, The Free Encyclopedia,* http://en.wikipedia.org/w/index.php?title=Franz_Kafka&oldid=603691043 (accessed April 13, 2014). Wikipedia cites two sources. Wikipedia also states that Kafka himself destroyed much of his work, so we can only wonder what was lost.

Regarding Frank Lloyd Wright's motto, "Truth against the world," we see on Wikipedia:
"After Wright's return to the United States in October 1910, Wright persuaded his mother to buy land for him in Spring Green, Wisconsin. The land, bought on April 10, 1911, was adjacent to land held by his mother's family, the Lloyd-Joneses. Wright began to build himself a new home, which he called Taliesin, by May 1911. The recurring theme of Taliesin also

came from his mother's side: Taliesin in Welsh mythology was a poet, magician, and priest. The family motto was *Y Gwir yn Erbyn y Byd* which means 'The Truth Against the World'; it was created by Iolo Morgannwg who also had a son called Taliesin, and the motto is still used today as the cry of the druids and chief bard of the Eisteddfod in Wales." Wikipedia contributors, "Frank Lloyd Wright," *Wikipedia, The Free Encyclopedia*, http://en.wikipedia.org/w/index.php ?title=Frank_Lloyd_Wright&oldid=61 6076262 (accessed July 12, 2014).

The Paul Goodman quote, "I do not write…," was spoken to the author in 1967.

2.2.2. A Hedgehog or a Fox . . . 121

Isaiah Berlin's essay on the hedgehog and the fox can be found in his 1953 book, *The Hedgehog and the Fox: An Essay on Tolstoy's View of History.*

For the quote from Archilochus, "The fox knows many things…," see Wikipedia:
Wikipedia contributors, "The Hedgehog and the Fox," *Wikipedia, The Free Encyclopedia*, http://en.wikipedia.org/w/index.php?ti tle=The_Hedgehog_and_the_Fox&oldi d=599579173 (accessed April 14, 2014).

The three quotes from John Updike, "We do not need…," "This age needs…," and "I set out to make…," are from an article titled "John Updike's Archive: A Great Writer at Work" by Sam Tanenhaus published in the *New York Times*, June 20, 2010.

Richard Feynman's 1959 talk, "There's

Plenty of Room at the Bottom: An Invitation to Enter a New Field of Physics," can be found at: http://www.zyvex.com/nanotech/fey nman.html

2.2.3. The Arc of your work . . . 124

2.3. HOW DO WE JUDGE CREATIVE WORKS? . . . 127
The quote from Arthur Schopenhauer, "Talent hits…" is an impressionistic translation. Find more at Wikiquotes:
Das Talent gleicht dem Schützen, der ein Ziel trifft, welches die Uebrigen nicht erreichen können; das Genie dem, der eines trifft, bis zu welchem sie nicht ein Mal zu sehn vermögen…
- Talent hits a target no one else can hit; Genius hits a target no one else can see.
- *Die Welt als Wille und Vorstellung, Zweiter Band, Ergänzungen zum dritten Buch*, Chapter 31
- As cited in *The Little Book of Bathroom Philosophy: Daily Wisdom from the Greatest Thinkers* (2004) by Gregory Bergman, p. 137
Wikiquote contributors, "Arthur Schopenhauer," *Wikiquote*, , http://en.wikiquote.org/w/index.php ?title=Arthur_Schopenhauer&oldid= 1775664 (accessed August 27, 2014).

2.3.1. Genius . . . 127

2.3.2. Changing Judgments . . . 127
The quote from Roger Ebert, "When I saw *La Dolce Vita*…," is from his 2002 book, *The Great Movies*. Although I re-see *La Dolce Vita* regularly, I have borrowed some of his thoughts and phrases in my description of the movie.

The quote from Gottfried Leibniz, "As for my own opinion…," is from Wikipedia.

Wikipedia contributors, "Gottfried Wilhelm Leibniz," *Wikipedia, The Free Encyclopedia,* http://en.wikipedia.org/w/index.php ?title=Gottfried_Wilhelm_Leibniz&ol did=613662056 (accessed June 22, 2014). Wikipedia cites H. G. Alexander, ed., *The Leibniz-Clarke Correspondence,* Manchester: Manchester University Press, pp. 25–26.

2.3.2.a. *Twain, Melville, and Fitzgerald* . . . 131

The Ernest Hemingway quote, "All modern American literature ..." comes from *Green Hills of Africa* (1935) ch. 1 Wikiquote contributors, "Ernest Hemingway," *Wikiquote,* , http://en.wikiquote.org/w/index.php ?title=Ernest_Hemingway&oldid=18 07383 (accessed November 25, 2014).

The quote, "Call me Ishmael...." is from Herman Melville's 1851 book, *Moby-Dick; or, The Whale.*

2.3.2.b. *Hedy Lamarr* . . . 134

Hedy Lamarr's work on advanced electronically controlled weapons is documented in several places, including Richard Rhodes's 2011 book, *Hedy's Folly: The Life and Breakthrough Inventions of Hedy Lamarr, the Most Beautiful Woman in the World.*

2.3.2.c. *Claude Shannon* . . . 135

"A Mathematical Theory of Communication," by Claude Shannon is cited in Wikipedia as follows: Shannon, Claude E. (July–October 1948). "A Mathematical Theory of Communication". Bell System Technical Journal 27 (3): 379–423. doi:10.1002/j.1538-7305.1948.tb01338.x. When it was published as a book, it

was retitled *The Mathematical Theory of Communication,* and is cited in Wikipedia as: Claude E. Shannon, Warren Weaver. *The Mathematical Theory of Communication.* Univ of Illinois Press, 1949. ISBN 0-252-72548-4 Wikipedia contributors, "A Mathematical Theory of Communication," *Wikipedia, The Free Encyclopedia,* http://en.wikipedia.org/w/index.php ?title=A_Mathematical_Theory_of_C ommunication&oldid=608966859 (accessed May 26, 2014).

You can find Claude Shannon's "A Symbolic Analysis of Relay and Switching Circuits" at: http://www.cs.virginia.edu/~evans/g reatworks/shannon38.pdf

The quote by Neil Sloane regarding Claude Shannon, "He's one of the great men...," is attributed by Wikipedia to a Shannon obituary: Bell Labs digital guru dead at 84 — Pioneer scientist led high-tech revolution (*The Star-Ledger,* obituary by Kevin Coughlin 27 February 2001) Wikipedia contributors, "Claude Shannon," *Wikipedia, The Free Encyclopedia,* http://en.wikipedia.org/w/index.php ?title=Claude_Shannon&oldid=60332 2012 (accessed April 19, 2014).

George Gilder's *Microcosm: The Quantum Revolution In Economics and Technology* was published in 1989.

2.3.2.d. *Hugh Everett III* . . . 137

The quote about John Archibald Wheeler, "...there was a tiger loose... " is by Robert Wilson and can be found in William H. Cropper's 2004 book, *Great Physicists: The Life and Times of Leading Physicists from Galileo to Hawking.*

The "undescribably stupid…" quote regarding Hugh Everett is from Wikipedia: Wikipedia contributors, "Hugh Everett III," *Wikipedia, The Free Encyclopedia*, http://en.wikipedia.org/w/index.php ?title=Hugh_Everett_III&oldid=5995 96230 (accessed April 14, 2014).

The introductory quote by Vincent van Gogh, "Wings, wings to fly…," is from a letter from Vincent van Gogh to his brother, Theo van Gogh, written 12 September 1875 in Paris. Translated by Mrs. Johanna van Gogh-Bonger, edited by Robert Harrison, number 037.URL: http://webexhibits.org/vangogh/lette r/3/037.htm.

The quote, "We hold these truths…," is from the 1776 American Declaration of Independence, original draft by Thomas Jefferson. It can be found online at: http://www.archives.gov/exhibits/ch arters/declaration_transcript.html

The quote from Alexander Pope, "Nature and Nature's laws…," can be found on Wikipedia at: Wikipedia contributors, "Isaac Newton," *Wikipedia, The Free Encyclopedia*, http://en.wikipedia.org/w/index.php ?title=Isaac_Newton&oldid=6080622 10 (accessed May 28, 2014).

The quote from Van Gogh, "La tristesse …," is from *Van Gogh: His Life And His Art* by David Sweetman, published in 1990.

Shawn Achor's book, *Before Happiness: The 5 Hidden Keys to Achieving Success, Spreading Happiness, and Sustaining Positive Change*, was published in 2013.

The quote, "Fostering social cohesion…," was made up by the author as a parody.

The quote, "Feeling good…," comes from the *Journal of Personality and Social Psychology*, vol 52, p 1122). It is quoted in article titled "How to be happy (but not too much)" in *New Scientist*, September 28, 2010.

The Happy Planet Index ranking is from 2012. Wikipedia contributors, "Happy Planet Index," *Wikipedia, The Free Encyclopedia*, http://en.wikipedia.org/w/index.php ?title=Happy_Planet_Index&oldid=6 03420523 (accessed April 14, 2014).

There is a formula used in many of today's happiness, self-help and business management books. Authors scan academic journals in the social sciences, find studies that confirm their preconceptions (ignoring those that don't), and present their preconceptions as scientifically confirmed approaches to increasing worker happiness, productivity, and weight loss.

The Hugh Laurie quote, "I equate happiness..," comes from an article in the *New York Times* titled "Hugh Laurie Sings the Blues" by Gavin Edwards, published September 2, 2011.

2.4.4. The Visionary Creative and Joy ... 153
The Arthur Brooks quote, "Earned success...," comes from a column he wrote titled: "America's new culture war: Free enterprise vs. government control," published in the *Washington Post*, Sunday, May 23, 2010; B01. http://www.washingtonpost.com/wp-dyn/content/article/2010/05/21/AR 2010052101854_pf.html

The David Brooks quote, "The graduates are also told...," comes from a column titled "It's Not About You," published in the *New York Times* on May 30, 2011. http://www.nytimes.com/2011/05/3 1/opinion/31brooks.html

The sitcom *Seinfeld* appeared from 1989 to 1998.

The 2002 movie featuring Jerry Seinfeld, *Comedian*, was directed by Christian Charles.

The Louis Kahn quote, "'How am I doing...," is from John Lobell's 1979 book, *Between Silence and Light: Spirit in the Architecture of Louis I. Kahn.*

2.4.5. The Flow of Energy ... 157
The quote from William Blake, "As I walk among...," is from his poem, "The marriage of Heaven and Hell." He did several versions, including one in 1790. Digital scans of the poem

can be found at: http://www.blakearchive.org/exist/bl ake/archive/work.xq?workid=mhh&j ava=no

From Wikipedia: "'Vincent and the Doctor' is the tenth episode in the fifth series of British science fiction television series *Doctor Who*, first broadcast on BBC One on 5 June 2010. It was written by Richard Curtis and directed by Jonny Campbell and featured an uncredited guest appearance from actor Bill Nighy."

Wikipedia contributors, "Vincent and the Doctor," *Wikipedia, The Free Encyclopedia*, http://en.wikipedia.org/w/index.php? title=Vincent_and_the_Doctor&oldid =604294895 (accessed April 18, 2014).

The quote by Vincent van Gogh, "Wings, wings to fly...," is from a letter from Vincent van Gogh to his brother, Theo van Gogh, written 12 September 1875 in Paris. Translated by Mrs. Johanna van Gogh-Bonger, edited by Robert Harrison, number 037. URL: http://webexhibits.org/vangogh/lette r/3/037.htm.

The Egon Schiele quote, "All things beautiful..." is from a letter he wrote to his mother in 1913. http://www.artchive.com/artchive/S/ schiele.html

The Egon Schiele quote, "The war is over..." is from a biography of the artist.

The Joseph Campbell quote, "People say that..." comes from a lecture he gave in New York in 1972. Joseph Campbell, lecture notes, 1972, New York, NY.

284

The Jose Ortega Y Gassett quote, "[T]he political or cultural aspects of history...," is from his book, *The Revolt of The Masses*, published in Spanish in 1930 and in English in 1932. Mihaly Csíkszentmihályi's book, *Flow: The Psychology of Optimal Experience*, was published in 1990.

André Gide published *The Immoralist* in 1902. In 1909 he published *Straight is the Gate*, which, he said, was to balance the moral position of *The Immoralist*.

Wolf is a 1994 movie directed by Mike Nichols, staring Jack Nicholson and Michelle Pfeiffer.

The Joseph Campbell quote, "Myth is the secret opening..." is from his 1949 book, *The Hero with a Thousand Faces*. Joseph Campbell, *The Hero with a Thousand Faces*. Novato CA; New World Library, 2008.

PART THREE: CREATING THE FUTURE

3.1. HOW THEY CREATED THE 20TH CENTURY . . . 165
The introductory quote by Erich Fromm, "Sanity is only..." can be found on the Internet, but is not sourced.

The introductory quote by Joseph Campbell, "... our meaning is now... " is from his essay, "The Symbol Without Meaning," published his 1968 book, *Flight of the Wild Gander*. Joseph Campbell, *The Flight of the Wild Gander*. Novato CA; New World Library, 2002, p. 154, 155.

3.1.1. The Loss of Fixed Frames of Reference . . . 165

3.1.2. Social Upheavals . . . 166

3.1.3. Some Developments in 20th Century Science . . . 167

3.1.3.a. *Geology* . . . 168

3.1.3.b. *Cosmology* . . . 168

3.1.3.c. *Physics: Relativity* . . . 169

3.1.3.d. *Physics: Quantum Theory* . . . 171
If you want to delve a bit into quantum theory, I find the most accessible book to be *Quantum Reality: Beyond the New Physics*, by Nick Herbert, published in 1985.

The quote from John Archibald Wheeler, "No phenomenon is a real phenomenon...," is widely referenced online, but without citation.

The quote from John Archibald Wheeler, "We are participators...," is from a transcript of a radio interview on "The anthropic universe," *Science Show*, 18 February 2006. It is cited in Wikipedia: Wikipedia contributors, "John Archibald Wheeler," *Wikipedia, The Free Encyclopedia*, http://en.wikipedia.org/w/index.php?title=John_Archibald_Wheeler&oldid=609531045 (accessed May 26, 2014).

3.1.3.e. *Mathematics* . . . 173

3.1.4. Loss of Frames of Reference in Modern Art . . . 174

3.1.4.a. *Cubism* . . . 174
The Ray Kurzweil quote, "Although we experience...," is from his 2012 book, *How to Create a Mind: The Secret of Human Thought Revealed*.

While the neuroscience that Ray Kurzweil is referencing in *How to*

Create a Mind is just now unfolding, these processes in seeing were long ago addressed in Gestalt psychology, and were addressed in Marshall McLuhan's 1964 *Understanding Media: The Extensions of Man.*

These processes are also extensively addressed by Anton Ehrenzweig in his 1953 book, *The Psycho-Analysis of Artistic Vision And Hearing: An Introduction to a Theory of Unconscious Perception,* and his 1967 book, *The Hidden Order of Art.* The depth of Ehrenzweig's analysis remains unmatched even by a half century of neuroscience due to his realization that art can reveal much about how we perceive.
Oliver Sacks's book, *The Man Who Mistook His Wife for a Hat,* was published in 1985.

Claude Monet painted his Rouen Cathedral series from 1892 to 1894.

The quote from Oscar Wild, "Where, if not...," is from his essay, "The Decay Of Lying—An Observation" that he included in his collection of essays titled *Intentions,* published in 1891. It is a significantly revised version of the article that first appeared in the January 1889 issue of *The Nineteenth Century.*
Wikipedia contributors, "The Decay of Lying," *Wikipedia, The Free Encyclopedia,* http://en.wikipedia.org/w/index.php ?title=The_Decay_of_Lying&oldid=6 08949932 (accessed July 9, 2014).

3.1.4.b. *Frank Lloyd Wright* . . . 178

3.1.4.c. *Other 20ᵗʰ Century Art Forms* . . . 179
With reference to the wildly asynchronous beat of Igor Stravinsky's 1913 *The Rite of Spring,* Edward Green

writes: "Technically this is what Stravinsky does: he begins with a series of identical chords in the strings—32 chords in all—moving in a strict and steady rhythm of eighth notes. To his series of chords he brings six sharp accents, produced by the sudden sound of eight French horns. But the accents divide the 32 pulses not into any regular or predictable pattern, but into the highly irregular pattern of 9 2 6 3 4 5 and 3 counts."
http://www.edgreenmusic.org/Stravins-a.htm

The quote from Marcel Proust, "No sooner had the warm liquid...," is from his novel *Remembrance of Things Past,* which he worked on between 1909 and 1922. Translated by C. K. Scott Moncrieff and Terence Kilmartin. (There are more rescent translations and updates of previous translations, and the title *In Search of Lost Time* is now also used.)

3.1.5. Internalizing Archetypes . . . 180
James Joyce's novel, *Ulysses,* was published in book form in 1922.

James Joyce's novel, *Finnegans Wake,* was published in book form in 1939.

Giambattista Vico's *New Science* was published as *Scienza Nuova* in 1725.

A Skeleton Key to Finnegans Wake by Joseph Campbell and Henry Morton Robinson was published in 1944.

The quote, "The latest incarnation of Oedipus...," is from Joseph Campbell's 1949 book, *The Hero with a Thousand Faces.*
Joseph Campbell, *The Hero with a Thousand Faces.* Novato CA; New World Library, 2008, p. 9.

The quote from Lao Tzu, "Without

desire...," is from the *Tao Te Ching*, a classic Chinese text with origins as far back as the late 4th century BC. It is attributed to a legendary figure, Lao Tzu, which means "Old Master." Impressionistic translation.

3.1.6. How Did the World Come Apart? . . . 184
Marshall McLuhan presented these insights in his 1964 book, *Understanding Media: The Extensions of Man.*

"The War of the Worlds" radio drama was adapted from H. G. Wells's novel of the same name by Orson Welles's *The Mercury Theater of the Air* and broadcast in 1938. It gained fame due to the fact that its realism led some to think that the Earth really was being invaded by Mars.

I Love Lucy was the most popular television sitcom of its day, and was broadcast from 1951 to 1957.

3.1.7. What Was the 20th Century All About? . . . 185

3.1.8. Marcel Duchamp . . . 186
The quote, "Whether Mr. Mutt made...," is from "The Richard Mutt Case," an anonymous article published in *The Blind Man* # 2, May 1917. It is believed to have been written by Beatrice Wood, H. P. Roché, and/or Marcel Duchamp. It can be found at: http://sdrc.lib.uiowa.edu/dada/blind man/2/05.htm

3.2. CREATING THE 21ST CENTURY . . . 191
You can find a description of Indra's net in many places, including Wikipedia. This is my rendition.

3.2.1. A Continuation of the

Twentieth Century . . . 191

3.2.2. Science and Technology . . . 192

3.2.2.a. *Information Theory* . . . 192
"A Mathematical Theory of Communication," by Claude Shannon is cited in Wikipedia as follows: Shannon, Claude E. (July–October 1948). "A Mathematical Theory of Communication". Bell System Technical Journal 27 (3): 379–423. doi:10.1002/j.1538-7305.1948.tb01338.x.
When it was published as a book, it was retitled *The Mathematical Theory of Communication*, and is cited in Wikipedia as: Claude E. Shannon, Warren Weaver. *The Mathematical Theory of Communication*. Univ of Illinois Press, 1949. ISBN 0-252-72548-4

Wikipedia contributors, "A Mathematical Theory of Communication," *Wikipedia, The Free Encyclopedia*, http://en.wikipedia.org/w/index.php ?title=A_Mathematical_Theory_of_C ommunication&oldid=608966859 (accessed May 26, 2014).
The John Archibald Wheeler quote, "It from bit...," is from Wikiquote: Wikiquote contributors, "John Archibald Wheeler," *Wikiquote*, , http://en.wikiquote.org/w/index.php ?title=John_Archibald_Wheeler&oldi d=1668404 (accessed April 12, 2014). Wikiquote credits: From the paper "Information, Physics, Quantum: The Search for Links" which appeared in *Complexity, Entropy and the Physics of Information* edited by Wojciech H. Zurek (1990), p. 5.

The Richard Dawkins quote, "What lies at the heart...," comes from his 1986 book, *The Blind Watchmaker.*

The David Chalmers quote, "We are led to…," is from his article, "Facing Up to the Problem of Consciousness," published in the *Journal of Consciousness Studies* 2(3):200-19, 1995.

3.2.2.b. *Chaos Theory* . . . 194
Chaos theory is described by James Gleick in his 1987 book, *Chaos: Making a New Science.*

The source of the title, "Does the flap…," is described on Wikipedia: "According to Lorenz, when he failed to provide a title for a talk he was to present at the 139th meeting of the American Association for the Advancement of Science in 1972, Philip Merilees concocted "Does the flap of a butterfly's wings in Brazil set off a tornado in Texas?" as a title." Wikipedia contributors, "Butterfly effect," *Wikipedia, The Free Encyclopedia,* http://en.wikipedia.org/w/index.php ?title=Butterfly_effect&oldid=612453 115 (accessed June 17, 2014).

3.2.2.c. *DNA and Genomics* . . . 195
You can find a description of a virologist designing a virus in an essay by William McEwan, "Molecular Cut and Paste: The New Generation of Biological Tools," published in the 2011 book, *Future Science: Essays from the Cutting Edge,* edited by Max Brockman.

Stephen Wolfram presents his rule-based approach to science in his 2002 book, *A New Kind of Science.*

3.2.2.d. *Bell's Theorem and Entanglement* . . . 197
The question from John Bell to Alain Aspect, "Do you have tenure…," is from Amir D. Aczel's 2002 book, *Entanglement: The Greatest Mystery in Physics.*

3.2.2.e. *Symbiogenesis* . . . 198
Niles Eldredge and Stephen Jay Gould put forward the theory of punctuated equilibrium in a paper: "Punctuated equilibria: an alternative to phyletic gradualism" (1972) pp 82-115 in "Models in paleobiology", edited by Schopf, TJM Freeman, Cooper & Co, San Francisco. Eldredge, N. & Gould, S.J.

The quote from Lynn Margulis, "All visible organisms…," is from an interview in *Discover Magazine,* April 2004.

The quote from Lynn Margulis and Dorion Sagan, "Life did not take over…," is from Wikipedia. Wikipedia contributors, "Endosymbiotic theory," *Wikipedia, The Free Encyclopedia,* http://en.wikipedia.org/w/index.php ?title=Endosymbiotic_theory&oldid= 600498351 (accessed April 12, 2014). Wikipedia credits: Margulis, Lynn; Sagan, Dorion (2001). "Marvellous microbes". Resurgence 206: 10–12.

3.2.3. Paradigms and Metaphors . . . 201
The quote from Steven Hawking and Leonard Mlodinow, "Strict realists often argue…," is from their 2010 book, *The Grand Design.*

3.3. A NEW SELF . . . 205
The introductory quote, "Today, after more than…" is from Marshall McLuhan's *Understanding Media: The Extensions of Man,* published in 1964.

3.3.1. Social Media . . . 205
Google's mission "to organize the world's…," can be found at: http://www.google.com/about/comp any/

288

The Marshal McLuhan quote, "After three thousand years…," is from his 1964 book, *Understanding Media: The Extensions of Man.*

The Gizmodo quote, "… your entire existence…," can be found at http://gizmodo.com/tag/facebook-timeline

3.3.2. Books . . . 210
The quote, "Another of those damned…," is variously attributed to King George III or Henry, Duke of Gloucester.
Wikiquote contributors, "The History of the Decline and Fall of the Roman Empire," *Wikiquote*, , http://en.wikiquote.org/w/index.php?title=The_History_of_the_Decline_and_Fall_of_the_Roman_Empire&oldid=1704748 (accessed May 27, 2014).

The Anna Quindlen quote, "In books I have traveled…," is from her 1998 book, *How Reading Changed My Life.*

Marshal McLuhan refers to the printed book and the private, fixed point of view in his book, *The Medium is the Massage: An Inventory of Effects*, by Marshall McLuhan and Quentin Fiore, published in 1967.

The Janet Maslin review of Russell Banks' *Lost Memory of Skin* appeared in the *New York Times* on September 25, 2011. It can be found at: http://www.nytimes.com/2011/09/26/books/russell-bankss-novel-lost-memory-of-skin-review.html?_r=0

The Matt Richtel's article, "Growing Up Digital, Wired for Distraction," appreared in the *New York Times* on November 21, 2010. It can be found at: http://www.nytimes.com/2010/11/21/technology/21brain.html?pagewanted=all

Plato presents Socrates' position on writing and memorization in his dialogue, "Phaedrus." Socrates' position is actually nuanced. His two concerns, after the loss of the ability to memorize, are first, that one cannot achieve mastery through reading alone. And second, that written notes should call up what one already knows. Here we see his idea that education does not teach us, but reminds us of what we already know.

"Electronacy" is, of course, the author's play on "literacy."

Cloud Atlas, a 2012 film directed by Lana and Andy Wachowski and Tom Tykwer, and starring Tom Hanks and Halle Berry, was adapted from the David Mitchell's 2004 novel of the same name.

The quote, "How is it possible…," is from Arthur Schopenhauer's 1837 essay, "On the Basis of Morality." Impressionistic translation.

3.3.3. A New Self Beyond Humanism . . . 215

3.3.3.a. *Is Humanism Anachronistic?* . . . 215
The full title of Joseph Wright of Derby's 1765 painting is *A Philosopher giving a Lecture on the Orrery in which a lamp is put in place of the Sun.*

The Edvard Munch quote, "I was walking along a path…," comes from Wikipedia.
Wikipedia contributors, "The Scream," *Wikipedia, The Free Encyclopedia*, http://en.wikipedia.org/w/index.php?title=The_Scream&oldid=603178455 (accessed April 19, 2014).
Wikipedia credits "Quick Facts".

Becoming Edvard Munch. The Art Institute of Chicago. Retrieved 6 May 2012.

3.3.3.b. *A Mixed Metaphor* . . . 216
Georges Seurat's painted his pointillist *A Sunday Afternoon on the Island of La Grande Jatte* in 1884-86 in France.

3.4. HUBRIS . . . 219
The introductory quote from F. T. Marinetti, "Standing on the world's summit...," comes from his *The Futurist Manifesto* of 1909.

The introductory quote from Stephen Wolfram, "I think when I find the code...," comes from various of his lectures and discussions.

3.4.1. Global Problems . . . 219
The quote from Charles Dickens, "It was the best of times...," is from his 1859 book, *A Tale of Two Cities.* Here is the full opening sentence: "It was the best of times, it was the worst of times, it was the age of wisdom, it was the age of foolishness, it was the epoch of belief, it was the epoch of incredulity, it was the season of Light, it was the season of Darkness, it was the spring of hope, it was the winter of despair, we had everything before us, we had nothing before us, we were all going direct to Heaven, we were all going direct the other way—in short, the period was so far like the present period, that some of its noisiest authorities insisted on its being received, for good or for evil, in the superlative degree of comparison only."

The quote from Lionel Trilling, "Life presses us so hard...," comes from his 1950 book, *The Liberal Imagination.*

The William Katavolos parable comes from his lectures

3.4.2. Expanse . . . 222
"Star Trek: Voyager" was one of several television series in the *Star Trek* franchise. It was created by Rick Berman, Michael Piller and Jeri Taylor, and starred Kate Mulgrew as Captain Kathryn Janeway. It was broadcast from 1995 to 2001.

3.4.3. The Singularity . . . 223
The notion of the Singularity as used here is from Ray Kurzweil as described in his 2005 book, *The Singularity Is Near: When Humans Transcend Biology.* He also describes this notion in many of his lectures, which can be found online.

The Ray Kurzweil quote, "The explosive nature...," is from his 2005 book, *The Singularity Is Near: When Humans Transcend Biology.*

The full Daniel H. Burnham quote is "Make no little plans; they have no magic to stir men's blood and probably themselves will not be realized. Make big plans; aim high in hope and work, remembering that a noble, logical diagram once recorded will not die, but long after we are gone be a living thing, asserting itself with ever-growing insistence. Remember that our sons and our grandsons are going to do things that would stagger us. Let your watchword be order and your beacon beauty."
Wikiquote cites: Burnham (1907) quoted in: Charles Moore (1921) *Daniel H. Burnham, Architect, Planner of Cities.* Volume 2. Chapter XXV "Closing in 1911-1912;" p.147.
Wikiquote contributors, "Daniel Burnham," *Wikiquote*, , http://en.wikiquote.org/w/index.php?title=Daniel_Burnham&oldid=1734004 (accessed May 28, 2014).

Daniel Burnham (1846–1912) was a Chicago School architect, and while in this book we describe his rival, Louis Sullivan, as the more innovative of the two, Burnham was a major figure in American architecture, coordinator of the Chicago Plan and architect of some of our most admired buildings, including New York's Flatiron Building and Washington D.C.'s Union Station. In addition he was partially responsible for the design of the Mall in Washington, D.C.

3.4.4. Values and Technology . . . 225
The quote, "Do you believe you can conquer ..." is from Lao Tzu's *Tao Te Ching.* Impressionistic translation.

PART FOUR: POSTSCRIPT

4.1. CREATING YOURSELF . . . 229
The introductory quote from George Bernard Shaw, "Life isn't about finding...," is online but is not sourced.

The introductory quote from Steve Jobs, "Oh, wow..." can be found in the article, "Steve Jobs's last words: 'Oh wow. Oh wow. Oh wow:' Mona Simpson, sister of the late Apple co-founder, reveals details of the final moments Jobs spent with his family," published in the *Guardian,* October 13, 2011.
http://www.theguardian.com/technol ogy/2011/oct/31/steve-jobs-last-words

4.1.1. Is it Time for Visions to be Born in You? . . . 229
The Nietzsche quote, "I will tell you of the three metamorphoses..." is from his 1883 to 1885 *Thus Spoke Zarathustra: A Book for All and None.* Impressionistic translation.

4.1.2. Over and Over . . . 230
The movie *Groundhog Day* was released in 1993, was directed by Harold Ramis, and starred Bill Murray and Andie MacDowell.

The Harold Ramis quote, "At first I would get mail..." is from an article titled "Groundhog Almighty" by Alex Kuczynski in the *New York Times,* December 7, 2003.

The Friedrich Nietzsche quote, "What, if one day or night..." is from his 1882, 1887 book, *The Gay Science.* Impressionistic translation.

The Steve Jobs quote, "I have looked...," is from his Stanford University 2005 commencement address and can be found at:
http://news.stanford.edu/news/2005 /june15/jobs-061505.html

The Roger Ebert quote, "We see that life...," is from his essay on *Groundhog Day* in his 2002 book, *The Great Movies.*

4.1.3. Stand in the Sun . . . 234
The Alexander McQueen quote, "This is the birth...," was included in the 2011 exhibit of his work titled "Savage Beauty," at New York's Metropolitan Museum of Art

The quote, "98 3/4% guaranteed." is from the 1990 book, *Oh, the Places You'll Go!* by Dr. Seuss.

A NOTE ON GENDER USAGE

There is no consensus in the usage guides on how to handle something like: "An artist must first master the tradition within which he is going to work." Some writers switch between "he" and "she," but I find this jarring, wondering if someone has been introduced that I missed. In this book I avoid "he," and thereby lose some concreteness. In some cases I make the statement plural: "Artists must first master the traditions within which they are going to work." This solves the problem at the cost of vagueness. In a few cases I use "he or she," but that is a problem when it, along with "his or hers" appears several times in the same sentence. I occasionally write: "An artist must first master the tradition within which they are going to work." This gets singular and plural mixed, but hey, "Shakespeare and the Bible do it." I await a more satisfactory solution from our usage gurus.

ACKNOWLEDGEMENTS

Quotation from *The Historical Atlas of World Mythology. Volume I: The Way of the Animal Powers*, by Joseph Campbell, copyright © 1991; reprinted by permission of Joseph Campbell Foundation (jcf.org).

Quotation from *The Flight of the Wild Gander* by Joseph Campbell, copyright © 2002; reprinted by permission of Joseph Campbell Foundation (jcf.org).

Quotation from *The Hero With a Thousand Faces* by Joseph Campbell, copyright © 2008; reprinted by permission of Joseph Campbell Foundation (jcf.org).

ABOUT THE AUTHOR

John Lobell has a widely ranging mind looking at culture, art, and science throughout history, and at how new technology leads to cultural changes affecting every corner of our lives.

Lobell studied architecture at the University of Pennsylvania and is a professor of architecture at Pratt Institute in Brooklyn, New York. He has studied with some of the most important creative and cultural figures of the twentieth century, including mythologist Joseph Campbell; architects Louis Kahn, Robert Venturi, and Edmund Bacon; Buddhist masters Chogyam Trungpa, Robert Thurman, and the Dalai Lama; shaman Michael Harner; and Tai Chi master Cheng Man-Ch'ing.

He consults on cutting edge technology projects, is the author of numerous articles, and has lectured throughout the world. His books include *Between Silence and Light: Spirit in the Architecture of Louis I. Kahn* and *Joseph Campbell: The Man and His Ideas.*

Lobell is a cofounder of the website CinemaDiscourse.com which looks at mythology and movies, and is Director of Research for the biotech organization, Timeship (Timeship.org). You can find more at JohnLobell.com. Asked to describe his approach to creativity, Lobell responds:

I have always been interested in where our ideas, our arts, our sciences come from. We usually approach each of the arts and sciences as separate disciplines so that our understanding of one sheds little light on any of the others. And we are told that the arts grow out of individual expression while the sci-

ences grow out of an objective attempt to understand nature. Yet neither the world, nor our experience of it, are divided into disciplines. And the approaches with which we are usually presented do not explain the underlying unities that we see in the arts and sciences.

What is unique about my approach is that I start with cultures as symbolic constructs. Most approaches today are materialist, assuming that all people and all cultures are the same, differing only in their material resources, not in how they experience themselves and the world. As I show in this book, our Western notion of a material world centered around the individual is not universal.

Creativity takes place in cultural context. As I say in this book, Visionary Creatives swim in the culture of their day and manifest in their work the spirit of their age. The things they create—in art, design, science, technology, business—embody that spirit, and at the same time are a little off center for us, somehow not what we anticipated, presenting discontinuities that stretch us, re-form our neural paths, and pull us into the future.

Asked about his next book project, Lobell responds:

I am now working on a book on Visionary Creativity in business. We see a constant stream of books on business management, but while good management is necessary, it is not sufficient for a successful business today. Also needed are Visionary Creative leaders who are immersed in, swim in, are native to, the spirit of the day, who wonder why others do not experience what they experience. They are driven to create products or services that allow others to experience what they experience.

296

www.ingramcontent.com/pod-product-compliance
Lightning Source LLC
Chambersburg PA
CBHW072113270326
41931CB00010B/1539